Churchill's Headmaster

The 'Sadist' Who Nearly Saved the British Empire

Edward Dutton

Churchill's Headmaster: The 'Sadist' Who Nearly Saved the British Empire
Edward Dutton

© Manticore Press, Melbourne, Australia, 2019.

Thema Classification:
NH (Histories), 1DDU (Britain)

978-0-6484996-3-3

MANTICORE PRESS
WWW.MANTICORE.PRESS

'. . . he was, I think, kind-hearted on the whole.'
Roger Fry, on Churchill's headmaster.

In memory of Dr Tony Harvey (1945-2010).

Contents

List of Illustrations

1. Rugby School (Wikipedia Commons).
2. Loxley Hall (Courtesy of Mrs Katherine Cox).
3. Charles Sylvester, Joseph Sandars and George Stephenson by Spiridione Gambardella (Courtesy of the Liverpool and Manchester Railway Trust).
4. The Sneyd-Kynnersley Coat of Arms (Courtesy of Mrs Katherine Cox).
5. Thomas Clement Sneyd-Kynnersley by Henry Turner Munns (Courtesy of the Birmingham Museums Trust).
6. North Gate, Salisbury (Wikipedia Commons).
7. The Rev. Douglas Macdonald (Macdonald & Macdonald, 1904)
8. Frederick Temple by James Russell and Sons (Wikipedia Commons).
9. Trinity College, Cambridge (Wikipedia Commons).
10. Queensmere, Slough (Wikipedia Commons).
11. Aldin House, Slough (Courtesy of Mr Adrian Giddens of the Datchet Village Society).
12. Thomas Alfred Sneyd-Kynnersley (Courtesy of Mrs Patricia Hunt of Reefton, New Zealand).
13. St George's, Ascot (Courtesy of Mrs Susan Van der Veen).
14. Thomas Jex-Blake by John Everett Millais (Wikipedia Commons).
15. Charles Walter Sneyd-Kynnersley (Courtesy of Mr Winson Saw).
16. Herbert William Sneyd-Kynnersley (Courtesy of Mr Michael Kousah).

17. Herbert Sneyd-Kynnersley's Gravestone (Courtesy of Mr Brian Bence)

18. Sir Edmund Backhouse (Wikipedia Commons - Hungary).

19. Roger Fry. Self-Portrait (Wikipedia Commons).

20. St George's, Ascot (Photograph by the author).

21. Maurice Baring (Sketch by the author).

22. The Rev. Sherard Statham (Courtesy of Cottisford and Hardwick PCC).

23. Aubrey Jay, OBE (Courtesy of the Hon. Peter Jay).

24. Arthur Bonham Carter, KC (Courtesy of the Warden and Scholars of Winchester College).

25. Richard Blagrove (Courtesy of Mr. Robert Gaskins).

26. Winston Churchill (Wikipedia Commons).

27. Harry Kessler (Wikipedia Commons).

28. Claude Schuster by Alfred Ward (Courtesy of Mr. Luke Hughes).

29. Chartwell (Photograph by the Rev. Mirjami Dutton).

30. The View from Chartwell (Photograph by the Rev. Mirjami Dutton).

31. Bottlescape by Winston Churchill (Photograph by the Rev. Mirjami Dutton).

Acknowledgements

I WOULD LIKE TO thank a rector, theologian and amateur Churchill historian, who wishes to remain anonymous, who has kindly read through and commented on earlier drafts of this manuscript. In addition, I wish to acknowledge the assistance of my wife, the Rev. Mirjami Dutton, for taking me to Ascot, Chartwell, Slough, Eastbourne, and other places relevant to this book, and taking many photographs.

I am grateful to the fantastically enthusiastic and extraordinarily helpful Mr Michael Kousah, of Ely Books, who managed to locate what seems to be a photograph of Herbert Sneyd-Kynnersley; the Hon. Peter Jay, who sent me parts of his grandfather's unpublished memoir as well as photographs of him; the Rt. Hon. The Lord Jay of Ewelme for sending me extracts from his grandfather's diary; the Rev. Christopher Turner who sent me an unpublished English translation of Harry Kessler's memoir and provided a valuable interview; the late Mrs Barbara Marke, who gave me a useful interview; Mrs Liz Moloney of the Eastbourne Local History Society who kindly assisted with my research on H. Martin Cooke, sent me her article about him, and drew my attention to an auction of Sneyd-Kynnersley family heirlooms; Mrs Susan Van der Veen, Alumnae Officer at St George's, Ascot, who scoured the school's archives for me; Dr Laird Easton, biographer of Harry Kessler, who answered my various questions; Miss Helena Brackenridge, WS, for her help with legalese; Dr John Smith, Archivist of Rugby School, who checked through relevant editions of *The Meteor*; Mr Winson Saw, local historian of George Town, Penang, Malaysia, for providing a photograph of Charles Walter Sneyd-Kynnersley and for his helpful correspondence; and Dr Mikko Lähdesmäki for his medical opinion regarding the Cooke family.

A number of people have helpfully responded to my inquiries, notably: Miss Gabriella Wilke, Publishing Assistant at *Commonweal Magazine*; Mr Charles Jackson of Cottisford and Hardwick PCC; Mrs Louise Kirk, great-great niece of Herbert Sneyd-Kynnersley; Mrs Katherine Cox, distant cousin of Herbert Sneyd-Kynnersley; Miss Graine Lenehan, Archivist of Marlborough College; Mrs Suzanne Foster, Archivist of Winchester College; Mr Michael Stansfield, Deputy Archivist of Durham University; Miss Aisling Lockhart of the Manuscripts and Archive Research Library at Trinity College, Dublin; Mr Charles Sale of Gravestone Photographic Resource, Mrs Jacqueline Wadsworth; Mrs Nadine Lees of the Birmingham Museums Trust; the Ven. Dr Sue Groom, Archdeacon of Wilts; and Sir George Arbuthnot, Bt.

Sections of this book paraphrase or are direct quotations from, *At Our Wits' End: Why We're Becoming Less Intelligent and What It Means for the Future* by Edward Dutton and Michael Woodley of Menie (2018). I would like to acknowledge Dr Woodley of Menie's valuable theoretical discussions as they relate to the book. Other sections of the book draw upon research of mine conducted with Prof Guy Madison (Dutton & Madison, 2019, Dutton & Madison, 2018; Dutton et al., 2016). I would, thus, also like to acknowledge my intellectual debt to Prof Madison. An expanded version of the sections on H. Martin Cooke and Sherard Statham is in press with the journal *Eastbourne Local Historian* as 'Demystifying Churchill's Tutor: The "Mysterious Headmaster" of St Vincent's, Eastbourne.'

Edward Dutton
8th March 2019
Oulu, Finland

Chapter One

The Demon Headmaster?

Monday Morning in the School Library, February 1883

THE 40 BOYS, all of them in black morning suits and white ties, sat in the school library as they finished hearing the report that Monday morning. The headmaster, in academic gown and mortarboard, stood behind his lectern at the front. Every week or so he gathered the entire school in this way to read out each boy's report. Boys with particularly poor reports would be punished.

When he'd finished reading, there was a tense silence. The 8-year-old boy whose report had just been read froze to the spot. Vomit rose up in his throat. He felt pulled down to the floor by an impending sense of doom. The boy began to pray — not the Lord's Prayer which the headmaster made them recite every morning — but his own prayer, from the heart; the kind of prayer his Nanny had taught him. Most of the other boys stared at him angrily, glared at each other with looks of exaggerated disbelief, shook their heads disdainfully, sighed or tutted.

The headmaster stroked his long sideburns. This report wasn't just poor. It was disgraceful . . . again. Starting scrapes with other boys. Coarse talk. Insolence to his masters. Obstinate refusal to do any work at all. Stealing another boy's food during luncheon. But then, thought the headmaster, he'd flogged this boy before and it had achieved nothing. So what was the point of doing it again?

Well, it would be unfair on all the well-behaved boys if he didn't. And he shouldn't forget who this boy was. The son of an influential Conservative MP. The grandson of a Duke. This boy had no ambition at all, but even in spite of this he'd probably be sitting in parliament a few decades hence. Running the Empire. Ruining the Empire. What would the headmaster of Eton think of him personally if this boy behaved anything close to this appallingly having been through *his* school? This little brute had to be broken down.

'Churchill,' he said, calmly. 'You will come up to my study afterwards.' And he moved on to reading the next report.

The Nuts and Bolts of History

Most people who become famous have done something important. They've helped to govern a country; they've written an immensely popular book; they've made some vital scientific breakthrough. But if they're extremely eminent then we become inquisitive about those who influenced them; the people who helped, or possibly hindered, them in reaching their lofty heights: their spouses, their parents, perhaps even their school teachers. These kinds of people — especially if the person whom they influenced is sufficiently admired or infamous — end up achieving a sort of fame by association. They are the nuts and bolts of history.

There are those who play a key part in moulding those who go on to be particularly eminent. Margaret Thatcher strongly admired her father; the grocer, Methodist preacher and Mayor of Grantham Alfred Roberts (1892-1970). What kind of father raised a daughter as unusual and driven as was Britain's first woman Prime Minister? (Campbell, 2011). If he had been a less strident character perhaps there would have been no Mrs Thatcher, meaning there's something inherently fascinating about Alderman Roberts.[1] And then there are those who bring down the mighty. If the obscure Welsh esquire Rhys ap Thomas (1449-1525) hadn't killed Richard III at Bosworth Field (Fern, 2014), English history may have been very different. There'd have been no Tudors, no Georgians, no Victorian Era . . . England might still be Catholic. In fact, one chronicler insists ap Thomas merely *led* the group of soldiers who brought down the hunchback king; the man who struck the fatal blow being the (even more mystery-shrouded) knight Sir William Gardner (1455-1506) (Baldwin, 2015, p.79), though there remains debate over which relative unknown despatched Richard of York (Fern, 2014).

Then there are the great 'What ifs?' of history. People who could have changed history, in a dramatic way, but for one fateful decision. In 1907, Hitler applied to Vienna's Academy of Fine Art. He passed the first stage of the entrance exam by presenting a satisfactory portfolio. He then had to sit the 'drawing' exam, in which he had to draw subjects such as 'Expulsion from Paradise.' Unfortunately for the future Führer, his drawings just weren't regarded as quite good enough, especially considering the fierce competition for places in the prestigious institution (Hamann, 2010, p.32). The dean of the Academy, Siegmund L'Allemand (1840-1910), was apparently sympathetic to the artistic dropout from the Austrian-German border. He thought Hitler was good at drawing and even asked him if he had previously attended an architecture school (Hamman, p.134). Had he been slightly more sympathetic, and able to persuade the other committee members, then Hitler's days as a drifting artist would have come to an end (Fuchs, 2000, Ch. 22). Less embittered and with a clearer purpose in life, Hitler may well never have become involved in the German Worker's Party. So, the director of the academy at the time played a walk on part — but a central one — in twentieth century European history.

---

[1] Until 1972, councils had two tiers: The Aldermen and the Common Councillors. The common councillors were elected by the electors. The Aldermen were elected by the common councillors. The Mayor was elected by the Aldermen. Grantham is a town in the east Midlands county of Lincolnshire. This is the first of a series of footnotes primarily aimed at non-British readers who may be less familiar with British honours, qualifications, ranks and historical idiosyncrasies.

It is just such a figure that will be the focus of this book. Specifically, it is a late Victorian school teacher. To the extent that he is known of at all, he has 'gone down in history as a wild-eyed sadist' (Perry, 2010, p.10), not least because his adversary prophetically stated, 'History will be kind to me, for I intend to write it' (Williams, 2007, p.156). However, as I will show, this school teacher very nearly 'broke down' the boy who would go on to destroy the British Empire and do very serious damage to Britain itself. Had this headmaster been slightly less violent or slightly more conscious of his pupil's physical health, this boy would likely not have been withdrawn from his school. If the boy had not been withdrawn, it would have allowed this teacher to completely break the rebellious spirit of this child who, in modern times, would almost certainly have been classed as a 'special needs' pupil, due to his monumental levels of 'conduct disorder.' This was clear from pretty much the moment this boy arrived at the school; St George's, Ascot, in Berkshire in the southeast of England. The child would grow up to show every sign of being high on the 'psychopathic personality spectrum' — something we will explore in detail in Chapter Nine — made all the more dangerous by the fact that he was highly intelligent, a quality already perfectly clear to his teachers at St George's, and extremely privileged.

But along with that intelligence were such psychopathic traits as shambolic finances, a fantastic sense of entitlement, dishonesty, untrustworthiness, and not caring about the suffering of others. Worst of all, this individual took his country into an avoidable war, bankrupted it, and so lost that country its Empire and left it too exhausted to defend itself. This commenced the process of mass-immigration from developing countries which, though it brought some benefits, also led to many difficulties, such as rising distrust, Islamic terrorism, and the destruction of other traditions vital to holding the country together (Murray, 2017). That boy was Winston Leonard Spencer-Churchill (1874-1965). And that teacher was his prep school headmaster, the Rev. Herbert William Sneyd-Kynnersley (1848-1886).

The Churchill Myth Factor

As so often happens with those who play any kind of a role in history, myths have built up around both men. The mythology surrounding Winston Churchill is captured in the widely held belief that he is the greatest Englishman ever to live; the Bulldog; the best of British. He presciently realised that Germany was rearming and that there was going to be a disastrous war, with the potential for Britain to be invaded. He bravely led his country as it stood alone in its 'finest hour' against the Nazi aggressors, as these belligerents simultaneously began the mass murder of Jews in concentration camps.

'Winnie' courageously and cleverly directed the war until England was victorious; inspiring the British with his hypnotic oratory, broadcast live over the wireless: 'We will fight them on the beaches . . .' A jovial enjoyer of life, with cigar in one hand, his other formed into a 'V' for 'Victory,' this people's aristocrat liked a tipple or three, but who doesn't? Winston was a selfless hero; inexplicably turfed out by the British people in the General Election of 1945. When he died twenty years later, the nation wept as one. And this was all in spite of the miserable two years he'd had to endure under the tutelage of his prep school headmaster, the 'perverted sadist' Herbert Sneyd-Kynnersley.

The Fall and Rise of Public Schools

Before turning to the mythology that has built up around Churchill's headmaster, it would be useful to understand the education system in which he played such a prominent part. Preparatory ('prep') schools are primary ('elementary') schools, usually for children aged between 8 and 13. They prepare children for public schools, which they attend aged 13 to 18. There is no clear definition of what constitutes a 'public school.' In theory, public schools are a group of particularly prestigious private secondary schools[2]; those whose Headmasters are members of the Headmasters' Conference. In many

---

[2]   These are schools attended by pupils between the ages of roughly 12 and 18.

cases, they are also boarding schools. However, the Headmasters' Conference includes assorted little known institutions, such as fee-paying grammar schools — such as Guildford Royal Grammar School or Manchester Grammar School — which are purely day schools. These grammar schools are usually ancient, often having been established in the sixteenth century when all schools were private, with 'grammar schools' distinguished by their focus on Latin. With the setting up of government-funded education in the late nineteenth century, many state-run, and thus free, grammar schools began to be set up, meaning that the ancient 'grammar schools' are really just private day schools.

As private schools, some of these 'grammar schools' have been accepted into the Headmasters' Conference, thus officially making them 'public schools.' However, in reality the term 'public school' is far from precise, because to a great extent it is really just a means of denoting prestige. In 1866, the Captain of the Westminster School XI refused to play a cricket match with the team from Shrewsbury School on the grounds that Westminster's cricket team only played teams from 'public schools.' This is despite the fact that the Clarendon Commission (1861-1864), which was tasked with investigating public schools, regarded Shrewsbury as a public school. Since 1866, a school has been officially a 'public school' if its headmaster is a member of the Headmasters' Conference. Throughout the nineteenth and twentieth centuries, many private schools run for profit ('proprietary schools') were gradually accepted into the public school fold, as their pupils attained university scholarships, attended Officer Training Corps (OTC), entered the higher echelons of the army and civil service, and were accepted by established public schools as worthy of a cricket match (Leinster-Mackay, 1981, p.54). So becoming part of the Headmasters' Conference was often only a step towards acceptance. There is a difference between being theoretically a public school and being accepted as one. Sociological studies of public schools restrict themselves to boarding schools within the Headmasters' Conference.[3] In that the reforms at Rugby turned public schools around (as we

---

[3]   It is the headmaster—not the school—that is elected to the conference, meaning that the official number of public schools fluctuates. In 2001, the conference became known as The Headmasters' and Headmistresses' Conference.

will see shortly), it has been suggested that the term 'public school' essentially means a school that is 'something like Rugby' (Walford, 2012, p.10). Colloquially, when people refer to a 'public school' they tend to mean a particularly prestigious boarding school that perhaps numbers children of the nobility among its pupils; Eton being the archetype. These especially august institutions include Eton, Harrow, Winchester, Rugby, Charterhouse, Marlborough, Westminster and Wellington. In addition, there are many 'minor public schools' that are similar to Eton except that they are little known and tend to have very few pupils from upper class backgrounds (McKibbin, 1998, p.235). Nevertheless, they are accepted as 'public schools.' But few people would accept that Guildford Royal Grammar School or Manchester Grammar School — all private day schools — are public schools at all, no matter what the Headmasters' Conference might say. It has been suggested, for this reason, that some schools should be termed 'Quasi-Public Schools' (Leinster-Mackay, 1981).

Rugby School

'Public Schools' haven't always been associated with the nobility. In the early seventeenth century, many children from noble backgrounds were still educated by private tutors as part of the household system, where they would be sent away to another noble household, or at grammar schools (Abbott, 1993). However, by the mid-eighteenth century, it had become increasingly fashionable,

21

among the nobility, for children to be packed off to one of the public schools. Among the children of peers, born around 1680, 16.2% attended Eton, Westminster, Winchester or Harrow. Among those born around 1740 this had risen to 72% (Cannon, 1987, p.41). Even so, public schools, more generally, were in decline, as, by the beginning of the nineteenth century, there was an increasing demand for high academic standards and modern subjects, rather than just Classics. It was the proprietary and grammar schools which offered these, where the public schools were merely rites of passage into adulthood for the upper class (Wardle, 1970, p.119), notorious for their poorly maintained discipline (Rose, 2002, p.177) and even for student riots (Mitchell, 2009, p.177).

For example, the November 1797 Rugby School Rebellion was sparked by a pupil being flogged by the headmaster for supposedly lying when he named a particular local shop as the place from which he had purchased gunpowder. The shopkeeper denied that he had sold the boy gunpowder, resulting in the boy being beaten for dishonesty. Infuriated by what they saw as the shopkeeper lying to the headmaster, the boy and his friends smashed the windows of the shop. The headmaster demanded that all fifth and sixth formers (aged 17-18) contribute to paying for the damage. They collectively refused, so the headmaster threatened further punishment. In consequence, the next day, the gang blew a school door off its hinges. The day after that, a Saturday afternoon when most of the masters had left the grounds, they set off the fire alarm as a rally call to other boys. The massed pupils then rampaged through the school, smashing windows, and removed the books, furniture and fittings, which they burnt in a huge bonfire on the school field, having previously barricaded the headmaster into his house. He somehow managed to get a message to a local Justice of the Peace (JP),[4] via a military recruiting party who were staying at Rugby at the time. The JP turned up with armed soldiers and read the boys the Riot Act. The mutineers retreated to a moated island on the school grounds but the troops managed to surround and overcome them. With order restored, the ringleaders were expelled — nevertheless one of them

---

[4] A Justice of the Peace is a lay-magistrate, usually with no legal qualifications, appointed from upstanding members of the community.

went on to be a bishop — and many of the mutineers were flogged (Bradby, 1900, pp.44-46).

However, the public schools were turned around by certain ambitious headmasters, especially Thomas Arnold (1795-1842), from the 1830s onwards, with the introduction of modern subjects and a more systematic regime of discipline (Rose, 2002, p.177). By the 1860s, it was the day schools that were aping the public schools rather than the other way around (Wardle, 1970, p.119). By Sneyd-Kynnersley's time, a lucrative industry had developed in preparing the sons of affluent families for public school, an industry in which Sneyd-Kynnersley was a particularly successful player. As testimony to how highly regarded his school was, Winston Churchill, the grandson of a Duke,[5] was sent there in 1882. By the twentieth century, Britain was effectively run by old boys from prominent public schools. For example, almost all cabinet members during the period of Conservative government between 1951 and 1964 had been to public school (Scott, 2014), despite only 7% of the population attending private schools at the time and less than 4% attending public schools (Halsey et al., 1972, p.155). Prime Minister Harold MacMillan's (1894-1986) first cabinet — between 1957 and 1959 — had 18 members of which 17 had attended public school, and one a state-funded grammar school, which would have had an entrance exam. Eight members of this cabinet, including MacMillan himself, had been to Eton.

---

[5]   Ranks of the British nobility in ascending order of precedence: Baron/Lord (Baroness/Lady), Viscount (Viscountess), Earl (Countess), Marquis (Marchioness) and Duke (Duchess). The younger sons of Dukes and Marquises are accorded the prenominal 'Lord.' The unmarried daughters of Dukes, Marquises and Earls are accorded the prenominal 'Lady.' The peerage passes to the oldest legitimate male heir. Until 1999, all peers whose family had been ennobled as English or British peers sat in the House of Lords by hereditary right. The last Prime Minister to sit in the Lords for the whole of his premiership was the 3rd Marquess of Salisbury (1830-1903) whose third term as Prime Minister was from 1895 to 1902. From 1911 onwards, the House of Commons became formally dominant over the Lords. The last time a hereditary peer served as a senior cabinet minister was in the person of Lord Carrington (1919-2018) who was Foreign Secretary from 1979 to 1982.

'An Old Perv'?

Insomuch as Churchill made a point of writing History, the myths surrounding Sneyd-Kynnersley paint him very much as the Anti-Churchill. Anyone with even the slightest interest in Churchill knows that Sneyd-Kynnersley was an archetypal sadist and child abuser who administered frequent and extremely severe floggings to the bare bottoms of the terrified boys, mainly aged 8 to 13, in his charge. In his book *The English Vice: Beating, Sex and Shame in Victorian England and After*, Irish historian Ian Gibson (1978, p.69) writes of Sneyd-Kynnersley that 'even his name sounds sadistic.' Public schools, finds Gibson, and the preparatory schools that prepared children for them, were rife with ferocious beatings, but Sneyd-Kynnersley was somehow in a league of his own.

This reaction to Sneyd-Kynnersley is unsurprising. Churchill is England's national hero. As we will see, many of the biographies of Churchill are nothing more than hagiographies that rehash and exaggerate the adulation for him in earlier hagiographies. Churchill has become central to a model of England — which begins with World War II — as a 'modern,' outward-looking country which stood alone against the evil Nazis. This 'Cult of Churchill' means that enemies of Churchill are Devil-like figures, anathematized by the Church itself. Sneyd-Kynnersley is just such a figure. Churchill, and Churchill's son Randolph, and other Churchill relatives, have proclaimed Sneyd-Kynnersley as demonic and, therefore, he is. No story about his sadism and perversion is too unbelievable. This hideous picture of him does not need to be calmly assessed; the sources about him do not need to be held up to scrutiny. To do so would be akin to questioning the Churchill Cult itself.

This has led to numerous myths, even with regard to Sneyd-Kynnersley's age. British politician Boris Johnson, himself an Old Etonian, in his book The Churchill Factor (2014), refers to Sneyd-Kynnersley as 'a High Anglican old perv who used to give the boys twenty strokes of the cane — drawing blood on the third — for the slightest infraction.' The idea, though not necessarily inaccurate, that such headmasters gained some kind of sexual pleasure out of these beatings has been articulated more and more as spanking has become decreasingly socially acceptable — and increasingly illegal — in Europe, currently being banned in every European country except the UK, the Czech Republic and Switzerland (Samuel, 3rd January 2017). Johnson's description, however, reflects and adds to misunderstandings about Sneyd-Kynnersley. Johnson has presumably garnered his knowledge from certain secondary sources (specifically Roger Fry's recollections, which have been paraphrased in numerous Churchill biographies without reference to Fry's name) which he has amalgamated with his own memories of the 1972 film Young Winston (Attenborough, 1972). The film was based on Churchill's son's extensive biography of his father (Churchill, 1966). This was itself partly based on Churchill's autobiography My Early Life: A Roving Commission (Churchill, 1930), which was published in 1930; Churchill already being a household name by then as a war hero, writer, former Chancellor of the Exchequer,6 and influential cabinet minister during World War I. In this film, Sneyd-Kynnersley was played by Robert Hardy (1925-2017), a Rugby old boy who was, at that time, 47 years old, looked older, and, in one scene, wielded a cane to a pupil's bare bottom. In fact, Sneyd-Kynnersley died at the age of just 38, used the (far more painful, and likely to draw blood) birch, but, as we will see, did not use it for 'the slightest infraction,' at least not by the standards of the time.

In this book, the myths surrounding both Sneyd-Kynnersley and his colossus of a pupil will be dissected and found to be seriously wanting. I will show that Churchill was essentially a high functioning psychopath who led Britain into the abyss and I will demonstrate that Churchill's 'demon headmaster' should be differently appraised. He likely suffered from some form of arrested development. However, he was not an archetypal sadist but rather a fetishist and a non-practicing pederast. There perhaps was a sublimated homosexual element to his flogging. But we will see that these remarks could be made about many prep and public school headmasters until relatively recently and many masters beat their charges far more harshly than did Sneyd-Kynnersley, sexually abused them as well, and, unlike Churchill's headmaster, treated pupils extremely unfairly. I will show that Sneyd-Kynnersley did not flog his pupils for 'the

---

6 Finance Minister.

slightest infraction' (which many other headmasters did), he did not beat children with anything like the severity that people now believe; Churchill was not withdrawn from St George's, Ascot, simply due to the harshness of the beatings, as many have argued; the school did not close because rumours of these supposedly uniquely harsh thrashings got out; and the worst (and most commonly believed) stories about Sneyd-Kynnersley's supposed brutality come from the most unreliable sources.

From the most reliable sources, we will find that Sneyd-Kynnersley was a highly educated, inspiring and devoted educationalist. I will demonstrate that, to some extent, Sneyd-Kynnersley's methods can be understood as an example of the profound conservatism which he believed was vital to saving civilization itself. We will see that he was right, and that they almost did. If Churchill had not been withdrawn from St George's, then Sneyd-Kynnersley would have broken him down and rebuilt him as a gentleman, with greater self-control and selflessness. Consequently, there likely would have been no World War II, no collapse of British influence, and no descent into nihilism. This eccentric and much maligned headmaster very nearly saved the British Empire and Britain itself.

The Way Ahead

In this chapter we will see how much worse than Sneyd-Kynnersley many other teachers were, especially in terms of corporal punishment, and how, unlike many such teachers, Sneyd-Kynnersley did not sexually abuse his pupils. In Chapters Two and Three we will explore Sneyd-Kynnersley's background, family and life in depth: his daredevil MP elder brother, his involvement in radical reactionary church politics, and his part in the scandalous removal of a leading headmaster. Chapter Four will involve a detailed assessment of what Sneyd-Kynnersley was like as a person and of experiences of life at his school, based on the available primary sources. We will also get to know some of the other intriguing men who attended or who taught at the school. These will include Sneyd-Kynnersley's brother-in-law, the Rev. Robert Estcourt Macdonald (1854-1923); sportsman and

British Vice-Consul in Austria who contracted two failed marriages to wealthy women, dispensed with the mess of flogging in favour of electrocution, and whose heinous behaviour forced him to flee the country. In Chapter Five, we will assess the reliability of these different primary sources, and find that Sneyd-Kynnersley's infamy as a sadist is as a result of the least reliable of them.

In Chapter Six we will analyse Sneyd-Kynnersley's psychology, and in particular evidence of personality and sexual disorders such as arrested development and sadism. In Chapter Seven, drawing upon research in anthropology and psychology, we will make sense of the less congenial aspects of the public school system as being part of a latter day tribal rite of passage, aimed at fostering a warrior class. In Chapter Eight, we will debunk the myths about Churchill's time at St George's and note that his behaviour showed every indication of a high placing in terms both of intelligence and psychopathic personality. Chapter Nine will involve an objective assessment of Churchill's psychology. We will find, just as was predicted by his childhood, that he was, in effect, a highly intelligent Narcissist and psychopath. In Chapter Ten, we will show that the war which Churchill spearheaded, underpinned by this psychology, was unnecessary, ruinous and directly led to the collapse of the British Empire, to Britain's decline, and to all that has stemmed from that, including the Balkanization of Britain itself.

Finally, in Chapter Eleven, we will see that Sneyd-Kynnersley's life was motivated by a desire to halt, or at least slow down, this decline, and we will show that had he been given just a little more time with Churchill, he likely would have been able to do so. Had Sneyd-Kynnersley acted very slightly differently then there may well have been no Winston Churchill and no Second World War. But let us begin by examining some seriously terrible schoolteachers, against whom Sneyd-Kynnersley's severity pales in comparison.

Some Truly Dreadful Teachers

The first myth, then, is that Sneyd-Kynnersley was a uniquely 'perverted sadist' (Leslie, 1969, p.97) – a myth strongly promoted by Churchill himself as we will see below. Let's compare Sneyd-Kynnersley to some of his brother schoolmasters. Doing so immediately places Sneyd-Kynnersley in a far more positive light.

There is no evidence that Sneyd-Kynnersley ever engaged in what we would now call statutory rape of a boy, though, as we will see, one particularly unreliable ex-pupil makes this claim. However, in his book on abuse at prep and public schools, *Stiff Upper Lip*, journalist Alex Renton (2017), himself an Old Etonian, introduces novelist Evelyn Waugh's (1903-1966) colleague W.R.B. 'Dick' Young (1894-1971), who taught with him at Arnold House, a prep school in Llanddulas in North Wales. This man's teaching career was entirely motivated by a desire to have access to prepubescent boys with whom he could have anal intercourse. As Renton quotes from Waugh:

'. . . Expelled from Wellington [*in Berkshire*], sent down from Oxford, and forced to resign his commission in the army. He had left four schools precipitately, three in the middle of term, through his being taken in sodomy and one through his being drunk six nights in succession. And yet he goes on getting better and better jobs without difficulty.'

When Waugh went for a drink with this pederast prep school teacher in 1926, Young 'seduced a garage boy in the hedge.' Renton provides us with cases of men who suffered so terribly at the hands of their schoolmasters that they never got over it and ultimately committed suicide. Historian Jonathan Gathorne-Hardy (1978, p.111) also notes many cases of prep school boys being so frightened and unhappy that they took their own lives. I can find no evidence of this among Sneyd-Kynnersley's known pupils from the 1881 census, although suicide was so socially unacceptable in the late nineteenth and early twentieth centuries that the coroner would have been more likely to direct the jury towards an open verdict to avoid bringing shame on the grieving family (Cox & Luddy, 2010, p.84). Renton gives many other examples, such as a master found to have been 'feeling a child's penis.'

Many 'old boys' actually describe their prep school days in rather more unpleasant terms than do former pupils at St George's, whose descriptions will be presented later. In *The Old School Tie,* Jonathan Gathorne-Hardy (1978, p.111) gives us the poet Stephen Spender's (1909-1995) wry summary of his own prep school: 'They might as well have had me educated at a brothel for flagellants.' Gathorne-Hardy, who attended the public school Bryanston, also observes that being beaten made you very popular among your classmates. It meant you were brave and there was an extent to which you had 'taken one for the team' as a kind of scapegoat: everyone was naughty but you had been found out and you hadn't grassed. Children would proudly show off the wounds from their thrashings (p.112). As we have seen, the standard Sneyd-Kynnersley flogging was, assuming the recollections of the art critic Roger Fry (1866-1934) are accurate (which is doubtful, as we will discover later), between 15 and 20 strokes of the birch. There is evidence that many prep schools exceeded this level of violence. At a prep school in Clapham in south London in around 1870 a boy of twelve, who would not submit to a birching, was given, by his headmistress, 'a sound caning across his shoulders' for disobedience until he bent over. This was followed immediately by six strokes of the birch on his bare bottom, after which the boy jumped up and refused to let her continue. She caned his shoulders until he bent over again. She finished her birching and then had her sister, also a teacher at the school, birch him again the next day for the original offence, presumably re-opening the previous day's wounds in the process. The sisters administered this treatment many more times until the boy learnt to obey them without question (*Appleton's Journal,* 1870, p.498).

There is also no suggestion that Sneyd-Kynnersley's beatings were sufficiently harsh as to have broken the law of the time. Edward Lockwood (1834-1903) wrote, in 1893, of a flogging administered to him at Marlborough (in Wiltshire) that: 'A village schoolmaster now-a-days would get a month at the treadmill, with a sinister caution as to his future behaviour, if he beat a boy as I was beaten at school . . .' (Lockwood, 1893, p.26). Sneyd-Kynnersley's floggings were nowhere near as cruel as one meted out by a particular East Sussex headmaster. In 1860, at 'a private school of the highest class' in Eastbourne, on England's southern coast, 'a mentally deficient boy of good family, Reginald Cancellor, was beaten to death by

Mr. Hopley' (Gibson, 1978, p.70). According to literature scholar Jenny Holt (2016), Thomas Hopley (1819-1876), the headmaster, was known as a humanitarian. He had campaigned for 'reduced working hours for the poor' and had even published a few scientific papers. However, he wasn't a very good special needs teacher. On 21st April 1860, Hopley had beaten Reginald Cancellor (1844-1860), who was 15, with a thick stick, and also with a skipping rope, continuously for two hours, having the boy bent over a staircase. When he'd finished, Hopley had carried Cancellor — who was unconscious but, claimed Hopley, alive — to bed, before he set about cleaning up his stairs, which were covered in blood. When Hopley discovered, supposedly the following morning, that the boy was dead, he wrapped up the corpse and had it conveyed to the boy's father, telling the boy's father — who was a lawyer — that his son had died of a heart attack. Hopley's maids, however, reported the blood-drenched sheets.

Hopley was put on trial for murder. The defence argued that the beating was justified because Cancellor, who had hydrocephalus ('water on the brain') and was thus mentally retarded (Cinalli et al., 2012), had been unable to do some arithmetic and was 'obstinate' and 'slow.' The father had given written permission for his son to be beaten, if the headmaster deemed it necessary, two days prior to the incident. And, anyway, Hopley was 'a gentleman.' The prosecution noted that Cancellor's limbs had been beaten to a 'pulp.' The judge reduced the charge to manslaughter because Hopley was in a position of parental responsibility, and the headmaster was sentenced to 4 years' penal servitude. Based on this precedent, the Lord Chief Justice,[7] Sir Alexander Cockburn (1802-1880) later asserted that parents and those in loco parentis had the right, under English law, 'to inflict moderate and reasonable corporal punishment – always with this condition, that it is reasonable and moderate' (Holt, 2016). After his release, Hopley's wife managed to obtain a divorce and Hopley moved to Bloomsbury in London where he worked as a private tutor and campaigned against the rise of spiritualism (Moore, 2018). Hopley was, briefly, a media hate figure in the UK. But only a month after his trial had concluded, the newspapers'

[7] The Lord Chief Justice was, at that time, the second most senior judge in England and Wales, after the Lord Chancellor who was head of the judiciary.

attention turned to a school mistress who had punished a pupil by badly burning her arms (Middleton, 2005).

Sneyd-Kynnersley, as we will see in more detail later, had a dark side to his character, but it pales almost into insignificance compared to some of the people who have taught at English boarding schools, particularly during the Victorian Era. Not only is there no evidence Sneyd-Kynnersley sexually abused anyone, there is also no evidence that he broke the law, let alone beat someone to death and then tried to cover it up, nor did he burn anybody. We also have to remember how violent late nineteenth century England was. Almost everybody beat their children, usually with a stick, a slipper, or a strap, yet they would still be considered, in most cases, loving parents (Frost, 2008). Flogging was not an uncommon punishment for criminals. It was only abolished as a judicial punishment in 1948 and was last used to punish an errant prisoner in 1962 (Leslie, 2014). Until 1861 a master could legally whip his servant (Gleadle, 2001, p.12), until 1878 a husband had the right to beat his wife (Shanley, 1993, p.170), and Mid-Victorian school punishments included roasting: holding a boy in front of a fire until he fainted (Marshall, 2013, p.114). It is against this kind of background that somebody like Sneyd-Kynnersley needs to be understood.

In addition, as we will see below, although Sneyd-Kynnersley had 'favourites,' as most teachers do, he did not let this influence what his pupils would regard as 'justice.' Algernon Ferguson (1867-1943), whom we will meet shortly, was one of the headmaster's favourites, as is clear from the fact that he was one of the current pupils who received a bequest in Sneyd-Kynnersley's will. But, clearly, nevertheless, when this favourite — who, as we will see, bullied another boy — did something for which other pupils would be flogged then, despite being a favourite, he was still flogged. It has been demonstrated empirically that children have a particularly strong sense of justice (Conry-Murray, 2015). Research has found that where corporal punishment, such as spanking, is the norm and children have transgressed the rules they often accept that they deserve the punishment and regard it as just (Addington-Dawson & Gettys, 1935, p.91). However, they find unjust punishment, or unjust absence of punishment, acutely intolerable. In that sense, from a child's perspective, Sneyd-Kynnersley was far more reasonable than the Rev. Charles William Hunt (1859-1935), headmaster of Cordwalles School near Maidenhead, also in Berkshire. Sneyd-Kynnersley was fair; he even beat boys he particularly liked if they deserved it. Hunt indulged in obvious favouritism and treated some boys unfairly 'which although less of a crime to humanitarian reformers of corporal punishment, to the school boy, is an even more serious offence than wielding justice with the cane' (Leinster-Mackay, 1971, p.94).

The Talented Mr Sneyd-Kynnersley?

To those who can be relied upon, Sneyd-Kynnersley was apparently an inspiring teacher; he did all that he could to instil these upper class children — these one-day rulers of the Empire — with a sense of responsibility and with boundaries. He steered them well away from ways of thinking that would damage his beloved British Empire. And he perhaps understood that the son of a household name, the Old Etonian Lord Randolph Churchill (1849-1895), would likely end up with power. So, it had to be ensured that Winston was instilled with a sense of acceptable behaviour, or there could be serious consequences.

As I will show as the book progresses, we cannot compare Sneyd-Kynnersley even to a modern day prep school headmaster, let alone to one of a non-private ('state') school. It was understood at the time that schools such as Sneyd-Kynnersley's — which was the most expensive prep school in the country — aimed, as did public schools, to do more than simply teach children to read, write and do sums. Part of their purpose was to mould extremely privileged boys, who had materially never really wanted for anything, into suitable men to run the British Empire. In many respects, the schools were akin to the brutal rites of passage into adulthood that are undergone by boys, as they turn into men, in many tribal societies. These boys, like almost all boys in such tribes, were their societies' future warriors and they had to be *made* into warriors: people who would obey authority, keep their emotions under control, endure physical pain, be mentally resilient, live for the future rather than the now, make sacrifices for others and deeply empathise with them, but have the ability to act lethally towards the enemy at the precisely appropriate moment. Though there is much that may now repulse us about Sneyd-Kynnersley's regime, this 'rite of passage' dimension needs to be borne in mind and we will later explore it in depth.

But now that we have debunked the myth that Sneyd-Kynnersley was a uniquely aberrant school master, let us turn to the man himself. Who was the Rev. Herbert William Sneyd-Kynnersley? How did he end up as Churchill's headmaster?

Chapter Two

Aristocratic Background,

School Days & Cambridge

St George's Day, 1848

ERBERT WILLIAM SNEYD-KYNNERSLEY was born on 23rd April — St George's Day — 1848 at Loxley Hall, his father's family's eighteenth century mansion just outside Uttoxeter.[8] Mentioned in the Domesday Book,[9] Uttoxeter is a picturesque market town in Staffordshire in the English West Midlands. This small settlement – the population on the 2011 census was just over 13,000 - is best known as the site of the last Royalist surrender during the English Civil War, this capitulation having taken place on 25th August 1648. The town centre retains a number of Elizabethan buildings which would have been standing at the time, though it is now dominated by Georgian and Victorian red brick houses. Uttoxeter is the nearest town to the popular Alton Towers theme park.

---

[8]   On the 1881 census, Sneyd-Kynnersley gave his place of birth as 'Loxley Park' and thus, by implication, Loxley Hall.

[9]   This was a census of land and population, conducted in 1086.

In 1848, however, themes in the UK were rather more serious. 1848, as in much of Europe, was a year of high drama, marked by serious food shortages. Amid an uprising, the French king abdicated and escaped to England. An enormous rally was held in Kennington Park, in London, demanding the extension of the franchise. Famine swept Ireland, while the, only recently fully emancipated, Roman Catholics in England began to assert themselves with the establishment of the first ever English-speaking oratory. More prosaically, the railways continued to expand, with London's famous Waterloo Station being officially opened on 11th July. In piecing the life of Churchill's headmaster together, I have drawn upon various unpublished primary sources, such as parish records of christenings, marriages, and burials; public records of birth, marriage and death; the English census, which has occurred every decade since 1841;[10] wills; probate summaries; and documents in the national and relevant county and school archives.

Ancient Ancestry

Herbert Sneyd-Kynnersley was christened at the church in Uttoxeter on 24th May 1848, almost exactly a month after his birth. He was the sixth of nine children of Thomas Clement Sneyd-Kynnersley (1803-1892), then of Highwood, near Uttoxeter and his wife (Eliza) Rose Sandars (1813-1860). Like Churchill, Sneyd-Kynnersley was from an aristocratic background. His father's family were armigerous gentry. The gentry were a kind of lower nobility of gentleman farmers. The 'armigerous gentry,' which included baronets,[11] had the hereditary right, by legitimate male-line descent, to use a coat of arms, whereas the non-armigerous gentry merely had the lifestyle of the gentry, being regarded as 'gentlemen' by public renown. The armigerous gentry also included the younger sons of peers who, having no title,

---

[10]   Due to the War, there was no census in 1941. There was, however, a *de facto* census, the 1939 Register, in September 1939, conducted precisely because the country had just gone to war.

[11]   A baronetcy is a hereditary knighthood which is beneath the rank of baron but above the rank of knight.

became part of the gentry. The wealthier armigerous gentry, as well as barristers (who were mostly from gentry backgrounds), had, until the mid-nineteenth century, exclusive use of the post-nominal 'Esquire,' unless they happened to be knighted (Coss, 2003). By the mid-nineteenth century, however, all gentry were 'Esquire' and coat armour was widely misappropriated (Fox-Davies, 1900).

Loxley Hall

The headmaster's ancestry was far less illustrious than Churchill's, unless you count being a proven descendant of King Edward III as part of his background, a fact which was published in 1907 in the genealogical book *Plantagenet Roll of the Blood Royal* (Raineval, 1903).[12] However, Sneyd-Kynnersley's pedigree was also far more ancient than Churchill's. Churchill — whose surname was actually Spencer-Churchill — was the son of the future Chancellor of the Exchequer and the grandson of the 7th Duke of Marlborough, who had himself been a cabinet minister. The Churchill family rose to prominence under the general John Churchill (1650-1722), a member of the armigerous gentry who was made Duke of Marlborough for his military efforts. As Marlborough had no sons, the peerage was created such that it could pass through the female line if necessary. John Churchill's daughter, Lady Anne Churchill (1683-1716), had

---

[12] This series of volumes attempted to record every known living descendant of the fourteenth century king.

married Charles Spencer, 3rd Earl of Sutherland (1675-1722). Their son, another Charles Spencer (1706-1758), had succeeded his aunt to become 3rd Duke of Marlborough. Presumably in honour of his illustrious ancestor, in 1817, the 5th Duke of Marlborough, George Spencer-Churchill (1766-1840), changed the family surname to Spencer-Churchill.

The Spencer family emerged from obscurity in 1504 when the non-armigerous Northamptonshire gentleman John Spencer was granted a coat of arms. His background was that of 'yeoman.' Yeomen were wealthy farmers directly beneath the gentry (Round, 1901), who engaged in some labour themselves. Together with husbandmen (who would likely take to the plough themselves), merchants, professionals and craftsmen, they made up the 'middling sort' (see Dutton, 2015, Ch. 2). Although a corrupt herald from the College of Arms, which regulated the use of coat armour, produced a pedigree connecting John Spencer to the ancient family of the same name during the reign of James I (r. 1603-1625) (Pearson, 2011), this has been shown to be bogus; an attempt by the Spencer family to disguise its parvenu origins (Round, 1901). The heralds were notoriously corrupt, happy to dig up (that is, forge) long lost documents 'proving' ancient lineage if the price was right (Corfield, 1996). Many families, like the Spencers, emerged from the 'middling sort' to join the ranks of the gentry in the wake of the chaos of the Wars of the Roses (Round, 1901).

Sneyd-Kynnersley's family, by contrast, had been aristocratic, in the male line, all the way back to the end of the Dark Ages. As a Victorian armigerous gentleman, Sneyd-Kynnersley would have known about his family history in detail and, indeed, according to his ex-pupil Roger Fry, he was very proud of it; ancient lineage being an important status symbol in Victorian England (Abbott, 1993, p.41). Sneyd-Kynnersley's grandfather was Thomas Sneyd-Kynnersley the elder (1774-1844), Lord of the Manor of Loxley.[13] He was a gentleman

---

[13] 'Lord,' in this context, was a form of semi-defunct feudal ownership whereby if you purchased an ancient manor, which had existed since the Medieval era, you were its 'lord.' You held the manor either from a 'tenant-in-chief' or, if you were a tenant-in-chief, directly from the monarch, traditionally in return for performing knightly service or paying a fee. Around the thirteenth century, the wealthiest

farmer, Justice of the Peace and Deputy Lieutenant[14] of Staffordshire (Burke, 1882, p.915). Thomas had been born plain Thomas Sneyd, but he had changed his surname when he inherited a large estate from his maternal uncle. Thomas' mother was Penelope Kynnersley (1740-1776), daughter of the gentleman farmer and naval officer Thomas Kynnersley of Loxley Park (1714-1755). Loxley Park was inherited by Thomas Kynnersley's son, Clement Kynnersley (1744-1815). Clement, who lived in Carshalton in Surrey, had no children. So he willed Loxley Park, as well as his estate in Surrey, to his nephew Thomas Sneyd (later Sneyd-Kynnersley), grandfather of the headmaster (Burke, 1847, p.1261; London Borough of Sutton, LG6/8/1/11).

Thomas Sneyd-Kynnersley's life was marred by tragedy, with him outliving many of his children. His family is a poignant testimony to the extent of child and more general mortality at the time and is thus worth briefly exploring. On 10th December 1795, Thomas Sneyd-Kynnersley married Maria Stokes Kynnersley (1774-1800), who was presumably some kind of cousin, though I cannot find her christening record. Cousin marriage was 'quite common' among the Victorian nobility and gentry because there was such a strong desire to 'marry within one's own social circle' that although 'some concern about the potential negative effects of inbreeding existed, xenophobia often outweighed it' (Nelson, 2007, p.135). They had two sons, Clement Sneyd (1796-1797) and Clement John Sneyd-Kynnersley (1800-1840) whose own son eventually inherited Loxley Park. They also had two daughters (Burke, 1879, p.945), both born in London: Matilda Sneyd-Kynnersley (1797-1816) and Eliza Sneyd-Kynnersley (1799-1873), a spinster.

In 1802, Thomas Sneyd-Kynnersley married again, to Harriet Potts (1778-1860), a watercolourist whose paintings reveal that the couple holidayed in Croatia, Austria, Italy, Switzerland and France (Somerset & Wood, 2018). With Harriet, he fathered a further three sons, all of whom had the middle name Clement, in honour of his

---

tenants-in-chief (or barons), who had court connections, evolved into the peerage. The lesser lords evolved into the gentry (Coss, 2003). The head of a prominent nineteenth century armigerous gentry family was usually a 'lord of the manor.'

14 The Lord Lieutenant is the sovereign's representative in a county. A Deputy Lieutenant (DL) is his deputy.

uncle. The eldest was the headmaster's father. The Head's father was followed by John Clement Sneyd-Kynnersley (1807-1836), who was a solicitor (*Observer,* 1ˢᵗ June 1835, p.1), and the Rev. Edmund Clement Sneyd-Kynnersley (1812-1841), who was rector[15] of Draycott in Staffordshire (*The Gentleman's Magazine,* 1841, p.215). According to *Burke's Landed Gentry* (Burke, 1879, p.945), Thomas had five daughters by his second marriage but I can only find evidence of four, so one may have died before being christened, likely Sarah Sneyd (1813-1814) who was buried at Uttoxeter. Regarding the four sisters: Mary Anne Sneyd-Kynnersley (1808-1832) married her distant relative the Rev. Henry Sneyd (1804-1859), vicar of Wetley Rocks in Staffordshire, in February 1831, and died in March the following year, possibly due to complications caused by giving birth to their daughter Jane Sneyd (1832-1848), who was christened in February that year. Harriet Sneyd-Kynnersley (1811-1889) married the Rev. Prof John James Blunt (1794-1855) in 1852 but was soon widowed by the Cambridge University Lady Margaret Professor of Divinity. Barbara Clementina Sneyd-Kynnersley (1814-1829) died as a teenager and Catherine Sneyd-Kynnersley (1817-1868) married the Rev. Christopher Smyth (1813-1897), vicar of Little Houghton in Northamptonshire in the East Midlands, in 1850 and had two children.

In 1815, Thomas finally inherited Loxley Park from his maternal uncle, Clement Kynnersley, but only on condition that he add Kynnersley to his surname. He was duly allowed to quarter his coat of arms, to reflect both armigerous family names (Burke, 1835, p.166). This tradition - of gentry families dying out in the male line with the final male representative bequeathing the estate to his sister's son on condition of that son continuing the surname – had begun in the eighteenth century and is the origin of many English double-barrelled surnames (Coates, 1998, p.349). Herbert Sneyd-Kynnersley's grandfather was heavily involved in local Tory (Conservative) Party politics (Warwickshire Archive, CR 2747/88).

---

[15] By 1868, *Rector* was synonymous with *Vicar* and simply meant the priest in charge of a parish and its church. Prior to that, a *Rector* was a priest to whom all the parish tithes passed, whereas a *Vicar,* upon receiving the tithes, had to pass them to a religious house or manorial lord.

Indeed, the Sneyd family had been running parts of England all the way back to the Norman Conquest.

Thomas-Sneyd-Kynnersley was the grandson of William Sneyd of Bishton in Staffordshire (1693-1745), who was Tory MP for Lichfield in 1718. William Sneyd was descended from William Sneyd of Keele, near Stoke-on-Trent (c.1614-1695), who had been High Sheriff of Staffordshire under Charles II (r. 1660-1685) (Burke, 1835, p.168) and MP for Staffordshire in 1660 (Helms & Mimardiere, 1983). In a period where political power was far more localized and parliament far less influential, William Sneyd's father and grandfather were also sheriffs of Staffordshire, the latter, Ralph Sneyd of Keele, having built Keele Hall around 1590. Ralph's father, Richard Sneyd, was the Recorder of Chester, in the north west close to Wales, from 1518 to 1533 (Thornton, 2000, p.92). Following this Sneyd male line back, we eventually reach Henry de Sneyd of Tunstall, Staffordshire, who was alive in 1310 (Ward, 1843, pp.82-83) and inherited Tunstall in right of his wife (Ward, pp.78-79). Henry de Sneyd descended from Richard de Sneyd, who was living at the beginning of the thirteenth century, and from there back the surname was de Auditheley or de Audley, which can be traced all the way back to the Norman Conquest (Hatcher, 1910, pp.6-8), Audley being a village in Staffordshire feudally held by a Norman.

While Winston Churchill's ancestors were tilling the soil in Northamptonshire, Sneyd-Kynnersley's were running Staffordshire and Cheshire. While Winston Churchill's ancestors were milking cows, Sneyd-Kynnersley's were helping to engineer the fall of Cheshire's *de facto* ruler, William Brereton (c.1490-1536), who was executed for adultery with Anne Boleyn (Thornton, 2000, p.206). While Winston Churchill's ancestors were busily engaged in bribing a herald to concoct a more impressive family tree (Pearson, 2011), Sneyd-Kynnersley's were enforcing law and order in Staffordshire.

Joseph Sandars and a Difficult Year for the Family

Thomas Clement Sneyd-Kynnersley (1803-1892), father of the headmaster, was a barrister, judge, and magistrate. He had married (Eliza) Rose Sandars on 4th June 1834 at St Mary's, Edge Hill, in Lancashire. Significantly, this was an Anglican church. Rose, however, was the daughter of corn merchant Joseph Sandars (1785-1860) and his wife Anna McKenzie Richards (1781-1853), a Liverpool girls' boarding school mistress whom Sandars married in 1812 (Rideout, 1991). Joseph Sandars was a Liverpool Unitarian, and Rose was christened in Liverpool's Paradise Street Unitarian Chapel on 17th November 1813. This form of extreme-liberal non-Conformist Christianity — which rejects the Trinity couldn't have been much further from the traditionalist High Church Anglicanism which Herbert was later to adopt. The High Church tends to stress ritual, sacraments and Anglican continuity with the Catholic Church, whereas the Low Church emphasises Protestant belief, evangelicalism, personal conversion and morality (Reed, 2000), as we will explore in more detail shortly.

On the night of the 1851 census, which was 30th March, Joseph Sandars was living in Taplow in Buckinghamshire, coincidentally a village where Churchill would attend a party as a relatively old man, where he 'let himself be pushed into the river and swam about in a top-hat with much composure' (Leslie, 1966, p.27). However, Taplow was also where Joseph Sandars had his estate in 1851 and his young grandsons, Herbert and Charles Walter Sneyd-Kynnersley (1849-1904), were staying with him. Sandars marked his occupation as 'Merchant,' but Sandars was a remarkably important merchant. His money had been vital to enabling civil engineer George Stephenson (1781-1848) — known as the 'Father of Railways' — to construct the first English railway. Sandars had underwritten the project: 'In 1824 he was a Deputy Chairman of the Liverpool & Manchester Rail-road Company and in 1826 he was elected a Director of the Liverpool and Manchester Railway Company' (Liverpool Record Office, 385 JAM/2/1).

Joseph Sandars (Centre)

Herbert Sneyd-Kynnersley stressed his aristocratic credentials, emblazoning his school with the Sneyd-Kynnersley coat of arms. Roger Fry was a pupil at St George's, Ascot under Sneyd-Kynnersley between 1877 and 1880, after which he attended Clifton School in Bristol and then Cambridge University. According to Fry:

'Mr Sneyd-Kynnersley had aristocratic connections. His double name was made even more impressive by an elaborate coat of arms with two creats, one of the Sneyd and the other of the Kynnersley, which appeared in all sorts of places about the house and was stamped in gold on the bindings of the prizes' (Woolf, 1940, p.31)

The Sneyd-Kynnersley Coat of Arms

Here we find a point in common with Churchill. The war-leader's nobleman father — a younger son, unlikely to ever inherit the Dukedom — had married Jennie Jerome (1854-1921), the daughter of an American financier. Socially, he had 'married down' and he had married money. Sneyd-Kynnersley's father had followed the same well-worn path of the younger son of the aristocrat who marries 'trade'. Thomas Sneyd-Kynnersley was, like Lord Randolph Churchill, a second son, unlikely to ever inherit Loxley Park, so he had married the daughter of a Non-Conformist Lancashire merchant.

Herbert Sneyd-Kynnersley was the antithesis of his grandfather in many fundamental ways. Joseph Sandars was a Unitarian and later a Quaker, as, incidentally, was Roger Fry. Quakers tended to oppose corporal punishment and in 1839 it was abolished in all Quaker schools (O'Donnell, 2013). Sandars was a Whig (Liberal), in favour of extending the voting franchise, and he was a wealthy corn merchant (Thomas, 1980, p.13). By contrast, Sneyd-Kynnersley was a High Church Tory and a conservative who was obsessed with Latin, Greek and books rather than money. Interestingly, Sandars' namesake son, Joseph Sandars, MP (1824-1893), was a Tory, rather than Whig, MP (Disraeli, 1982, p.231; Dell, 2007, p.120). Cementing his father's social ascent, Joseph Sandars, MP, went to Cambridge, became a barrister and married the daughter of the 2nd Marquess of Headfort, an Irish peer.[16]

The brothers were seemingly staying with their grandfather because their family had been plunged into crisis. The family's eldest son, John Clement Sneyd-Kynnersley (1837-1851) had died, aged 13, on 18th February 1851 at Budleigh Salterton, a small town on the south Devon coast then in the parish of East Budleigh, 15 miles from Exeter (*North Devon Journal,* 27th February 1851, p.8). He was presumably attending prep school there. As Gathorne-Hardy (1977, p.110) has pointed out, 'Death in Victorian schools was extremely common, particularly in the first twenty years of the reign;' the chief causes being disease, primitive medicine and suicide (p.111). When John died it was definitely term time because his older sister Barbara Sneyd-Kynnersley (1835-1895) and younger sister (Anna Catherine) Emily Sneyd-Kynnersley (1843-1922) were both, according to the 1851 census, at Southlands, a girls' boarding school in Heavitree, near Exeter, and John's younger brother, Edmund McKenzie Sneyd-Kynnersley (1841-1933), was at the 31 pupil Rodwell Academy in Weymouth. On the 1851 census, Herbert's older brother, Thomas Alfred Sneyd-Kynnersley (1839-1874), was the only sibling with his parents. They were staying at the house of Herbert's paternal grandmother, Harriet Potts. In that it was term time, this would potentially be consistent with Thomas Alfred Sneyd-Kynnersley

---

[16] An Irish Peer is a peer who was not (unless elected) entitled to sit in the House of Lords. When the Irish House of Lords was abolished in 1800, prior to the 1801 Act of Union, Irish peers began to elect 28 'Irish Representative Peers' to represent them in the British House of Lords. However, Irish peerages continued to be created as honours until 1868. This meant that someone could be granted a peerage but still sit in the House of Commons. Viscount Palmerston (1784-1865), who was twice Prime Minister in the mid-nineteenth century, was an Irish Peer who sat in the Commons. Until 1963 it was impossible to disclaim a peerage.

having been allowed home from school because his brother had recently died at that same school.

As if this tragedy wasn't enough for Herbert's mother to worry about, Rose Sneyd-Kynnersley was about six months pregnant at the time. Herbert's younger brother, Henry Francis Sneyd-Kynnersley (1851-1900) was born in Exeter on 22nd June 1851, presumably when his mother was returning one of his siblings to school. In 1857, it seems that history repeated itself. Harriet Virginia Sneyd-Kynnersley (1857-1936) was born near Exeter on 14th June that year (*Morning Chronicle*, 18th June 1857), probably when her mother was returning Emily Sneyd-Kynnersley to school. Southlands took pupils until at least the age of 16 according to the 1851 census.

Sneyd-Kynnersley's Father

Just as Churchill's father was an eminent politician, reaching the second highest office of state; Thomas Clement Sneyd-Kynnersley was successful in the Law. After Rugby, Thomas went to St John's College, Cambridge, in 1821, graduating in 1825. In 1824, he began training as a barrister at Middle Temple, a so-called Inn of Court, before being called to the bar in 1828. There is then a 4-year gap where all that is known is that he spent April to September 1830 on a 'Grand Tour' of Belgium, the Netherlands, Germany and Austria (Unpublished Primary Sources: Grand Tour), the 'Grand Tour' of Europe being popular among young gentry at the time (Mullen & Munsen, 2009, p.xii). Between 1832 and 1856, Thomas practiced on the Oxford circuit. Under the system of Assizes, the courts would travel around a particular area, trying serious crimes in various towns. In one of his more bizarre cases, Thomas was the prosecuting counsel in March 1848 at the Stafford trial of '*Francis* Bennett' whom the newspaper report implies was charged with bestiality: 'the day was occupied with cases of an abominable and most disgusting nature [some of which seem to involve bestiality], the details of which are totally unfit for publication.' An eye witness testified that he had seen Bennett engage in an 'unnatural offence' — unlike in other cases that day, no human is named as the one with whom the offence occurred — on 29ᵗʰ August 1847. The jury found Bennett guilty and the judge sentenced the prisoner to death (*Staffordshire Advertiser*, 18ᵗʰ March 1848, *cf.* Norton, 30ᵗʰ April 2017). In that there is no record of a Francis Bennett's death in Staffordshire in this period, the prisoner was likely a woman, Frances Bennett (1779-1851), who was in a 'lunatic asylum' on the 1851 census and died in December that year.

Thomas Clement Sneyd-Kynnersley by Henry Turner Munns

Thomas became a full-time stipendiary magistrate — a judge over less serious offences — in Birmingham in 1856, moving to 'The Leverets' on Soho Street in Handsworth on the outskirts of Birmingham. He was 'introduced to the town council' the same year (*The Eagle*, 1893, p.320). This meant that he became an Alderman, as this is how he is described on a painting of him which is held by Birmingham City Council. In 1858, Thomas was appointed a judge in the higher courts; the Recorder of Newcastle-Under-Lyme in Staffordshire. Then, in 1863, he was made Vice-Chairman of the Warwickshire Sessions. These 'Quarter Sessions' — transport being so much slower and less reliable back then — were also mobile, trying cases which required a jury, rather than simply magistrates, but which were not sufficiently serious to go before the Assizes (Foster, 1885). By 1871, he had moved to Moor Green in Kings Norton, just outside Birmingham. In his spare time, Thomas Clement Sneyd-Kynnersley was an active member of his local Masonic Lodge (*The Freemason's Chronicle*, 13th October 1883, p.229). He was also Deputy Lieutenant of Staffordshire and Worcestershire (*The Eagle*, 1893, p.320) and a history enthusiast, giving a talk to members of the 'Literary and Scientific Institution' on 'Robin Hood and His Times' in Uttoxeter Town Hall in 1859 (*Derbyshire Advertiser and Journal*, 4th March 1859).

The 'Spinster Crisis' and Evolutionary Psychology

When he died, in 1892, Thomas Clement was living with his two spinster daughters Emily and Harriet Virginia Sneyd-Kynnersley. Upon their father's death, these sisters moved in with their bachelor brother Edmund McKenzie Sneyd-Kynnersley in Chester. Due to upper class males marrying later in order to first develop their careers and also due to opportunities for upper class males in the Empire, and the deaths of males in industrial accidents, there was something of a 'spinster crisis' in Victorian England (Jarvis, 2012, p.299). By 1901, women outnumbered men by approximately one million and there were 421,549 females, who had never been married, who were over the age of 45. This 'crisis' was particularly pronounced among the upper class because the women didn't want to 'marry down,' and it was higher status men who tended to delay marriage and then marry down and marry a younger woman, being more interested than females in beauty and youth in a partner than in status (Buss, 1989). Also, the higher a woman's social status was, the fewer acceptable jobs there were for her (Nelson, 2007, p.133), rendering her a drain on her family.

It is widely accepted in evolutionary psychology — the study of the evolution of the human mind — that females are evolved to select for male status, as in prehistory this bias would have ensured that they and their offspring, benefiting from the male's resources, would have been more likely to survive. Males, by contrast, select more for youth and beauty, as this is evidence of fertility and genetic health. The an essential aspect of beauty is symmetry, so if you've maintained a symmetrical phenotype in the face of childhood disease you must have a good immune system (as well as few asymmetry-causing mutations) meaning you're genetically healthy (Woodley of Menie et al., 2018a). Losing nothing from the sexual encounter, as they do not carry the child, it makes sense for males to be more promiscuous, place relatively little value on the females' resources, and to select for her fertility and health as evidenced in beauty and youth (Dutton, 2018).

The Elderly Archdeacon of Wiltshire and Clergyman-Tutors

The 1861 census took place on 7th April and there is every reason to think it was term time as the houses at Rugby school had their scholars in residence. Henry Francis Sneyd-Kynnersley was home with his father at the Leverets but he was at King Edward's School, Birmingham (*Marlborough College, School List*, 1865, p.38), so probably lived at home. The Leverets was 4 and a half miles from King Edward's School. Twelve year-old Herbert, and his 11-year-old brother Charles, however, were 'visitors' at 37 to 38 Liberty of the Close, near Salisbury Cathedral. This was the home of the Ven.

William Macdonald (1783-1862), who was Archdeacon[17] of Wiltshire, residentiary canon[18] of Salisbury Cathedral and vicar of Bishops Cannings. Also present were Macdonald's eldest son Frederick William, his younger son Robert Estcourt, and his daughter Flora Georgina.[19] These three siblings, there were five siblings in all,[20] all played important roles in Sneyd-Kynnersley's life, with him marrying the latter.

Entrance to Liberty of the Close, Salisbury

---

[17] An Archdeacon is a kind of deputy bishop with responsibility for clerical discipline in an area within a diocese. He is addressed as the Venerable rather than the normal clerical prenominal of Reverend.

[18] A Canon is either a priest who works at a cathedral (other than the Dean, who is in charge) or a priest who has been made an honorary canon of a cathedral in recognition of his service to the Church of England.

[19] Flora had presumably been named in honour of Flora Georgina Hadow (1814-1881), the cousin and wife of her half-brother the Rev. Douglas Macdonald who was vicar of West Alvington in Devon. Perhaps her half-sister-in-law was also her godmother.

[20] Also living there in 1861 were Flora's two sisters Eleanor Frances Macdonald (1851-1935) and Marion Kinneir Macdonald (1856-1940), neither of whom ever married.

In that it was term time, it appears that the Sneyd-Kynnersley brothers were being educated by Macdonald along with his own children. To be 'home educated' was not unknown for younger members of the nineteenth century gentry. The philosopher John Stuart Mill (1806-1873), for example, never went to school at all but was tutored at home by his father (Wilson, 2010). In addition, it was extremely common in Mid-Victorian England for clergymen to take-in boarder-pupils or run small boarding schools from their houses (Davidoff & Hall, 1987). Consistent with the hypothesis that the Sneyd-Kynnersley brothers were at Liberty of the Close to be educated, Macdonald's household in 1861 included a governess, Amelie Weber (b. c. 1839) from Wingen in France (close to the border with the Kingdom of Bavaria), as well as 'nursery governess' Minna Moyer (b. c. 1841) who was from Hanover.[21] Hiring German or French governesses was popular because it helped the children learn a foreign language, their foreignness was novel, it reduced the kind of social class tensions that might exist if a British governess was employed, and there were, at the time, many middle class refugees in England who had fled unrest in Germany and France (Hughes, 2001, p.105). Clearly, the 1861 census described the Sneyd-Kynnersley brothers as 'visitors,' but there were many mistakes on this census, including 'servants' being described as 'visitors' (Christian & Annal, 2014).

William Macdonald, an Oxford University educated Scotsman, was, at 77 years of age, one of the oldest clergymen in the diocese (Urban, July-December 1862, p.233). He had been ordained by his maternal uncle in 1806; this uncle, John Douglas (1721-1807), Bishop of Salisbury, being another Oxford-educated Scot (Chisholm, 1911, p.446). Macdonald was from a gentry background himself. His ancestors did not simply adopt the surname Macdonald because they were loyal to the head of the *de facto* protection racket that was the Clan MacDonald (Herman, 2007, Ch. 4), as so many members did in the lawless Highlands (Sellar, 2011, p.93). He was a linear

---

[21] Until German Unification in 1871, Germany was composed of various states, some of whom were in economic union with each other.

descendant of Archibald Mor MacDonald, Laird[22] of Sanda, and of Archibald's son and heir Alexander, both of whom were killed by Covenanters at Dunaverty Castle in Kintyre in 1647 (MacKenzie, 1881, p.475)[23] and who descended from Alexander MacDonald, 5th Chief of the MacDonalds of Dunnyveg (c.1480-1538) (Macdonald & Macdonald, 1904, p.387). The Archdeacon was brother and heir of Madras and Persia-based Lt. Col.[24] Sir John MacDonald-Kinneir (1781-1830) (MacKenzie, 1881, p.476), from whom the Archdeacon inherited the lairdship of Sanda, an island off the Mull of Kintyre.

William Macdonald had first married, in 1810, to Frances Goodman (1785-1838), by whom he had 9 children, beginning a dynasty of clergymen. His sons included the Rev. Douglas Macdonald (1811-1865), the vicar of West Alvington in Devon, and the Rev. William Macdonald (1814-1880), a rector in Wiltshire (MacKenzie, p.477). The Archdeacon married again in 1847 to Frances Dawson of Wakefield in Yorkshire (1814-1904). By her he fathered the five children with whom Sneyd-Kynnersley was staying on 7th April 1861.

The Rev. Douglas Macdonald

---

[22] A Laird is the owner of a long established Scottish estate, as recognised by the Scottish heraldic authority, the Lord Lyon.

[23] This took place as part of the Dunaverty Massacre in which about 300 MacDonalds and members of allied clans were slaughtered by Presbyterian supporters of Cromwell; the MacDonalds being Catholic and Royalist (see Campbell, 1885).

[24] British army officer ranks in ascending order of superiority: 2nd Lieutenant, Lieutenant, Captain, Major, Lt. Colonel, Colonel, Brigadier-General, Major-General, Lt. General, General and Field Marshal.

Rugby Under Frederick Temple

In July 1861, Herbert's sister Barbara married Irishman Edward Ashley Scott (1830-1905) who was an assistant master at Rugby. Scott was a former Rugby pupil and a former Fellow of Trinity College, Cambridge. The son of a Dublin QC[25] (Urban, 1862, p.224) and the brother of the future Archdeacon of Dublin. In his study of the heritability of talent — essentially an enquiry into eugenics — the scientist Sir Francis Galton (1822-1911) actually explored the example of the Scott family of Dublin (Galton, 1906, p.61).

In August, Sneyd-Kynnersley went to Rugby himself (Mitchell, 1902, p.207), following in his family's tradition. The school, established in 1567, is in the market town of the same name in Warwickshire in the West Midlands. Unlike Churchill, Sneyd-Kynnersley did quite well academically. In his will, which he wrote in 1880, he bequeathed such items as 'my Rugby prize Shakespeare,' 'my Rugby prize Boswell's Life of Johnson' and 'my Rugby prize copy of Tennyson's poems in four volumes.' He was clearly committed to Rugby, with the school's magazine *The Meteor* recording that 'Kynnersley, Rev. H. S.' had made a donation of £10 to the school in 1885, a donation which was on the high side of those listed and which would have been about £1100 in 2018.[26] His father only donated £5 (*The Meteor*, 21st February 1885, p.19).

Sneyd-Kynnersley's housemaster, according to the school's register, was the Rev. Thomas Jex-Blake (1832-1915) who was headmaster of Rugby between 1874 and 1887 and was eventually Dean of Wells in Somerset. Sneyd-Kynnersley's headmaster at Rugby was the Rev. Frederick Temple (1821-1902) who was Archbishop of Canterbury from 1896 until his death. It was not uncommon in the nineteenth century, and even in the first half of the twentieth century, for the professions of schoolmaster (at least at prestigious

---

[25] QC/KC: Queen's Counsel/ King's Counsel – a senior barrister; this being a lawyer employed to prosecute or defend the more serious cases.

[26] Until decimalization in February 1971, there were 20 shillings (s) to the pound ˚and 12 pennies (d) to the shilling, meaning 240 pennies to the pound. The coin known as the 'half crown' was worth 2s 6d (so one eighth of a pound). A guinea was 21 shillings – £1, 1s.

schools), academic, and clergyman to be intertwined. For much of the nineteenth century, the three English universities — Oxford, Cambridge and Durham — were dominated by the Church of England, something which only changed as the government attempted to make these universities more useful to society as a whole by having them teach a wider variety of subjects (Williams, 2016, p.99). Fellows at Oxford and Cambridge colleges had to be ordained as deacons (the most junior ordained rank in the Church of England) and often unmarried if they wanted to remain fellows for longer than a few years (Melnyk, 2008, p.19). Graduates might be fellows for a short time, often doing no actual teaching, before training as barristers or entering into the relatively lucrative world of educating the children of the wealthy as private tutors, while still being fellows (*Reports from Commissioners*, 1872, p.352). If they wanted to remain fellows long-term then they would become deacons. However, fellows were not allowed to marry, so many might still eventually migrate into school teaching if they found the right woman. They would often have no experience of being priests in the pastoral sense, because, at the time, providing education was a function of the Church of England and thus of its clergy. Only in 1877 was the requirement that fellows be ordained in the Church of England and remain unmarried abolished (Young, 2015, p.46, Lynd, 1968, p.372). Many college statutes restricted certain numbers of fellowships to graduates from areas where the college owned land, to members of certain families, or to pupils from specific schools, meaning there was an enormous variation in the emolument paid to fellows and in their academic standards (Haig, 1984).

Public schools had close ties with the Church of England and the headmasters were usually, by tradition, clergymen. A number of Archbishops of Canterbury were first headmasters of English public schools, most recently Geoffrey Fisher (1887-1972), who was Archbishop between 1945 and 1961. A product of the public school Marlborough, Fisher began his career as a schoolmaster. He was ordained deacon in 1912, after having studied for the priesthood at Wells Theological College for one term during a long holiday in 1911. He was ordained priest in 1913. Fisher was appointed priest-headmaster of Repton in 1914. The children's author Roald Dahl

(1916-1990) was later one of his pupils at this Derbyshire public school. Without any experience as a parish priest, Fisher was consecrated Bishop of Chester in 1932. Service as an ordained headmaster was regarded as sufficient experience to run a diocese (Hein, 2008).

Temple's path to Canterbury was quite similar, though he was, very briefly, a full time pastoral clergyman. The son of an army officer of middle class background, Temple did not attend public school. After graduating from Oxford in 1842, he lectured Mathematics there for four years as a fellow, before being ordained and becoming the headmaster of a school for poor children. He resigned in 1855; appointed a school inspector. By 1856, Temple had gained the admiration of Prince Albert for his educational work and was made Chaplain-in-Ordinary to Queen Victoria. On the strength of this experience, he was offered the post of priest-headmaster of Rugby in 1858. A Liberal and later a supporter of Prime Minister William Gladstone (1809-1898), in stark contrast to the Sneyd-Kynnersleys, Temple arrived at Rugby determined to raise academic standards, particularly in Classics of which, as we will see later, Sneyd-Kynnersley was so fond. Though apparently liked by his pupils, Temple gained a reputation for being quite a rough character (Hinchcliff, 1998, p.195).

The Rev. Frederick Temple, Headmaster of Rugby

As with most public schools at the time, as headmaster Temple punished pupils with the birch across the bare buttocks (Hinchcliff, 1998, p.57). In 1904, a book called *Six Great Schoolmasters* (How, 1904) hit the shelves. It included a biography of Temple. The author explained that:

> 'Dr Temple hated flogging. There was very little of it in his day. When he did flog, he *did,* but there would not infrequently be tears in his eyes . . . Mr Hart Davis writes: ". . . I was one of the Sixth Form boys on duty to see fair play. The Headmaster seemed to feel his position more acutely than the culprit. But in spite of the tears coursing down his cheeks, Temple inflicted on the boy a good sound licking"' (How, 1904, p.204).

Thus, even a clearly positive source implies that when Temple birched pupils it was severe, something which was clearly not the case with the clergyman George Moberly (1803-1866), later Bishop of Salisbury, a Winchester College headmaster whose life was presented in the same volume. He administered four strokes of the birch 'or six for a very serious offence' (p.62). Perhaps Temple's practices in some way contributed to the nature of Sneyd-Kynnersley's floggings, a possibility we will explore anon.

Rugby's previous headmaster, Thomas Arnold, was, to a great extent, hero-worshipped as having turned around not just Rugby but, via imitation of his practices, *all* public schools. Arnold administered what he called a 'swishing' – a term presumably also employed by Sneyd-Kynnersley, as Roger Fry used it – to the exposed bottoms of errant pupils. Imitating Arnold, the clergyman headmaster of Harrow, Charles Vaughan (1816-1897), beat pupils very severely. 'He would deliver six, eight, or ten cuts and draw blood, leaving birch buds embedded in the wounds that could last for a fortnight' (Mangan, 2004, p.19). These boys would have ranged in age from about 13 to 18 and would have very much been 'boys.' Puberty arrived much later than today.[27] Public school headmasters

---

[27] The age of menarche, for example, in mid-nineteenth century Europe was roughly 17 compared to less than 13 in 2014 (Jones & Lopez, 2014, p.112). The beginning of male puberty is more difficult to precisely measure. However, based on the proxy of the age at which boys' voices break, this has fallen from 18 in the

were highly significant figures in Victorian and Edwardian society because the landed gentry still substantially ran the country and people like Temple prepared the children of the landed gentry to continue doing so. In addition, the children of, increasingly powerful, parvenu industrialists would also be sent to public schools. The fact that *Six Great Schoolmasters* (which included a biography of Vaughan) was put out by Methuen — a mainstream publishing house which had previously distributed Rudyard Kipling and Robert Louis Stephenson and would print Oscar Wilde's *De Profundis* the following year — is testament to public school headmasters' perceived importance in society in 1904: A book on that subject had popular appeal.

Life at Rugby during Sneyd-Kynnersley's time was Spartan, as it was at most public schools. In summarising his time at prep and public school, almost 50 years after Sneyd-Kynnersley was a pupil, George Orwell (1903-1950) talks of:

'squalor and neglect taken for granted in upper class schools of the period . . . it seemed natural that a little boy of eight or ten should be a miserable, snotty-nosed creature, his face almost permanently dirty, his hands chapped, his nails bitten, his handkerchief a sodden horror, his bottom frequently blue with bruises' (quoted in Mangan, 2004, p.23).

Food was foul and likely to be fought over, dormitories were cold with dominant boys stealing all the duvets, there was endemic bullying and fighting which staff did little to stop, and younger pupils acted as servants — 'fags' — to older pupils, who reserved the right to beat them. Sometimes, the deeply ritualistic, bloody floggings by the headmaster would be in public, as occurred at Eton, and the screams of miscreants would reverberate throughout the school; with such a system fully respected by the pupils as the accepted code of the institution. Pupils would gather to watch the beatings or listen to them outside the headmaster's study. Marlborough, in the 1850s and 1860s, was notoriously violent, but other public schools

mid-eighteenth century to 13 in the 1960s to about 10 and a half in 2014 (Steinberg, 2014, p.49).

were relatively similar. A Marlborough pupil in the 1840s, Edward Lockwood, whom we met earlier, recalled that, when he returned home from school, he was:

> 'undressed and put to bed by my tender-hearted nurse, she viewed my back with the utmost horror and indignation. But she was told that as the punishment had been administered by a reverend man called to ministry, I must have deserved every blow I got' (Lockwood, 1893, p.26).

'Back' was a widely understood euphemism for 'bottom' (Gibson, 1978, p.52). Lewis Carroll — the Rev. Charles Dodgson (1832-1898) — attended Rugby around 15 years before Sneyd-Kynnersley. Carroll had to sleep in a long, cold dormitory, whereas by Sneyd-Kynnersley's day each pupil had his own cubicle. This privacy, however, was accompanied by intense physical and psychological bullying and violent sports, such as rugby and boxing (Bakwell, 1996, Ch. 3). But these were schools approved of by the royal family and the nobility and they permitted children to make the right contacts and to have been through the right rituals. This is what seemed to matter to the parents (Mangan, 2004).

Cambridge University and Scholarship

Sneyd-Kynnersley matriculated at Trinity College, Cambridge – as a pensioner, meaning he did not have a scholarship, so his parents had to pay for board, lodging and his tuition fees – in July 1867, when he was 19 (Venn, 1911). Sneyd-Kynnersley was quite active at Cambridge and later boasted many intellectual attainments, though this information has, unfortunately, been successfully suppressed by a disgruntled former pupil.

Trinity College, Cambridge

Roger Fry, whom we met earlier, was relatively famous during his lifetime as part of the Bloomsbury Group of writers, academics, and artists that included Virginia Woolf (1882-1941). This group were bound together by the belief that life should be centred around love, aesthetic experience ('art for art's sake'), and the attainment of knowledge. They strongly questioned Victorian values such as patriotism, with group member the novelist E.M Forster (1879-1970) stating 'if I had to choose between betraying my country and betraying my friend, I hope I should have the guts to betray my country' (Forster, 1965, p.76). They even critiqued conventions such as monogamy, and were politically of the Left (Gadd, 1974). In other words, Fry was diametrically opposed to almost everything Sneyd-Kynnersley stood for, which should be borne in mind when using Fry as a source of information about his former headmaster. However, according to Fry, who was one of Sneyd-Kynnersley's favourite pupils:

'[*Sneyd-Kynnersley's*] intellectual attainments consisted almost entirely of having as an undergraduate at Cambridge belonged to a Dickens society which cultivated an extreme admiration for the great man, and tested each other's proficiency in the novels by examination papers, from which he would frequently quote to us' (Woolf, 1940, p.32).

Fry's reference to a lack of 'intellectual attainments' is perhaps rather confusing to a modern audience. At the time of writing, in the UK at least, teaching, and especially primary school teaching, is a decreasingly respected profession. It is dominated by females (Williams, 2017, p.19), something which tends to reduce the standing of an occupation (Heath, 2004), and its educational requirements have remained the same — a Bachelor's degree — since the 1980s when it effectively became a graduate profession (Mentor, 2016, p.6), as British society has become increasingly educated around it (Williams, 2017, p.18). As such, the teaching profession has 'comparatively low wages and perceived low status' (Williams, 2017, p.33). Evidence presented to the House of Commons' Education Committee in 2011 even referred to 'the relatively low status of teaching compared to other occupations' (House of Commons Education Committee, 2012, ev. 134).

This was far less the case in nineteenth century England, at least if the teacher had a degree. This made him part of the country's educational elite. In 1870, only 0.2% of the British population were university graduates. Even among barristers, a prestige profession, only 70% were university graduates in 1885 (Abel, 1998, p.47). The graduate teacher would often be in holy orders as well, in a society that was still strongly religious. Roughly 58% of the population attended Church every week in 1851 compared to 7% today (Kim, 2012, p.64). Also, at a time when universities were very much teaching institutions with little in the way of science facilities, a great deal of academic research was conducted outside of universities by gentleman scientists, such as Charles Darwin (1809-1882), scholar-rectors like the Rev. Thomas Malthus (1766-1834) or enthusiastic amateurs such as the Aberdeenshire shoemaker and naturalist Thomas Edward (1814-1886) (Williams, 2016, p.39). In line with this, there was a tradition whereby teachers at public schools —and especially headmasters — produced their own scholarship. The historian Thomas Arnold (1795-1842), for example, was headmaster of Rugby. In addition, some public school headmasters were part of the miniscule elite who had doctorates. The Rev. Dr Charles Vaughan wrote a number of academic books on theology while headmaster of Harrow. So, there was very much an expectation that a prep school headmaster would be able to boast intellectual achievements in a way that is no longer the case.

That said, despite Fry's denigration of his headmaster's academic accomplishments, Sneyd-Kynnersley was extremely highly educated by the standards of the time, and even by modern standards. Following in his father's footsteps, he read for a Law degree. He graduated in 1871 and promptly got a job as a prep school teacher. This, it should be noted, could be regarded as relatively low intellectual achievement insomuch as, unlike some future schoolmasters, he did not serve as a fellow of his college. However, he continued his education as a part-time student. In 1885, the year before his premature death, he was made an LLD; a Doctor of Jurisprudence. This would have been awarded upon the presentation of an acceptable portfolio of advanced research in English Law. In addition, Sneyd-Kynnersley's enthusiasm for Latin and Ancient Greek led to the publication of three educational books on Classical languages, which is a reasonable number, especially for a man of only 38 with a full time teaching job: *Greek Verbs for Beginners*[28] (Page, 1883, advert), *A Parallel Syntax: Greek and Latin for Beginners* (Sneyd-Kynnersley, 1877) and, in the year he died, *Latin Prose Composition* (Sneyd-Kynnersley, 1886). *A Parallel Syntax*, according to a critic, was 'not valueless' but still 'rather too mechanical to prove of any great service' (*The Westminster and Foreign Quarterly Review*, 1st April 1878, p.566). *Latin Prose Composition*, however, was warmly received: 'Dr Kynnersley seems to have done his work consciously and selected his examples judiciously' (*Knowledge*, 1886, p.259).

Thus, it is simply inaccurate of Roger Fry to claim that Sneyd-Kynnersley's only intellectual achievement was his involvement in the Dickens Society at Cambridge. Considering that Fry portrays Sneyd-Kynnersley as a braggart — who would quote from the Dickens papers he had written at Cambridge — it is unlikely that Fry wouldn't have known at least about Sneyd-Kynnersley's first two books. Indeed, Fry probably knew about all of 'Dr Sneyd-Kynnersley's' intellectual endeavours, in that he was a beneficiary in the headmaster's will. Sneyd-Kynnersley's LLD was even announced

---

[28] This book is not in the British Library and appears to be lost. Evidence of it is found in publisher's advertisements for *A Parallel Syntax*.

in *The Morning Post* (25th May 1885), a leading newspaper. So this should make us at least slightly cautious about the reliability of Fry as a source of information on Sneyd-Kynnersley. This is particularly important because, as we will see, Fry is the source of the most disturbing stories about the headmaster, which are repeated quite uncritically in so many popular Churchill biographies. Fry also claimed that Sneyd-Kynnersley had a pronounced sense of inferiority about his own intelligence, something which led him to continuously replace masters who displayed any intelligence with 'imbeciles.' As we will see below, two of these 'imbeciles' were highly respected by Maurice Baring, OBE[29] (1874-1945) and other pupils and most of the teaching staff, at any one time, were evidently highly qualified and obviously of considerable intellectual ability.

What is Intelligence?

There is currently controversy over the concept of 'intelligence' (Woodley of Menie et al., 2018b) so, in discussing it, let us be clear what we mean. Intelligence is defined as 'the ability to reason, plan, solve problems, think abstractly, comprehend complex ideas, learn quickly, and learn from experience (Gottfredson, 1997, p.13). In other words, it is the ability to solve complex problems and to solve them quickly. There are different kinds of intelligence — such as mathematical, linguistic and spatial — and these positively inter-correlate, meaning that if you're high on one you're normally high on all, though you will be higher on some than others. This means that there is a 'general factor' which underpins all of them. This is known as 'general intelligence' or g (Jensen, 1998). Proxies for general intelligence include general knowledge, something which is valued in all cultures and in all time periods (Buss, 1989). Intelligence is negatively associated with criminality, which is disliked in all cultures. It also robustly positively correlates with educational achievement, income, health, altruism, impulse control and the

---

[29]   OBE: Order of the British Empire. This is the second highest honour after a knighthood; the first being Commander of the British Empire (CBE) and the third being Member of the British Empire (MBE).

ability to delay gratification. It predicts openness to new ideas, an intellectual approach, and a questioning disposition (Jensen, 1998). In science, a 'correlation' refers to the relationship between two variables. If one predicts the other, then you have a positive correlation and if one predicts the absence of the other then you have a negative correlation. If one absolutely predicts the other, then you have a correlation of 1. Accordingly, 0.9 (or -0.9 if it is negative) is a very strong correlation while 0.1 is a weak one.

Intelligence cannot be dismissed as only relevant in the West or in modern times and nor can it be dismissed as unimportant. Intelligence cannot be argued to be too complex to understand, because, as science is in a constant state of progress towards greater understanding, this could be argued to be true of anything. Even though the modern definition of intelligence was only really clarified in about 1912, there is no reason whatsoever why the concept cannot be applied to people in the past. If it cannot be, then, presumably, we cannot assess historical characters in terms of mental illnesses which weren't understood at the time. Based on twin studies, intelligence is about 80% genetic, so it is overwhelmingly inherited from your parents (Lynn, 2011, p.101; Dutton & Woodley of Menie, 2018). Sneyd-Kynnersley obtained a doctorate in Law; an LLD. The thesis-based PhD did not exist at the time; it was only introduced to the UK in 1917 (Simpson, 1983). He also wrote three books on Classical languages and was the son of a successful barrister – intelligence being about 80% genetic. So it is most unlikely that Sneyd-Kynnersley was lacking in intelligence. Accordingly, we see another example of Fry denigrating Sneyd-Kynnersley in an unwarranted way.

Tractarianism and Irreverent Debates

Also, Sneyd-Kynnersley did far more than simply talk about Charles Dickens (1812-1870) novels while he was studying at Cambridge. He campaigned for High Church Conservatism even then. In 1868, Sneyd-Kynnersley was one of three Trinity undergraduates, along with one postgraduate, to put his name to what might seem to us like a rather obscure petition to the master of the college. But this was a formal petition; something relatively rare and noteworthy. It demanded that communion should be celebrated every Sunday, as well as on Ascension Day, before the usual service in the college chapel. It further insisted that communicants should receive communion kneeling at the altar rail, and that those receiving communion should not have to leave their name with the dean. The latter custom was a means of ascertaining how religiously committed undergraduates had been if and when they later wanted to become fellows of their college, which ultimately required them to be ordained as deacons (Smyth, 1940, p.146).

However, in the context of 1868, Sneyd-Kynnersley was espousing what might be called 'radical conservatism.' By 1868, there was vehement conflict within the Church of England. In the 1830s, John Henry Newman (1801-1890), an Anglican who later became a Catholic Cardinal, had led the Oxford Movement. The Oxford Movement, which began at the university, believed that Roman Catholicism, Eastern Orthodoxy and Protestantism were all ultimately branches of one Catholic Church and its members argued for a return to the ancient traditions of this Church, preserved in the practices of the Roman Catholic Church in particular. They were criticised as Romanising and secretive by evangelicals, in part because their movement was tremendously successful. Under their influence, Anglicanism became more like Roman Catholicism: The Eucharist became more central to worship and began to be taken more often, services became more ritualistic and symbolism-laden, vestments became more widespread, clergy began to dress distinctively, and Anglican monasteries and nunneries were established (Herring, 2010). There were various shades within this movement. The *Tractarians* were the most extreme. Named after the Oxford Movement's publications *Tracts of the Times,* they were generally highly sympathetic to Rome. The *Ritualists*, with whom Tractarians crossed-over, were more concerned with issues such as the form of worship and the use of vestments.

By the 1860s, Ritualist priests were fundamentally altering the nature of Church services, sometimes leading to violent disruptions from congregation members (Herringer, 2014, pp.13-14). The Tractarians evoked hatred among many evangelicals, in a society which was still strongly religious. Rugby headmaster Thomas Arnold wrote, in a letter to Queen Victoria, that, 'I look upon a Roman Catholic as an enemy in his uniform; a look upon a Tractarian as an enemy disguised as a spy' (Brown, 2002, p.540). For many Victorians, Catholicism was 'foreign' and associated with Britain's enemies; embracing it was a kind of treason, and Tractarians were fifth columnists, a view often extended to Ritualists and even to the entire High Church (Mazurek, 2017, p.88). Evangelicalism became more ardent, partly in response to the rise of the Oxford Movement (Bebbington, 1989). This, in turn, led to most Ritualists stressing that they were reviving a distinctly Medieval English form of Christianity — they were 'Anglo-Catholics' — which fitted with the late Victorian Romanticising of Medieval England (Welby, 2016). A minority, however, simply imitated the Roman Catholic Church (Morris, 2016, pp.22-23).

Taking communion while seated was a practice associated with the evangelical movement; the Low Church (Johnson, 1997), as was the infrequent taking of communion (Balmer, 2004, p.414). The evangelical movement became strongly influential in England during the nineteenth century. It was characterised by fervent religious belief in traditional doctrines, personal conversion, religious experience, conversion of non-evangelicals, puritanical attitudes, personal morality, and the rejection of perceived Catholic aspects of the Church such as pedantic ritual observance, clerical dress and church adornment (Bebbington, 1989). Britain's main student evangelical movement — known as the Christian Union — was established at Cambridge University in 1877, six years after Oxford, Cambridge and Durham Universities were compelled to open their doors to non-Anglican students. The Christian Union had long been preceded by informal student evangelical meetings, which the authorities termed 'enthusiasm' (Barclay & Horn, 2002). Sneyd-Kynnersley's petition can be understood as a pre-emptive strike — on behalf of the High Church — against the growing evangelical movement. The symbolism of this petition was important and we will see why in a later chapter.

However, despite being fiercely religious and conservative, Sneyd-Kynnersley clearly had a sense of humour and did not take himself too seriously, even though one Churchill biographer has termed him 'humourless' (Farrell, 1964, p.12). While at Cambridge, he was an active member of Trinity College's Magpie and Stump Debating Society; their records revealing that he gave a speech (Ferguson, 1931, p.59). This joke debating society, though with very occasional serious debates, met on Friday evenings (Weston-Smith, 2013). Members had to give speeches on ludicrous topics for 4 minutes. Those who failed to do so were fined half a crown. The chamber's centre piece was a stuffed magpie on a tree stump and all speeches had to be addressed to 'My Lord, the Bird' (Piper, 2006, p.14). The topics of debate at this 'irreverent' society included 'This House prefers an English sense of humour to an American' (Hunter, 2007, p.12). Sneyd-Kynnersley would also have needed a sense of silliness in order to succeed in what he chose to do next.

Chapter Three

'A Man Among Boys . . .'

Assistant Master in Slough

UPON GRADUATING FROM Cambridge in 1871, Sneyd-Kynnersley took the post of assistant master at St Michael's School, Aldin House, Slough. This Berkshire town is 1 mile from Eton College and about 3 miles from Windsor. It has since become notorious for being one of the least attractive towns in England. The British poet laureate John Betjeman (1906-1984) infamously wrote in his poem 'Slough' (Guest, 1989, pp.24-25):

'Come friendly bombs and fall on Slough!
It isn't fit for humans now,
There isn't grass to graze a cow.
Swarm over, Death!'

The town was developed after World War I, expanded into what Betjeman regarded as a bland urban sprawl of near-identical red brick houses. It became home to, as far as Betjeman was concerned, a certain kind of lower middle and working class type that he couldn't abide. This happened in many small towns, but Slough — with the Slough Trading Estate, founded in 1921 — epitomised it. At remarkable speed, Slough transformed from a sleepy, rural, railway town into a highly industrialized one, dominated by hideous factories churning out everything from Mars Bars to Chappie Dog Food to Black and Decker Work Tools (Rowley, 2006, pp.141-142). This led to the population not only growing hugely — from 11,000 in 1911 to 60,000 in the late 1930s when Betjeman published his poem (Rowley, p.142) — but changing in its nature.

'It's not their fault they do not know
The birdsong from the radio,
It's not their fault they often go
To Maidenhead

And talk of sport and makes of cars
In various bogus-Tudor bars
And daren't look up and see the stars
But belch instead.'

Its reputation only got worse when it became the setting for the popular 2001 sitcom *The Office*, which was focused around the tedium of life as an office worker. It was set in Slough precisely because Slough is widely regarded as a particularly dull and featureless town (Moran, 2005, p.41). Visiting Slough, as part of research for this book, I can attest that it is a truly hideous place. A bland early twentieth century High Street sits uneasily alongside brutalist post-War buildings with aestheticism bypasses, early twentieth century detached houses, estates of various kinds and recent, gleaming, asymmetrical monstrosities.

Queensmere, Slough Town Centre

This, however, was not the Slough where Sneyd-Kynnersley was a prep school master. His Slough had a population of just 6,000, a little industry based around its brickfields, a railway station with some large houses close to it, and only one church (Rowley, 2006, p.141). The headmaster of Aldin House at the time was the Rev. John Hawtrey (1818-1891), who had previously been assistant master for the lower school at Eton (Leinster-Mackay, 1971, p.76; *The Royal Calendar*, 1846, p.331), just down the road. Until 1869, Eton had taken pupils as young as seven and Hawtrey had been their housemaster. But, in that year, Eton's lower forms were moved to a separate school, Hawtrey's, run out of John Hawtrey's own Slough home (Cust, 1899, pp.208-209).

Coincidentally, also in 1871, Herbert's older brother Edmund McKenzie Sneyd-Kynnersley (1841-1933) was appointed an inspector of schools. After Rugby and Oxford, Edmund had become a school teacher and then a barrister. However, he made neither much progress nor much money and by 1871, having just returned from a year in Australia, he was desperate for work. His father's neighbour's son, back in 1854, had been a school inspector and this neighbour was the cousin of Sir Francis Sandford (1824-1893) who was the civil servant in charge of schooling by 1871. Through these connections, Edmund managed to get a job as a school inspector himself (Sneyd-Kynnersley, 1908, pp.1-2). He was eventually appointed one of the chief school inspectors and wrote a book on this subject: *HMI: Some Passages in the Life of One of Her Majesty's Inspectors of Schools* (Sneyd-Kynnersley, 1908). It says something about how different early twentieth century readers were from those today that a major publisher would consider there to be a market for such a book. *HMI* 'brims' with humorous anecdotes and was well reviewed. 'Those who remember across the twenty years the wit, wisdom and fun of *H.M.I* will welcome with special zest his new volume *H.M.I.'s Notebook*' wrote a reviewer in 1930 (*Dundee Courier,* 12th August 1930).[30] It

---

[30] Edmund also wrote, in 1910, *A Snail's Wooing: The Story of an Alpine Courtship* (Sneyd-Kynnersley, 1910) of which it was reported, 'A man as brimful of anecdote as the author of H.M.I. has proved himself to be, could hardly fail to write an entertaining book of any kind. In A Snail's Wooing Mr. E. M. Sneyd-Kynnersley brightens the record of an Alpine courtship . . .' (*Bexhill-On-Sea Observer,* 25th February 1911).

would have been fascinating to read what Edmund would have made of Rugby if he had inspected it in 1871.

A Rumpus at Rugby

In 1872, Herbert Sneyd-Kynnersley was involved in a legal case which gives us an insight into the childishness of many school masters, an issue we will turn to later. December 1872 saw the culmination of a two-year long feud between the Rev. Dr Henry Hayman (1823-1904), headmaster of Rugby 1869-1874, and Rugby assistant master and former pupil Edward Ashley Scott (1830-1905), who was Sneyd-Kynnersley's brother-in-law. Hayman had merely been to the day school Merchant Taylor's School in Hertfordshire. Hayman's headmastership of Rugby was a disastrous interlude. His predecessor, Frederick Temple, took the unprecedented step of openly opposing Hayman's appointment, which had been made by outgoing governors (Hinchcliff, 1998, p.131). The other Rugby masters also reacted with uproar to Hayman's becoming headmaster, a decision which was widely discussed in the national press and even queried in the House of Commons. The hostility towards him came to Hayman's attention before he arrived, so he tried to sack Scott, who was his chief critic among the masters, but ultimately failed to secure the support of the school's trustees to do so (Gronn, 1999, p.142). In the meantime, he had sent Scott on leave.

According to a report in *The Leeds Mercury* (27th December 1872), Hayman had sent Scott a letter stating that he could once again teach at Rugby, but that this needed to be decided by the governors, as Hayman had no confidence in Scott. This was because, so claimed Hayman, beginning in 1870, Scott had written letters to Sneyd-Kynnersley — then still an undergraduate — saying that none of the teachers at Rugby had any confidence in Hayman. If they saw him in the street they would blank him, hide, or run away. They also believed he'd likely be forced to resign within 3 months. Somehow, a 'Miss A.' had become aware that Sneyd-Kynnersley was receiving these claims and she stated that Sneyd-Kynnersley was excited about this conflict, because he thought it would end up being discussed in the House of Commons. He was disappointed and silent when it was not. This is an indication of just how important the headmasters of leading public schools were at the time. This intelligence got back to Hayman who raised it with Scott and accepted Scott's explanation that Miss A. must have misunderstood something. However, in July 1871, one 'Mr J.W. Fletcher' had told Hayman that he was a teacher at Epsom College in Surrey alongside Sneyd-Kynnersley and that Sneyd-Kynnersley would, having read letters sent to him from Rugby, describe Dr Hayman in terms which were 'ungentlemanly and unfair in any society.' Based on this testimony, Hayman tried to get Scott fired from teaching at Rugby.

So vital was Rugby that a file on the case was passed to the attorney general, Sir John Coleridge (1820-1894) in addition to there being an internal investigation by the Rugby governors. As part of this investigation, John Hawtrey stated that Sneyd-Kynnersley had never even taught at Epsom College and that he was teaching at Aldin House in 1871. This is confirmed by consulting the *Epsom College Register* which lists all staff at the school between 1855 and 1905. 'J. W. Fletcher' is listed as having been an assistant master there between 1871 and 1872 (Essex Winter & Chetwood, 1905, p.vi). Sneyd-Kynnersley is not listed at all. Fletcher left Epsom College in 1872, perhaps because his dishonesty had been publically exposed. Consulting the 1861 census permits us to understand why Fletcher was prepared to lie for Hayman. In 1861, Fletcher was a pupil at Cheltenham Grammar School — of which Hayman was headmaster — and was actually lodging with Hayman's family. In other words, he had concocted a story about Sneyd-Kynnersley, perhaps in order to protect his former headmaster and, presumably, current friend, from a problematic employee.[31]

---

[31] Fletcher actually went on to gain some prominence. John Walter Fletcher (1847-1918) had matriculated at Pembroke College, Oxford, in 1865, was training to be a barrister at Inner Temple in 1867, but was then awarded his History degree in 1869. By 1874, he was teaching at a school in New South Wales, possibly having left the UK due to the negative publicity. Flourishing Down Under, Fletcher established his own boys' school in Sydney in 1877. In 1880, he organised the first recorded football match in Australia and is consequently known as the 'Father of Australian Soccer.' By the 1890s, Fletcher was a barrister and eventually became a magistrate (Mosley, 1995).

But returning to the Hayman case, in his testimony, Hawtrey added that it was quite normal for assistant masters to express negative views about the headmaster. Sneyd-Kynnersley stated that Fletcher was, for some reason, 'in the habit of abusing the Rugby masters and accusing them of disloyalty without any knowledge of the facts.' Both Coleridge and the Rugby governors concluded that Edward Ashley Scott had done nothing wrong and nor had Sneyd-Kynnersley. As far as they were concerned, Hayman was simply being unreasonable and it was felt that his behaviour towards Scott showed that he wasn't capable of being headmaster. In 1874, Hayman was finally sacked by the governors for his incompetent running of Rugby (*Oxford Undergraduate's Journal*, 29th January 1874).

Life at Aldin House

In 1874, Sneyd-Kynnersley was ordained a deacon at Oxford, continuing to teach at Hawtrey's. The Rev. R. H. Quick (1831-1891) visited Hawtrey's prep school in about 1875 and certainly while Sneyd-Kynnersley was still there. He does not date his visit in his journal, but it sits between visits to other schools in 1875 and 1877. According to Quick (1899, p.189), 'The boys are worked on a system which knocks Latin and Greek into them most effectually (does it knock all else out of them?).' Quick described the food as 'sumptuous for everyone' and also noted the rather stressful working conditions for masters such as Sneyd-Kynnersley. They were paid £200 per year, in addition to board and lodging. However, if their pupils performed poorly in end of year exams then they could be sacked 'without notice' (p.189).

While Sneyd-Kynnersley was at Aldin House, which had 150 boys, pupils included the Scottish poet, translator and diplomat Douglas Ainslie (1866-1948), later an acquaintance of Oscar Wilde and Marcel Proust (Ainslie, 1922, Ch. 5 & 15). Ainslie recalled that Hawtrey was so short-sighted that they called him 'the Beatle' (p.43) and that there would be a 'weekly reading out' of reports, a tradition Sneyd-Kynnersley took, in some form, to his own school. Ainslie felt that he never learnt very much (p.42) and that the classes were too large (p.44), but his brother seemed to enjoy himself at Hawtrey's (p.43) and he presents a generally positive account of his own experiences. Another pupil contemporary of Sneyd-Kynnersley's was socialite Arthur Sebright (1859-1933) who believed that there couldn't possibly be another school where the children were 'so well cared for, so well fed . . .' (Sebright, 1922, pp.14-15), his having had there 'a thoroughly happy and healthy life, both in body and in mind' (p.15).

Aldin House, Slough

Also in 1874, Herbert's brother, Lt. Thomas Alfred Sneyd-Kynnersley, RN, MP (1839-1874) died. After Rugby (Mitchell, 1902, p.112), Thomas Alfred had attended Naval College, joined the Navy and risen to the rank of Lieutenant.[32] But he had had to leave the navy due to his tuberculosis. He moved to New Zealand, where he became a gold prospector, local government administrator and eventually an MP. The former naval man was noted for his wit and daring. In 1867, the *Westport Times* published an article implying

---

[32] British naval officer ranks in ascending order of superiority: Midshipman, Sub-Lieutenant, Lieutenant, Lt. Commander, Commander, Captain, Commodore, Rear-Admiral, Vice-Admiral, Admiral, Admiral of the Fleet.

that he had attended the races with two prostitutes. He marched to the newspaper's offices armed with a whip and beat up the editor who had resigned by the next day. The following year, he and some friends were having a meal in Punakaiki when they heard gun shots and shouting from outside. 'Mrs Jarvis,' a revolver in each hand, was chasing a particular man. Thomas felt they should intervene. He persuaded Mrs Jarvis to come to a bar. A brandy was offered towards her right hand, leading her to drop one revolver, and another towards her left, causing her to drop the other. Thomas grabbed both revolvers and left the bar. He died aged just 35 (Hutchinson, 1990).[33] When his brother Herbert made his will he instructed that altar cloths at the chapel at St George's be given to a church in New Zealand.

Thomas Alfred Sneyd-Kynnersley

---

[33] Hutchinson (1990) states that Thomas was the twin brother of 'Mary Palmer Kynnersley.' The parish records show that she was in fact the daughter of 'Samuel Kynnersley.'

Sunninghill House and St George's, Ascot

Sneyd-Kynnersley taught at Aldin House for six years before he and another assistant master at Aldin House decided to establish their own school, in 1877. Sneyd-Kynnersley's partner in this venture was fellow Rugby old boy Hugh Fraser Thornber (1847-1910). However, they appear to have parted ways fairly quickly, as Thornber had left Sunninghill House by 1881 and by 1891 Thornber was a school master in Brighton.

Sneyd-Kynnersley advertised the new school in the *Saturday Review* (5th May 1877, p.504) on 5th May 1877 as well as in *The Pall Mall Gazette* (2nd June 1877). The advert described it as a 'high class prep school' which would be opening on 19th September for children aged between 8 and 15. The school would be in Ascot in Berkshire, close to the border with the neighbouring county of Surrey. Ascot is about 7 miles from Windsor and 25 miles west of London. The small town is famous for its race course and the annual set of races known as Royal Ascot, both of which began in 1711. The advertisement described the luxurious facilities, the system of individual cubicles, and how it aimed to prepare boys for major public schools - listing Eton, Harrow, Winchester, Rugby and Charterhouse – as well as for Naval College. Preparation for Naval College would explain why the school educated boys up to the age of 15. In the late nineteenth century, boys who wanted to be naval officers often did not go to public school. If they were already clear that they wanted to join the navy, they went straight from prep school, aged either 13 or 15, to naval college and would often be Midshipmen, the most junior officer rank, by the age of either 15 or 17 (Thompson, Ch. 1).

St. George's Ascot

The fees at Sneyd-Kynnersley's new school were to be £150 per year, all inclusive. The school was initially called Sunninghill House, but Sneyd-Kynnersley later changed the name, seemingly in 1880, to St George's, Ascot, because his birthday was on St George's Day. Roger Fry regarded this as 'a remarkably feeble reason' (quoted in Brendon, 2009, p.68). The list of referees, in the advert, prepared to vouch for Sneyd-Kynnerseley was very impressive; a veritable roll call of the great and the good in the late 1870s. Sneyd-Kynnersley's own former headmaster and future Archbishop of Canterbury Frederick Temple, at the time Bishop of Exeter, topped the list, after the obligatory reference from J.W. Hawtrey. Then there was 'the Headmaster of Rugby' – Sneyd-Kynnersley's old housemaster Thomas Jex-Blake; Canon Joseph Lightfoot (1828-1889), at that time Professor of Divinity at Cambridge, chaplain to Queen Victoria and, as the advertisement stated, 'Vice-Master of Trinity, Cambridge' which was Sneyd-Kynnersley's old college. The list included the 13th Earl of Strathmore (1824-1904); Lt. Col. Arthur Tremayne (1827-1905) who had commanded a troop at the Charge of the Light Brigade and became a Conservative MP the following year, and Walter Powell, MP (1842-1881). This Rugby-educated MP for Malmesbury in

The Rev. Thomas Jex-Blake, Sneyd-Kynnersley's Housemaster

Wiltshire forced a by-election in 1881 when he was carried out over the English Channel in a hot air balloon, never to be seen again. The new headmaster's own father was at the foot of the list. This would definitely have impressed parents. 'Lt Col. Tremayne,' for example, was something of a household name. The salaries that could be earned by clergymen who set up prep schools were substantial, and schoolmaster clergy were sometimes criticised for abandoning their churches in pursuit of money (Leinster-Mackay, 1971, p.94).

A Clerk in Holy Orders and Tory Activist

The following year, Sneyd-Kynnersley was effectively outed as an extreme High Churchmen – a Tractarian - in the political magazine *Truth*. A highly critical article published a list of every Anglican clergyman – over a hundred of them - known to be members of the Confraternity of the Holy Trinity; a fully Tractarian society which had been established at Cambridge University in 1857 (Sparrow-Simpson, 1933, Ch. 4). Sneyd-Kynnersley, as with all but one of the other clergy on the list, had joined the confraternity as a Cambridge undergraduate. The *Truth* article accused members of the confraternity of without doubt being 'engaged in endeavouring to subvert and destroy the Church of England as a Protestant establishment' and being part of a 'secret society' whose members are 'traitors to the Church' and 'corrupters of public morality' (*Truth*, 1878, p.407). In 1878, Sneyd-Kynnersley's widowed aunt, Harriet Blunt, 'a kind old lady' (Unpublished Sources: Jay, 1947, p.6), was living with him at the school and helping to look after the younger children, comforting them if they got upset.

In 1879, Sneyd-Kynnersley was ordained a priest. In the same year, in Bath, he married Flora Georgina Macdonald (1852-1925), the daughter of the Ven. William Macdonald (1783-1862) whom we met earlier. The *Dorset County Chronicle* (24th April 1879) ran an article on the wedding, headlined 'A Remarkably Good Tea' and Sneyd-Kynnersley's pupils bought the couple an aquarium, later kept in the school 'drawing room,' as a wedding gift (Jay, 1947, p.17). Sneyd-Kynnersley and Flora never had any children. Sneyd-Kynnersley was elected to the corporation of the Society for the Propagation of the Gospel in 1884 (*The Monthly Record of Church Missions,* 1884). This society organized missionaries to be sent around the world to convert Non-Christians. Roger Fry told his mother in a letter home that a missionary had visited the school and that, 'We are going to keep a nigger at Bishop Steer's [*sic.*] School . . . it will cost, I believe, £60 per annum . . . He seems to be getting on well in most things but his character is only fair' (Woolf, 1940, p.30). This would have been the school founded in Zanzibar by the Rt. Rev. Dr Edward Steere (1828-1882), colonial Bishop of Nyasaland, who ran a school for natives (Loimier, 2009, p.218; Heanley, 1888). Presumably, Sneyd-Kynnersley was using school fund money to pay for a boy to attend the school, as an act of mission work.

By the time of the 1881 census, on 3rd April that year, Sneyd-Kynnersley's flourishing school had 40 pupils, including many sons of the nobility. Herbert's younger brother, the Hon. Charles Walter Sneyd-Kynnersley, CMG[34] (1849-1904) was also staying with Herbert and his wife that night. After Rugby, Charles had entered the civil service and by 1881 he was attached to the Lieutenant-Governor's Office in the Malaysian state of Penang, specifically Resident Councillor of Malacca. Subsequently, Charles was Singapore's Acting Colonial Secretary. He married Ada Nash (1861-1934), daughter of the Rev. George Lloyd Nash (1827-1893), vicar of Tolpuddle in Dorset and canon of Salisbury Cathedral (Burke, 1898, p.855). However, in July 1904, Charles, then living in Kingston Upon Thames in Surrey, was at a friend's house in nearby Wimbledon when he died suddenly of a heart attack (*Cheshire Observer*, 16th July 1904). His widow married Sir Walter Egerton (1858-1947), Governor of Southern Nigeria.

Charles Walter Sneyd-Kynnersley

---

[34] Companion of the Order of St Michael and St George; an honour directly below knighthood.

In 1885, Sneyd-Kynnersley was not only awarded his doctorate but conducted the marriage of his youngest brother. Henry Francis Sneyd-Kynnersley (1851-1900) married Margaret Ethel Chapman (1856-1939), daughter of a County Durham wine merchant, in Silksworth, near Sunderland, in April 1885, with his ordained brother Herbert assisting the local vicar in performing the wedding (*The Morning Post*, 28th April 1885). They went on to have four daughters (see Wadsworth, 2014). Unlike his brothers, Henry had, aged 14, gone not to Rugby but to Marlborough, presumably partly because his father was friends with its headmaster, George Bradley (1821-1903), later Dean of Westminster (Heffer, 2013, p.25). They had become friends while pupils at Rugby together, Bradley had taught Thomas Clement Sneyd-Kynnersley's two elder sons at Rugby, and Thomas had been one of Bradley's many referees when he applied to be Marlborough's headmaster in 1858 (Bradley, 1858, p.54). According to Henry Francis Sneyd-Kynnersley's obituary in the school magazine, Henry had 'good brains . . . but not quite of scholarship class . . . not a school hero in any way.' He was, however, 'an unusually loveable man' (A.G.B., 1900, p.329). Henry trained as an engineer, becoming a railway engineer based in Newcastle Upon Tyne in the northeast of England, hence his wedding a woman from County Durham. He was sufficiently notable to warrant an obituary in *Minutes of the Proceedings of the Institution of Civil Engineers* (1901).

In autumn 1885, Herbert devoted his energies, as an active member of his local Conservative Association, to ensuring that the Conservative candidate, local judge Sir George Russell, Bart (1828-1898), was returned for East Berkshire (Wokingham) in that year's General Election. Sneyd-Kynnersley was a member of the Sunninghill Conservative Ward Committee[35] which aimed to ensure that this occurred (*Windsor and Eton Express*, 21st November 1885).[36] The election, held on 24th November, was a turning point because it was the first in which the majority of adult males could vote. Russell was duly returned and Gladstone's Liberal government lost

---

[35] The area which a British council or corporation administered was divided into wards each of which elected one or more common councillors.

[36] His brother, Edmund McKenzie Sneyd-Kynnersley, was elected a Conservative councillor in Chester in 1906 (*Manchester Courier*, 21st August 1906).

its majority, struggling on until the election of July 1886, when the Conservatives won a substantial victory. In the same month, the Head was campaigning to improve the quality of the water supply in Sunninghill and Ascot (*Windsor and Eton Express,* 10th July 1886).

Death and Mid-Victorian Health

Sneyd-Kynnersley died 'very suddenly, from heart disease' while staying at his father's house, Moor Green, near Birmingham, on the evening of Monday 1st November 1886. According to his death certificate, Sneyd-Kynnersley died in the presence of his father's housekeeper. His passing was announced in *The Morning Post* the following week (*The Morning Post,* 6th November 1886). He was buried on 6th November 1886 at All Saints Church, Ascot Heath. Consulting the death certificate confirms that Herbert Sneyd-Kynnersley died of heart disease, as stated in his death announcement, and specifically of 'syncope heart disease,' aged just 38.

Mid-Victorians were surprisingly healthy. Life-expectancy at 65 was about 10 years, a life expectancy which subsequently declined, as did other markers of health, such as height. Due to the Agricultural Revolution and improved transport, Mid-Victorians enjoyed an extraordinarily healthy, essentially Mediterranean, diet. It was very high in fruit, vegetables, whole grains and fish, and low in fat. Alcoholic drinks were far weaker than today, meat was mainly nutrient-rich offal rather than the less healthy but tastier cuts, and people did formidable levels of exercise, walking from place to place. Smoking as well as sugary and salty tinned food was still quite rare. People died of infections or in accidents. Deaths from strokes, cancer and heart attacks were 90% lower than is the case today; these degenerative conditions now being the leading causes of death (Clayton & Rowbotham, 2009, Dutton, July 2018). As such, it was very rare for anybody — let alone a man of just 38 — to die from heart disease.

Problems Picturing the Headmaster

Sneyd-Kynnersley's estate was worth £4,189 and he left a will, carefully distributing all of his favourite books, paintings and watches. On 18th November 1880, Herbert had made his way to a solicitor's in Windsor to make this will. He made his brother-in-law, the Rev. Frederick Macdonald (1848-1928), vicar of Stapleford in Wiltshire, one of the executors and his brother, Henry Francis Sneyd-Kynnersley, the other. Aged just 32, Sneyd-Kynnersley was clearly very young to be making a will. Perhaps he had recently been seriously ill, with syncope heart disease being associated with periods of fainting. Flora did not remarry after her husband's death. Instead, according to the censuses, she worked at a college in Bristol, training female teachers. She died in 1925 and was buried in Clevedon in Somerset alongside her brother Robert Estcourt Macdonald. Flora left her entire estate to her childless brother, the Rev. Frederick Macdonald, who was the Free Masons' Grand Chaplain of England (Rylands, 1906, p.194) and later Canon of Salisbury Cathedral, and an Alderman on Wiltshire County Council, among many other accomplishments (*Who Was Who*, 1967; *Wiltshire Archaeological and Natural History Magazine*, June 1929, p.375).

The canon's childlessness has made tracking down a picture of Sneyd-Kynnersley rather difficult; not even St George's, Ascot possesses one. However, a photograph in an album which belonged to the Sneyd-Kynnersleys of Loxley Hall (Unpublished Sources: Photograph of . . .) would appear to be Herbert Sneyd-Kynnersley. At least, it is very much in line with the converging primary source descriptions of how he dressed and of his physical appearance, which we will look at below. The photograph depicts a well-dressed youngish man, in late Victorian costume, with a flower in his buttonhole, in line with descriptions of his smartness and his being a 'dandy.' He is wearing a white tie with black cloth, strongly implying that he is a late Victorian clergyman, and, as we will see, a former pupil remembers him wearing precisely such a tie as the only marker of his ordained status. Congruous with convergent comments on Sneyd-Kynnersley's physical appearance, the photograph's subject is tall, has a long face, has a Roman nose, has slightly bulging eyes, and has prominent mutton chops. The subject of the photograph is not remarkably slim, as Sneyd-Kynnersley was described as having been in around 1880, but if the photo was taken towards the end of his life he may have been subject to a degree of 'middle age spread.' Consistent with it being Sneyd-Kynnersley, the same album also contains definite pictures of his father and of his brothers Thomas Alfred and Charles Walter (Correspondence: Kousah, 16th November 2018), as these can be compared to other known photographs or portraits of them.

The Rev. Dr Herbert William Sneyd-Kynnersley

The Death of the Sneyd-Kynnersleys of Loxley Park

Within less than 30 years of the Headmaster's passing, the gentry family to which he was so proud to belong died as well. The Sneyd-Kynnersleys of Loxley Park went the way of so many late Victorian gentry families. Herbert's Sneyd-Kynnersley's Eton and Oxford-educated half-cousin Clement Thomas Sneyd-Kynnersley of Loxley Park (1833-1876) was Deputy Lord Lieutenant of Staffordshire (*London Gazette*, 28th June 1859). Clement's heir, Captain Clement Sneyd-Kynnersley of Loxley Park (1859-1909), was a sugar and coffee planter in Hawaii from 1882 to 1902 (*Brasenose College Register,* 1909, p.655), introducing polo to the kingdom (Hoyt, 1983, p.78) before returning to Uttoxeter to marry the vicar's daughter. (Restarick, 1924). *His* son, (Clement) Gerald Sneyd-Kynnersley (1888-1912) died young after a long illness (*Staffordshire Advertiser,* 28th September 1912). Two lots of death duties so close to one another forced the widow to sell part of the estate. The family sold Loxley Hall in 1945 (Foley, 1998, p.93), signalling the end of the Sneyd-Kynnersleys of Loxley Park. Death duties, which began to become a heavy burden from around 1894, forced many gentry families to part with stately homes and estates which had been in their families for many generations (Mingay, 1976).

So, Herbert Sneyd-Kynnersley was evidently from an eminent family of high achievers, in the lower ranks of the Victorian upper class, descending from a judge and even from a man who worked with George Stephenson to create the railway system. Churchill, of course, was close to the summit of that class. So, now that we have an understanding of Sneyd-Kynnersley's background, life, and family, let us turn to the sources of evidence for his much criticised teaching methods.

Herbert Sneyd-Kynnersley's Gravestone

Chapter Four

Life at St George's & Sneyd-Kynnersley's

Behaviour

An Innovative School

DUE TO THE exclusive nature of St George's, Ascot, a relatively large number of boys who went on to be celebrities were educated there, duly leaving autobiographies or having biographies written about them based on their private papers. As such, considering it was only a small school, there are a relatively large number of sources to tell us what it was like to be taught by Herbert Sneyd-Kynnersley.

Most obviously, there is Winston Churchill who wrote of the school in *My Early Life* (Churchill, 1930) and has been the subject of numerous biographies. But there is also the art critic Roger Fry (1866-1934) (Woolf, 1940), whom we met earlier. His memoirs and letters were edited and presented by Virginia Woolf but the original documents have been checked for any evidence of censorship or rewriting (Briggs, 2007). Then there is the man of letters and war correspondent Maurice Baring, OBE (1874-1945) who tells of the school in his 1922 autobiography *The Puppet Show of Memory* (Baring, 1922). We also have the 'Red Count' Harry Graf von Kessler

(1868-1937), a German diplomat, writer and left-wing politician who left Germany when the Nazis took power (Easton, 2002), Sir Edmund Backhouse, 2nd Baronet (1873-1944), an Oriental scholar and sinologist (Backhouse, 2017) and the unpublished memoirs and diary of barrister (Edward) Aubrey Hastings Jay, OBE (1869-1950) (Unpublished Primary Sources: Jay, 1947, Diary of Aubrey Jay). In addition, we have two very brief recollections. In the case of the colonial judge Arthur Bonham Carter, KC (1869-1916), who was killed at the Battle of the Somme, this takes the form of a single letter home to his father. Finally, Claude Schuster, 1st Baron Schuster (1869-1956), long time permanent secretary to the Lord Chancellor's Office (Graham Hall, 2003), spoke to his grandson about an aspect of life at St George's.

St George's, Ascot is a redbrick country house, built in 1874 (as marked on one of its drains) as well as surrounding cottages. The school is on a hill just above Ascot railway station and is surrounded by pine trees. St George's boasted excellent facilities and attempted to be 'fashionable' in every way it could be. It was the first and, in 1877, the only school in England to have electric lights (*Electrical Review*, 18th December 1891, p.716). Churchill (1930, pp.9-10) recalled that:

'It was supposed to be the very last thing in schools. Only ten boys in a class; electric light (then a wonder); a swimming pond; spacious football and cricket grounds, two or three school treats, or "expeditions" every term; the masters all M.A.'s in gowns and mortar boards; a chapel of its own; no hampers allowed; everything provided by the authorities.'

The small school was composed of the headmaster and three assistant masters. The swimming pond was fed by a waterfall and there was a forest and a garden in which boys could grow their own vegetables (Easton, 2002, p.24). Indeed, 'Mr Richards' — Sneyd-Kynnersley's gardener, George Richards (1848-1918) — actually won awards for his horticultural skills (*Journal of Horticulture and Cottage Gardener*, 27th November 1884, p.488). Beyond the garden was 'the Wilderness' in which, according to Aubrey Jay, the boys 'used to spend many happy hours helping the Head construct rockeries, tunnels, grottoes and other fascinating things' (Jay, 1947, p.11).

The school had, and still has, breath-taking views of the Surrey Hills. It was divided into four 'divisions' — based on composition, translation, grammar and diligence — and the 'First Division,' which was taught by Sneyd-Kynnersley himself (Baring, 1922), enjoyed the best expeditions. The school was also divided into four 'sets' for Mathematics and French only. Expeditions, in general, included hikes to Bagshot (an ancient village in Surrey) or Virginia Water (a Surrey village close to a large lake) for a picnic or for tea, and trips to Bath, the Isle of Wight, the Great Western Works in Swindon, the Huntley and Palmer Biscuit Factory in Reading, the Bank of England, a Home Rule debate in the House of Commons and the Mint at the Tower of London (Baring, 1922, p.76; Spalding, 1980, p.13; Jay, 1947, p.12). According to Aubrey Jay's diary, on Monday 4th July 1881 there was a 'general expedition' to Haslemere in Surrey:

'... it was nearly 30 miles, a most dreadfully long drive, we started soon after 9 o'clock and did not get there till about 1. It was a most fearfully hot day ... Mrs Kynnersley came after us with some of the boys and one of their horses would not go. Unfortunately, they had the glasses in their carriage and so we had to wait; we were all dying of thirst.' The boys had a picnic, 'then went about catching butterflies for about an hour and a quarter. Then we drove back to the hotel and met Mrs Kynnersley and her boys there. We then had some tea and drove back home again, the comet was very bright indeed. We did not get home till nearly 12 o'clock ...'

Roger Fry remembers that the school served excellent food, 'a good deal better than what I was accustomed to at home' (Woolf, 1940, p.32), and at home Fry had 'sirloin' every Sunday (p.28). Maurice Baring concurs on the high food quality (Baring, 1922, p.77). In 1878, there were two school dogs – Taff and Fan. The latter, according to Roger Fry's letter home to his mother (Sutton, 1972, p.105), was 'a stray dog found by a policeman in Birmingham and bought by the Head for ten shillings while he is really worth five guineas. I don't think it quite fair as the policeman didn't know . . .' Five guineas amounted to 65 shillings, so Sneyd-Kynnersley got a very good deal. Sneyd-Kynnersley liked collecting pedigree animals. He kept 12 Angora rabbits, worth £1 10s, in a hutch in his garden, which were stolen on the night of 2nd March 1883 by labourer Stephen Turner (1857-1925), leading to Turner's prosecution and sentence to 4 months' hard labour (*Reading Observer*, 7th April 1883; *Windsor and Eton Express*, 7th April 1883). The hutch also contained 15 to 20 Belgian hares (*Berkshire Chronicle*, 7th April 1883). In addition, there were tortoises and lizards at the school, imported by Sneyd-Kynnersley (Jay, 1947, p.11).

Teaching methods were innovative as well. The boys never had to write lines (Woolf, 1940, p.30), which was common practice at many schools for minor misdemeanours, something very time consuming, with fountain pens not yet having been invented. The stereotypical Victorian school involves rows of desks full of frightened children learning facts by rote. This wasn't how things worked at St George's, Ascot. American Robert Pilpel (1905-1987) (Pilpel, 1978, p.6) has asserted that: 'St George's was run by a sexually perverted, social climbing Anglican clergyman and it exemplified the rote-learning, blind obedience approach to education that has stultified so many creative spirits.' He provides no reference, which makes sense because his assertion is historically inaccurate. Kessler recalled that they would learn about Shakespeare by acting out and miming the roles. He was similarly enthused by the way all subjects at the school were taught, and he regarded Sneyd-Kynnersley as a brilliant and inspiring teacher, going so far as to compare him to Plato (Easton, 2002, pp.24-25). If you did well, such as by writing a very good essay, the Head would give you a nice leather-bound book, which was a very expensive prize at the time. Baring won the prize for writing the best essay on the book they'd had to read during a holiday. For this he received a copy of *Half-hours in the Far South* (Baring, 1922, p.75). In the view of Claude Schuster's grandson, the Rev. Christopher Turner (b. 1930), Sneyd-Kynnersley was 'a truly terrible man – but he did give sumptuous prizes' (quoted in Graham Hall, 2003, p.3). Turner informed me, however, that his grandfather never talked about Sneyd-Kynnersley himself, only the wonderful prizes that he gave (Interview, Turner, 7th July 2018).

Sir Edmund Backhouse

Churchill, Churchill's son Randolph, and Roger Fry have helped to ensure that Sneyd-Kynnersley is remembered only for his supposed constant, pitiless floggings, apparently motivated by sadism. This has become so-well established that Sneyd-Kynnersley is named in Terry Deary's (2016, p.216) *Villainous Victorians* (part of the popular *Horrible History* children's book series) as the archetypal sadistic Victorian headmaster. It is surprising — especially considering Sneyd-Kynnersley's vicarious fame via Churchill — that nobody has yet dispassionately analysed all of the sources about him. So let us do so. They range from Sir Edmund Backhouse, who portrays Sneyd-Kynnersley as a flogging obsessed sadist and homosexual who had a heart attack while flogging a boy to the point of bleeding, to Harry Kessler, who remembered Sneyd-Kynnersley as an amazing man and a life-long inspiration.

Let us begin with Sir Edmund Backhouse. He is an extremely unreliable source. In his book *The Hermit of Peking*, historian Hugh Trevor-Roper (1914-2003) explores Backhouse's life, exposing his forgeries and the fantasies and exaggerations in his autobiographical works. Hugh Trevor-Roper (1977, pp.16-17) observes that Sneyd-Kynnersley has become famous because:

'the success of his school drew to it several boys who afterwards became either famous, articulate or both, and who described his least attractive features – his *snobisme*, his fanatical Toryism . . . and his sadistic passion for beating bare buttocks.'

In Backhouse's memoir, first published in 2017 as *The Dead Past* (Backhouse, 2017), the manuscript of which was quoted from by Trevor-Roper, the baronet describes the school as 'a nursery of stereotypical intellects' and 'prigs and snobs.' The headmaster was 'a sadistic tyrant of colossal self-adulation who loved to flog his pupils and had homosexual relations with some of them' (quoted in Trevor-Roper, p.145).

Sir Edmund Backhouse, Bart.

The baronet claimed that while he was at St George's the Head died of a heart attack in full flogging-mode, on 16th July 1886, beating a boy called 'Dermot Howard Blundell,' and so the school broke up early that year. Backhouse writes that:

'We boys were so thrilled by the tidiness of the fatal synope that, with the friendly cooperation of a kindly housemaid who laid him out on his coffin, we managed to have the broken rod inserted into his shroud . . .' (quoted in Trevor-Roper, p.145).

Backhouse goes on to compare this to the Ancient Egyptian custom of burying the dead with familiar objects. As Trevor-Roper (p.165) notes, this is complete nonsense. By July 1886, Backhouse was at school at Winchester, so he certainly wasn't party to this supposed incident. Furthermore, Sneyd-Kynnersley died at his father's house, Moor Green in Kings Norton, on 1st November 1886. However, Backhouse's memoir indicates, as we will see below, a great deal of hatred for Sneyd-Kynnersley, and in passages not quoted by Trevor-Roper, he goes into detail about his own floggings at Sneyd-Kynnersley's hands.

Captain Dermot Howard Blundell-Hollinshead-Blundell, MVO[37] (1874-1910), however, was a real person. The son of a Major-General, Blundell-Hollinshead-Blundell was a Captain in the King's Royal Rifle Corps. The younger half-brother of a colonel turned Conservative MP as well as of one of Queen Victoria's Chaplains, Dermot died as a young man, after a 'long illness,' though in Kensington rather than in action in the army (*The King's Royal Rifle Corps Chronicle*, 1911, p.213). Presumably, Backhouse had heard about this and so selected this name to make his lie more convincing and

---

[37] Member of the Royal Victorian Order.

also because the falsehood, therefore, could not be disputed. Hugh Trevor-Roper censored from his quotations from *The Dead Past* Backhouse's assertion that Sneyd-Kynnersley and Blundell were in a homosexual relationship. However, the unreliability of Backhouse is such that he should only be believed where he is congruous with other sources. All of the sources agree on Sneyd-Kynnersley's floggings being severe, while one other source cautiously concurs with Sneyd-Kynnersley being attracted to the (older) boys, though this source does not suggest this was acted upon. Yet another, as we will see, has probably heard the rumours but doesn't believe them. So, there is a case, if no more than that, for concluding that Sneyd-Kynnersley was a non-practicing 'pederast,' as there is no evidence that he had sexual intercourse with a pupil. As we have observed, and as we will explore further below, there is nothing particularly remarkable about men with this predilection being school teachers.

Backhouse's memoir provides many other fascinating details, but unless they can be independently corroborated it is difficult to believe them, due to the obvious lies in his writings, which Hugh Trevor-Roper has highlighted. Backhouse recalls how Sneyd-Kynnersley would work himself into fits of rage, something which is, in a less exaggerated way, confirmed by others, such as Maurice Baring, as we shall see. Also, according to Backhouse, the headmaster would have fainting fits and seizures, such that a 'Dr Ringe' had to regularly come up from London to treat him. No other source recalls this and there is no physician with the surname 'Ringe' (or anything similar) on the 1881 census living in London. Backhouse also states that these medical complaints were a product of Sneyd-Kynnersley's 'aortic heart disease.' The 'fainting fit' recollection, however, is likely correct, as Sneyd-Kynnersley's death certificate records that he died of 'syncope heart disease.' This is a condition whereby the heart cannot pump sufficient oxygen to the brain, leading to low blood pressure, fainting and, in extreme cases, a heart attack.

Backhouse's Memories of the Masters

Like Maurice Baring, as we will see shortly, Backhouse regarded a particular teacher, called Robert Estcourt Macdonald (1854-1923), as being especially unpleasant. The Estcourts were a prominent Wiltshire gentry family (Burke, 1852, p.381), so one of their number may have been MacDonald's godfather, explaining his unusual middle name. It is unclear where Macdonald went to school but it was not to a well-known public school. He probably attended Somerset College, Bath, as his elder brother did (*Who Was Who,* 1967). Macdonald matriculated at New College, Oxford, in 1873, but by 1874 he was training to be a barrister at Middle Temple (Foster, 1891, p.891). At some point, he returned to Oxford, graduating, according to *Alumni Oxonienses,* from St Alban Hall in 1882, though most other records, such as the staff list from 1883, indicate that it was New College. Macdonald likely joined St George's in autumn 1880, as he was definitely there by the end of that academic year in August 1881 (Diary of Aubrey Jay, 1st August 1881), meaning he had not yet graduated when he joined the staff. Backhouse writes of him: 'Mr Robert Estcourt Macdonald, BA of Oxon, the head's brother-in-law, with streaming sentimental eyes, sentencing a boy to be "sent up to the head" for posterior treatment' (Backhouse, 2017). Consistent with this memory, Aubrey Jay noted in his diary on Monday 1st August 1881 that Macdonald was responsible for reading half of the reports in that Monday morning's weekly ritual, known as the 'Reading Over,' wherein boys' 'reports' were read out and those with very poor reports were sentenced to be punished. On this occasion, however, there were no punishments. But if Macdonald 'read over' half the reports on other occasions as well, and passed sentence accordingly, then this would make sense of Backhouse's recollection of Macdonald 'sentencing' boys to be sent to the Head to be birched.

Another master, Herbert Martin Cooke (1858-1931), was by implication, fairly reasonable: 'Mr Herbert Martin Cook [*sic.*], BA, with his huge *piton* and favoured gesture of thumb biting toward a recalcitrant boy' (Backhouse, 2017). H. Martin Cooke was Churchill's division master and one of the two masters whom Baring liked, as we will see below. Cooke was the son of landowner Mason

Cooke (1827-1906) of the Lawns, South Downham, Ely (Fox-Davies, 1929) and Mary Jane Martin (1834-1897) who was the daughter of a Downham gentleman farmer. Cooke was the eldest of ten children, in a rather tragic family. The second sibling, Arthur Mason Cooke (1861-1946) became a farmer, married and had children. But life for the other eight was far from easy. According to the 1871 census, Mary Rebecca Cooke (1863-1925) was 'Blind from birth' as was Ada Cooke (1869-1915). By the 1881 census, where the catchall word 'blind' was used, these were joined by Ethel (1872-1933) and Bertha (1877-1927), both of them 'blind.' In adulthood these blind sisters were spinster gentlewomen, employing their sighted spinster sister Helen Emma (1866-1947) to care for them along with a paid 'companion.' Also, by 1881, Harold (1864-1881) had died aged just 17 and Martin Huntingdon Cooke (1867-1915), later a poultry dealer with his own family, was also 'blind,' meaning he had gone blind sometime between the ages of 4 and 14. In that neither of the parents were blind and both male and female children had the condition, this may have been an autosomal (relating to a non-sex chromosome) disorder caused by both parents carrying the recessive form of the relevant allele. A physician friend informs me that it may have been the very rare condition Leber's Congenital Amaurosis. Most sufferers are born blind, though some gradually go blind. Cooke had one other sibling: John A. M. Cooke (1870-1936), an architect, was accused of fraud sometime shortly before 1893 (East Sussex Records Office) and was likely guilty as he had left the country by 1893.[38] He died — a divorcé with children, born in Cambridgeshire, aged 65 and noted to be an architect — living at 43 East Superior Street, Chicago (Unpublished Sources: Illinois Cook County Deaths, 1878-1994).

According to the 1871 census, H. Martin Cooke attended Great Yarmouth College, run by Daniel Tomkins (1826-1902), a school which taught pupils of all ages. Tomkins' son, Oliver Tomkins (1873-1901), was a missionary in Papua New Guinea with the London Mission Society. He was killed by natives in 1901 (Langmore, 1981). Sneyd-Kynnersley, as we have seen, was very interested in

---

[38] According to John Cooke's death record his ex-wife was called 'Zina.' A John Cooke and a Zina Binderkneadt had a child in Polk, Iowa — the state which neighbours Illinois — in September 1893.

overseas mission work. Accordingly, he may have known Daniel Tomkins, would have been looking for a music master in 1877, and Cooke may well have been recommended. There must have been some connection of this kind because, otherwise, Cooke had little to recommend him to the headmaster of such a 'high class prep school.' Cooke had not been to a prominent public school and nor did he have a degree, no matter what Backhouse recalled. It was not uncommon for prep school masters to not have degrees. Many were university dropouts, had failed their degrees, such as Evelyn Waugh (Silvester, 1993, p.449), or had simply been to public school and had the right contacts. They would be taken on without any teaching certificate (Brendon, 1993, p.95). But Cooke had none of these factors in his favour. As Eastbourne local historian Liz Moloney (2015, p.16) has put it, Cooke's 'later career would be more understandable if he had moved on to a well-known public school. There is no evidence of this, however, nor of his having taken a university degree.'

Churchill recalled that the St George's masters all wore 'gowns and mortar boards.' A master would only have been entitled to wear a mortarboard if he had at least a Bachelor's degree. As far as I can see, Backhouse must have assumed Cooke had a degree because the other master's did and perhaps Churchill simply exaggerated to make his sentence flow better and avoid an aside. The evidence implying that Cooke did not have a degree is substantial. The 1881 census lists Cyril Scudamore (1856-1945), another master whom we will meet below, directly above Cooke and, under profession, states that Scudamore was 'BA Schoolmaster.' Cooke's profession is marked 'Do' ('Ditto') but this is only beneath the word 'Schoolmaster.' Cooke is not on the published alumni lists for Oxford or Cambridge, nor can he be found in Durham University's archives (Correspondence, Stansfield, 4th October 2018) nor those of Trinity College Dublin (Correspondence, Lockhart, 15th October 2018). The Scottish universities that existed at the time — St Andrews, Glasgow, Aberdeen, Edinburgh, and Heriot-Watt — can be eliminated because, at that time, a Master's degree in Scotland was an undergraduate qualification; Bachelor's degrees were *not* conferred on undergraduates. The university colleges in London — London only gained full university status in 1890 — offered degrees from 1836 onwards and various provincial colleges, including those in Wales (Lawrence, 1972, p.21), were affiliated to them (Marriott, 1981), but Cooke cannot be found in the records of the University of London (University of London, 2018). So Cooke definitely did not have a BA. In addition, a degree is not stated for Cooke on St George's 1883 staff list (though it is for the other masters); in any of the gentry reference books which record Cooke's marriage (*Burke's Landed Gentry* 1912, p.154; Fox-Davies, 1929, p.422; *Walford's County Families,* 1909, p.243); nor when Cooke was made a Fellow of the Royal Society of Literature in 1899, with the degrees of many other fellows placed after their names (Royal Society of Literature, 1907, p.39). No degree is mentioned for Cooke in Eastbourne local newspaper reports about the school he founded there nor in reports about Cooke's many civic activities, nor in local directories, but the degrees of other masters are recorded (Moloney, 2015).

Indeed, for Maurice Baring, Cooke's lack of education was something almost fascinating about him. How could Cooke have come so far — in a prep school teaching world populated by Oxbridge graduates — when he'd never been to university? In his autobiographical novel *C,* Maurice Baring presents a character called 'Mr Forsyth' who was clearly supposed to be Cooke. In the novel, C's 'Berkshire school' had broken up after the 'headmaster . . . died.' Mr Forsyth 'although the least intellectual [*of the Berkshire masters*] was considered to have great organising capacities, started a school near Brighton' – a coastal Sussex town like Eastbourne. This 'brisk, breezy, rather burly man' was '. . . not a scholar in any sense and he left the intellectual education of the boys to his staff . . . At the Berkshire school, he had only taught the smallest boys . . . as well as drawing and music to the whole school . . . Mr Forsyth was unmarried' (Baring, 1934, Ch. 5). All of this — Cooke set up a school on the Sussex coast, had taught the fourth division at Ascot which mainly included the youngest boys, had taught the whole school music, organized concerts, and was unmarried — implies that Mr Forsyth is Cooke, with Cooke being less educated than all the other masters at St George's. Cooke was a great organiser of concerts, such as a very well-reviewed one at the Corn Exchange in Ely in 1883 (*The Musical Standard,* 1883, p.58), for example.

Similarly regarded as amiable by Backhouse seems to have been the 'Reverend Thomas Cadwallader[39] Sanders, MA, bearded and high stomached, at the wicket plying the cricket ball which indeed he did with success . . .' (Backhouse, 2017). Sanders — whose actual name was Thomas Cooke Sanders (1843-1892) — was the son of the vicar of Moulton in Northamptonshire. He had attended Rossall School in Lancashire before going on to Oxford, where he was McBride Scholar (*The Morning Post,* 7th April 1862) and was also given a 'Lusty Scholarship' (Moody, 1863, p.226). Sanders was an experienced teacher by 1883. In 1871, he was assistant master at a school in Lucton in Herefordshire and in 1881 he was working as a private 'tutor' and 'clergyman without care of souls' in Minister in Kent. Sanders was at St George's in 1883 but had left by autumn 1884 when Maurice Baring arrived, as it is clear from Baring's memoirs that Sanders was not one of the three assistant masters. Backhouse, like his fellow-pupil Roger Fry, believed that Sneyd-Kynnersley was sexually aroused by flogging his pupils. Backhouse (2017) writes:

'. . . wan, blue as lead, with droopy whiskers and fishy eyes, wearing a ghastly sadistic grin, thin as a whipping post, salacious and lustful; probably boasting a Cyclopean orgasm, birch in hand, with flogging block draped in solemn black, with a spare rod intended to overawe and impress, with a hideous rug thoughtfully disposed for the doomed candidate of the *fessée* to kneel upon, his naked buttocks upturned for the encounter . . .'

Consistent with Maurice Baring, Backhouse tells us that it was absolutely forbidden to touch the electric light switches and that pupils who did so were immediately flogged. However, unlike Baring, Backhouse asserts that there was a sign prominently displayed stating that any pupil who disobeyed this rule would be subject to 'a most severe punishment across the bared breach.' That there existed such a bizarre sign — without it being remarked upon by others — seems most unlikely, especially as Baring recalls a child showing his visiting parents how the lights worked.

---

[39] 'Cadwallader' was not Sanders' middle name. It is unclear why Backhouse stated that it was.

Churchill's Experience: 'How I hated this school . . .'

Churchill attended St George's from 1882 to 1884. In his autobiography *My Early Life,* Churchill himself tells us that on the first day, just before turning 8, he was 'alone with the form master' who produced a book and said, 'You have never done any Latin before, have you?' He then handed Churchill a page on which were the declensions for 'Mensa,' the Latin word for 'table.' The 'form master' told Churchill to learn it and that he'd return 'in half an hour, to see what you know.' Churchill managed to commit it to memory but was confused that one of the declensions was, 'O table' and kept asking the form master 'what does it mean?' The form master explained that you would use that declension when 'speaking to a table.' 'But I never do!' blurted out Winston, to which the master responded, 'If you are impertinent you will be punished, and punished, let me tell you, very severely.' As we will explore later, the nature of memory, and its place in ensuring a positive sense of self (e.g. Bluck, 2003) may well mean that Churchill was far more 'impertinent' than he recollected in 1930.

In his biography of his father, *Winston S. Churchill: Youth, 1874-1900,* Randolph Churchill (1966) presents this incident in a very confusing way. He provides us with Churchill's recollection, quoted above from *My Early Life,* of how St George's was 'the very last thing in schools . . .' Randolph then completely misses out a section on the headmaster's floggings, which we will look at below, quotes the Latin incident verbatim and then states, 'The school which Winston discreetly camouflaged as St James' was St George's, at Ascot, and the headmaster was the Rev. H. W. Sneyd-Kynnersley.' However, up to this point in Randolph's text and in his quotations from Winston there has been no mention of the headmaster. Accordingly, Randolph presents this incident as if it were with regard to the headmaster, implying that Churchill has, for some reason, disguised him as the 'Form Master.' This is precisely what was assumed in the film *Young Winston,* where the script included this incident pretty much word-for-word with the scene involving Winston and the headmaster. But in *My Early Life,* Churchill finishes recalling the Mensa incident with his '*Form master*' and then goes on to discussing the '*headmaster*' and his beatings. Thus, it wasn't Sneyd-Kynnersley who snapped at Churchill on his first day at school at all. Based on Backhouse's descriptions of the three form masters it was almost certainly Robert Estcourt Macdonald, something which will be substantiated by Maurice Baring's recollections of Macdonald, below, as childish, petty, and quick to anger.

With regard to the *headmaster*, Winston Churchill (1930, pp.11-12) tells us in *My Early Life* that:

> 'The Form Master's observations about punishment were by no means without their warrant at St James' school. Flogging with the birch, in the Eton-fashion, was a great feature of the curriculum. But I am sure no Eton boy, and certainly no Harrow boy in my day, ever received such a cruel flogging as this headmaster was accustomed to inflict on little boys who were in his care and power. They exceeded in severity anything that would be tolerated in any of the Reformatories under the Home Office. My reading in later life has supplied me with some possible explanations for his temperament.'

Winston continues, informing us that:

> 'Two or three times a month the whole school was marshalled into the Library and one or more delinquents was haled off to an adjoining apartment by the two head boys, and there flogged until they bled freely, while the rest of us sat quaking, listening to their screams.'

This system of discipline was 'reinforced' by frequent High Church religious services in the chapel. Churchill states that, due to the influence of his Nanny, Mrs (Elizabeth) Everest (1834-1895), he was Low Church (see Sandys & Henley, 2016), and that he obtained, therefore, little religious comfort from these services but 'I experienced the fullest applications of the secular arm. How I hated this school . . .' In other words, he was frequently beaten, consistent with evidence of his very poor behaviour, which we will explore in more detail in a later chapter. Mrs. Everest wasn't merely Low Church; she was Non-Conformist. She was baptised on 17th August

1834 at the independent Clover Street Ebenezer Chapel in Chatham in Kent. 'Mrs. Everest' was never married and was probably given the honorific 'Mrs.' due to her status as the nurse to a noble family (Addison, 2017, p.94).[40] But, importantly, Churchill's brief description would appear to paint a portrait of Sneyd-Kynnersley as sadistic. Indeed, he pretty much states this to be the case when he refers to 'My reading in later life . . .'

It has been widely reported that Churchill only discovered Sneyd-Kynnersley's death many years after it occurred, having made his way to Ascot to beat the headmaster up. Peregrine Churchill (1913-2002), Winston's nephew, recalled that while Winston was at Harrow, and already an accomplished swordsman, 'he decided to settle the score,' embittered by the thrashings he had endured at Sneyd-Kynnersley's hands. Winston 'set out to St George's, Ascot, to tackle the headmaster, unaware that he had died of a heart attack the year after Winston left the school' (Lee & Lee, 2010, p.37). However, another biography, *The Churchills* by Mary S. Lovell, states that during Churchill's time at Sandhurst Military Academy, which was between September 1893 and December 1894, still seething after almost ten years, Churchill returned to his prep school to 'exact physical retribution' on Sneyd-Kynnersley. Churchill rode to the school and 'with mixed feelings received the news that Sneyd-Kynnersley was dead and the school was under new management.' No source is provided (Lovell, 2012, p.68).

The key question is: Did Churchill return to Ascot to confront Sneyd-Kynnersley and, if so, when? With regard to the second issue, St George's, Ascot did not acquire 'new management' until 1893, when it was auctioned off, as we will later see. This would mean that Churchill was at Sandhurst *not* Harrow at the time that he supposedly set out to confront his old headmaster. This would also make sense insomuch as Sandhurst is only 10 miles from Ascot, while Harrow is 25 miles away. As for whether the incident happened at all, tracing the sources back, it would seem that the original

---

[40] Until the nineteenth century, the title 'Mrs.' was reserved for gentry women — of just the kind who would be nannies to noble families — and was ascribed to them whether they were married or not (Erickson, 2002, p.99). By the 1880s, the Churchills were simply using the title in what was, by then, an old-fashioned way.

source for the anecdote that Churchill made his way to Ascot to beat up Sneyd-Kynnersley, thereupon discovering he had died, is his maternal cousin Sir Shane Leslie, Bart (1885-1971) who wrote in his autobiography *Long Shadows* (Leslie, 1966, p.21):

> 'Churchill realised in later life that he had been disciplined by a sadist. His early memories were so incensed that he went from Sandhurst as a cadet to settle matters but found his old enemy had suddenly died to the relief of his pupils. His double-barrelled name is best forgotten.'

Peregrine Churchill may have heard this second hand, with Sandhurst having somehow evolved into Harrow.

There is good reason, however, to doubt that the incident ever occurred. Firstly, Shane Leslie idolised his cousin: 'We admired Winston intensely . . . We children followed Winston' (Leslie, 1966, p.16) Leslie recalled of his childhood. Even when writing *Long Shadows,* Leslie seems to have felt something like veneration for Churchill: 'From his mother came determination, undeviating ambition, immense health-power and a clear vision into the future' (p.15), 'I can offer memories [*of Churchill*] from the preheroic period of nursery and schooldays,' (p.18), 'In History he must join Robert the Bruce whose patient investigation of spiders induced him to try and try again' (p.20). So we can imagine that Winston may have told his cousin-apostle a few self-aggrandising tales and may have done the same with regard to his younger brother, Peregrine's father. It is quite possible that Churchill did this even in later life, having somehow learnt that Sneyd-Kynnersley had died, possibly directly or indirectly via Maurice Baring's (1922) *The Puppet Show of Memory* or Virginia Woolf's (1940) *The Life of Roger Fry*. Churchill was certainly fabricating aspects of his life story in 1930. In *My Early Life,* Churchill stated that the Boer soldier who had personally taken him prisoner in South Africa in 1899 had been General Louis Botha (1862-1919) who went on to found the modern South African state. Botha, claimed Churchill, had revealed this to him in 1902 when they had met in London (Churchill, 1930, p.253). However, it has since become quite clear from primary sources that it was *not* Botha that captured Churchill at all. Botha *interrogated* Churchill, but he did not apprehend him. Nevertheless, Churchill insisted that Botha personally captured him and told him so in 1902 because Churchill didn't recognize him (Schoeman, 2013). Churchill (1930, pp.253-254) wrote:

> "'Don't you recognise me? It was I who took you prisoner, I myself," and his bright eyes twinkled with pleasure. Botha in white shirt and frock coat looked very different in all save size and darkness of complexion from the wild war time figure I had seen that day in Natal. But about the extraordinary fact there can be no doubt.'

The simplest explanation for this discrepancy is that Churchill was embroidering his life to make it a better read, something that would be unlikely to be challenged in 1930 due to Botha having died of Spanish flu in 1919 (Steyn, 2018). One wonders what else in Churchill's scintillating and brilliantly written *My Early Life* has been fabricated with this aim in mind.

Secondly, Churchill did not mention returning to Ascot in *My Early Life,* despite the book setting out many anecdotes about his bravery. So this would potentially mean that the return was a later invention. This story does not appear in Randolph Churchill's biography, either. Thirdly, it is difficult to explain why Churchill disguised St George's in his memoir. He called it 'St James" and didn't reveal even the county it was in, but he did not follow this course with his second prep school, clearly stating that it had been in Brighton. One possibility is that he felt that this disguise would allow him to engage in some artistic license — for example, with regard to the cruelty of the beatings — without being accused of exaggeration. But Churchill's fame by 1930, and the prominence of many of his St George's contemporaries, means that this obviously failed. A second possibility is that he was concerned about libel. He was, it might be argued, implying that Sneyd-Kynnersley's beatings were of sufficient severity to have broken the law. So, to avoid the possibility of being sued, he chose to name neither the headmaster nor the school nor even the county the school was in. Indeed, to really be on the safe side, he didn't even directly state that the headmaster was, in his judgement, a sadist. This would potentially mean that he had realised that he had hyperbolized the harshness of the beatings and that, as a public figure, he wanted to avoid the possible negative publicity — as well as financial loss — attendant on being sued. But in that a dead man cannot sue, this would imply that in 1930 Churchill was not certain that Sneyd-Kynnersley was dead. However, in 1896, when Churchill was an army officer, he became good friends with Major Hugo Baring, OBE (1876-1949) as they sailed together to Bombay, to the extent of sharing a bungalow with Hugo Baring in Bangalore (Churchill, 1930, p.106). Hugo Baring had been a pupil at St George's until the end of 1885 (see below) and he would definitely have known that Sneyd-Kynnersley was dead. It seems unlikely that Churchill and Hugo Baring would not have compared notes on their old school, meaning that Churchill surely knew of Sneyd-Kynnersley's passing by 1930.

Roger Fry's Trauma

Roger Fry's recollections of Sneyd-Kynnersley are more even-handed. He attended the school from 1877 to 1880. In terms of physical appearance, Fry recalls that Sneyd-Kynnersley was 'a tall, lose-limbed man with aquiline nose and angular features.' He also sported a pair of 'Dundreary whiskers, which waved on each side of his flaccid cheeks like bat's wings,' which he used to constantly stroke. With regard to dress, 'He was something of a dandy' (Woolf, 1940, p.32). He didn't wear a clerical collar, but marked himself out as a clergyman with 'the white tie and the black cloth.' 'He was decidedly vain' and he spoke of the sense of superiority which being a clergyman bestowed upon him. Fry remembers that Sneyd-Kynnersley '. . . read Dickens aloud to the whole school every evening before bed time.' As we will see later, this is an exaggeration, something to which Fry appears to be prone. Politically, Fry describes the headmaster as '. . . a bigoted and ignorant High Church Tory' (p.31-32).

Fry was part of a Quaker family from Highgate, a fashionable north London suburb. He was the son of a wealthy judge, Sir Edward

Fry (1827-1913). Roger Fry had first met Sneyd-Kynnersley in the summer of 1877 when he came to lunch at Fry's parents' house and Fry was asked to show him round the neighbourhood. Once he'd left, Fry's parents asked him whether he would like to go to school with 'Mr Sneyd-Kynnersley,' who was setting up a new school in Ascot, which had been built by Fry's maternal uncle Alfred Waterhouse (1830-1905) (Woolf, p.29). 'I answered in the manner that was expected of me that it would be very nice to go to school with the strange clergyman' (p.30). According to Virginia Woolf, who wrote Fry's biography and with whose married sister Fry had a sexual relationship, Fry's mother kept all of his letters home from school. They talk of cricket matches, visits from missionaries, school trips — such as to Eton, where they were treated to extravagant high teas — and how he was allowed to keep a pet snake. However, Fry also mentions being bullied at the hands of a boy called Ferguson (p.30). Woolf quotes various flogging anecdotes from Fry's letters:

> 'Mr Sneyd-Kynnersley had assured the Frys that there were to be no punishments. Yet "there were two fellows flogged yesterday and there is going to be one flogged tomorrow. He was only playing with another boy at dinner." Again, "the moon-faced boy" had been flogged because he threw some water on to the wall. Again, "Last night Ferguson went to Mr Kynnersley's room I don't know what for, but he was found out and I had to dress and go to the Head's room . . . Ferguson was so troublesome that Mr Holmes had to hold him down' (p.31).

Fry had to dress because he was the head boy, and it was therefore his duty, along with the deputy head boy, to bring the miscreant to the headmaster's study and hold him down during the flogging, with something similar occurring at most public schools at the time (How, 1900). He wrote to his mother on 17th February 1878 that:

> "'I intend to get leave not to bring the boys up to be whipped, as I don't like it" he told his mother; but the Head said that "it was the business of the captain of the school, but he hoped not to whip anyone"' (Sutton, 1972, p.105).

In later life, Fry provided more detail regarding Sneyd-Kynnersley. Woolf does not provide a date but she collected together various fragments of autobiography Fry had written. One of these refers to events in 1929 (Woolf, 1940, p.25), implying that Fry wrote these fragments no earlier than 1930, when he was 64 years old.

'[*Sneyd-Kynnersley*] was however genuinely fond of boys and enjoyed their company. He was always organising expeditions. During a cold winter he took the upper form boys for long afternoons skating on the Basingstoke canal. In summer we went to Eton and always we were treated very lavishly with high teas and strawberries and cream. The school was I think a very expensive one but everything was done in good style and the food a good deal better than what I was accustomed to at home. As the boys came mostly from rather aristocratic homes they were much easier to get on with than those which I met later at a Public school. They had not to the same extent the idea of good form, were much more natural and ready to accept things. Altogether my time at Sunninghill House might have been more than tolerable if it had not been for one thing which poisoned my whole life there' (Woolf, 1940, p.32).

Sarah Ferguson's Ancestor: The Boy Flogged Until He Excreted Freely?

This 'poison' was the apparently frequent and severe floggings.

'When my parents told me that there were no punishments it was quite true that the masters never set lines or kept boys in, but as Mr Sneyd-Kynnersley explained to us with solemn gusto the first morning that we were all gathered together before him he reserved to himself the right to a good sound flogging with the birch rod. How my parents who were extremely scrupulous about verbal inaccuracy reconciled it to their consciences to omit this fact I never made out, but I cannot doubt that they knew or else they would have expressed more surprise than they did when later on I revealed the horrid fact to them.

Anyhow the birch rod was a serious matter to me, not that I dreaded it particularly for myself because I was of such a disgustingly law-abiding disposition that I was never likely to incur it. But as I was from the first [*division*] and all through either first *or* second in the school I was bound *ex officio* to assist at the executions and hold down the culprit. The ritual was very precise and solemn. Every Monday morning the whole school assembled in Hall and every boy's report was read aloud.

After reading a bad report from a form master Mr Sneyd-Kynnersley would stop and after a moment's awful silence say "Harrison minor you will come up to my study afterwards." And so afterwards the culprits were led up by the two top boys. In the middle of the room was a large box draped in black cloth and in austere tones the culprit was told to take down his trousers and kneel before the block over which I and the other head boy held him down. The swishing was given with the master's full strength and it took only two or three strokes for drops of blood to form everywhere and it continued for 15 or 20 strokes when the wretched boy's bottom was a mass of blood. Generally, of course the boys endured it with fortitude but sometimes there were scenes of screaming, howling and struggling which made me almost sick with disgust. Nor did the horrors even stop there. There was a wild red-haired Irish boy, himself rather a cruel brute, who whether deliberately or as a result of the pain or whether he had diarrhoea, let fly. The irate clergyman instead of stopping at once simply went on with increased fury until the whole ceiling and walls of his study were spattered with filth. I suppose he was afterwards somewhat ashamed of this for he did not call in the servants to clean up but spent hours doing it himself with the assistance of a boy who was his special favourite.'

From a combination of this description and Fry's letters home, it is very probable that this unfortunate boy was Algernon Francis Holford Ferguson (1867-1943). He later attended Eton, became a

Brigadier-General and is the great-grandfather of Sarah Ferguson, who was married to Prince Andrew, Duke of York. St George's became a girls' private secondary boarding school in 1905 and was actually attended by Princess Beatrice — the daughter of Prince Andrew and great-great grand-daughter of Algernon Ferguson — who was elected the school's head girl in 2006 (*Mail Online*, 16th May 2006). Algernon Ferguson was at St George's on the 1881 census; Fry had every reason to call him a 'brute,' as he wrote home about how Ferguson bullied him, and 'Ferguson' was definitely flogged in Fry's presence, as Fry referred in a letter to Ferguson being so 'troublesome' that one of the masters had to hold him down (p.31). In addition, Ferguson's father was from Belfast; there was no other boy at the school on the 1881 census with Irish connections apart from Harry Kessler, who had been born in Wicklow. However, he was a nervous, depressed little boy, unlikely to bully anyone, he was never flogged (Kessler, 1935), and Fry would surely have referred to him as 'German.' And, of course, ginger hair famously runs in the Ferguson family. With regard to the flogging of Algernon Ferguson, Fry notes:

'I think this fact alone shows that he had an intense sadistic pleasure in these floggings and that these feelings were even excited by the wretched victim's performance or else he would certainly have put it off till a more suitable occasion. Monday morning thus was always a dreadful time for us. It nearly always resulted in one or two executions but sometimes no sufficient excuse could be found in the reports. Sunday in spite of its leisure and amusements was spoilt for me by the anticipation of next morning's session and I lay awake often praying feverishly, and nearly always futilely, that no one would get a swishing. But one was never sure not to be called on to assist.'

Ferguson — who was clearly flogged by Sneyd-Kynnersley and is very likely the boy who 'let fly' — was actually one of the beneficiaries in Sneyd-Kynnersley's will, receiving 'a book or picture to be selected by my wife.' Based on Sneyd-Kynnersley's will, it appears very probable that the 'special favourite' was George Hubert Olliver (1868-1944), who was, according to the 1871 census, the stepson of the rector of Ascot, the Rev. Beauchamp Kerr Pearse (1836-1900). Olliver, alone of the many pupils and former pupils who received bequests in Sneyd-Kynnersley's will, is referred to as 'my friend and pupil.' Also, his inheritance was far more generous than that of any other boy.

Roger Fry

Fry also tells us of another flogging:

One night just as I was going to sleep the Head, as we called Mr Sneyd-Kynnersley, called me to come to his study. We slept in cubicles, sometimes three or four were arranged in a single large bedroom and the Head had over-heard one boy say to another "What a bother, I forgot to pump ship: I must get out of bed." This indecent talk merited of course a ferocious flogging and my night's rest was spoilt by the agitation it had put me into (. . .) But whatever the cause, my horror of these executions was certainly morbid and it has given me all my life a morbid horror of all violence between men so that I can scarcely endure any simulation of it on the stage. . .' (pp.32-35).

In understanding why this boy was flogged, it must be remembered that the Victorians had an extreme abhorrence of bodily functions and of their discussion (Marshall, 2013, p.114). Even loo paper was not directly referred to, but euphemistically termed 'curling paper' (Ratcliffe, 2018).

However, Fry was not of the view that Sneyd-Kynnersley was necessarily homosexual. Instead, he felt that his interest in boys was due to his own child-like nature. We will see striking evidence of this from another source shortly, but Fry writes:

'You will no doubt long ago have come to the conclusion that Mr Sneyd-Kynnersley was at least an unconscious Sodomite but on looking back I feel fairly convinced that he was not and that his undoubted fondness for boys was due to his own arrested development. He was certainly very vain and his very meagre intellectual culture left him I suspect always with a feeling of slight humiliation among grown-up people. I attribute to that the care with which he got rid of any master of intelligence and supplied his place with imbeciles. It was natural therefore that he felt happiest among boys where he could more than hold his own and whose sense of humour was of his own elementary brand' (p.35).

Despite the trauma that Sneyd-Kynnersley caused Fry, the art critic seems to ultimately have liked him. When the headmaster died, Fry wrote: 'I am very sorry for it . . . as although he never inspired me with much respect he was, I think, kind-hearted on the whole' (p.35). Sneyd-Kynnersley left Fry a book of Thomas Arnold's sermons in his will. The fact that Fry could describe Sneyd-Kynnersley — in light of the trauma the headmaster's behaviour seems to have caused him — as 'kind-hearted on the whole' would surely imply incredible acts of kindness, sufficient to overwhelm what Fry clearly regards as, and what is surely to modern eyes, quite appalling behaviour towards children.

Maurice Baring's Time at St George's

The diplomat, war correspondent and author Maurice Baring (1874-1945) (Baring, 1922) provides us with the most detailed account of life in the Sneyd-Kynnersley kingdom, which began in September 1884, just after Churchill had left, and lasted until the end of 1885. Baring, who would go on to attend Eton, was the fifth son and eighth child of Edward Baring, 1st Baron Revelstoke (1828-1897), a senior partner in Baring's Bank, director of the Bank of England and chairman of Lloyds of London. Baring's resentment is often focused on masters other than the headmaster, as he recalls the way that the masters would mock his nasal accent (p.71). Masters would write denigrating reports of pupils who, for example, let the school down on the sports field and these would be published in the school newspaper, which was sent to parents (pp.72-73). 'It was the masters who every now and then made life a misery' Baring writes, rather than simply 'the headmaster' (p.74), his life at the school being 'marred and made hideous for the time being by unexpected dramas' (p.71).

One day, Baring's maths master — he was in Set Four for Maths — found that Baring had cheated in a test. Baring hadn't meant to cheat, but 'Duckworth' — likely Somerset vicar's son Major Arthur Campbell Duckworth (1870-1948) — had told him the answer so they could both hurry up and leave the classroom. Baring had scribbled the answer down, meaning that Baring's working out was wrong. The master said he would report this to the head. Then at chapel on Sunday — Baring was in the school choir — the same (clearly rather infantile) master snuck up behind Baring and pinned a sheet of paper with the word 'cheat' written on it to his gown. Later that day, when the children were writing their letters home, this master sarcastically told Baring that he must write in his letter that, 'I had done very well and I was his favourite boy' (p.73). When it came to the next 'Reading Over' — when the whole school was assembled in divisions, the reports were read out, and, according to Roger Fry, there'd usually be an 'execution' or two — Sneyd-Kynnersley told Baring, and the other boy involved in the cheating, that this would be mentioned in their half-term reports, which were sent to parents, and if it happened again then they would be flogged. Other boys were apparently horrified by this dishonesty, asking the two accused, aghast, 'How could we?' and both boys remained social pariahs for a while (p.73). This implies that the frequency with which floggings occurred has been exaggerated by Fry.

One master, in charge of Division Two, not the head, made a group of badly behaved boys hold hands while he jolted them with a strong electric current. This enraged one of the boys so much that he picked up the battery and threw it at the master, 'inflicting a sharp head wound.' The boys 'thought it jolly' of this master 'not to sneak' – not to tell the headmaster (p.77). Presumably the same master — as Baring states the only assistant master he didn't get on with was the Division Two Master — sentenced Baring to not be allowed to talk for a week at meals for using the term 'mighty good' to describe the food, a term which was presumably regarded as unacceptably colloquial (p.77). The Maths master's telling 'the head' implies that this master was Robert Estcourt Macdonald, as Sir Edmund Backhouse commented that he was known for threatening to 'tell the Head.' In addition, Macdonald was the only assistant master left behind at St George's when the two assistant masters whom Baring liked left to found a new school, as we will see below. So, this further confirms that the Second Division master was Macdonald.

St George's Ascot

Baring's Views on Sneyd-Kynnersley

Baring's attitude towards Sneyd-Kynnersley is rather ambiguous. Baring thoroughly enjoyed it when Sneyd-Kynnersley read them all stories, for example, and especially the Head's performance of *The Last Abbot of Glastonbury* 'which I revelled in' (Baring, 1922, p.71, see Crake, 1883). Baring says that the thing he 'enjoyed most' about the school were 'readings out by the headmaster which happened on Sunday afternoons and sometimes on ordinary evenings' (p.74). However, the headmaster's behaviour was seemingly erratic and childish. Not long after Baring had arrived there was 'the incident of the Spanish chestnuts' (pp.71-72). The boys had been told not to eat any of the chestnuts that were lying on the grass in part of the school garden, but some of them did anyway. At tea that evening, the Head suddenly rapped his knife on the table and commanded that 'All boys who have eaten Spanish chestnuts are to stand up.' Boys gradually stood up, at the Head's encouragement that the punishment wouldn't be so bad if they owned up, though most believed this spectacle 'portended dreadful things.' The boys were told that they were guilty of the sins of 'greed, disobedience and deceit' and they were sentenced to 'two hours' extra work on half-holiday' (p.72), that is Saturday, which was a half-working day at the time rather than a full day off. Again, we note an example of wanton disobedience, yet no corporal punishment.

In *Boy* (Dahl, 1984), Roald Dahl recalls being caned at Repton merely for talking during class. However, at St George's, boys who cheated at Maths received no corporal punishment at all. Nor did a boy who received a message from the head, while the Head was away, with some instruction or other, and sent a much younger boy, who had conveyed the message to him, back to ask if the instruction was 'genuine.' This joker merely had to apologise for his behaviour in front of the entire school (p.76). However, one day a boy whose parents were visiting couldn't resist showing his parents how the electric lights (at that time extremely rare) worked, by turning them on and off. This was expressly not allowed, as only the 'head engineer' — a particularly exalted pupil — was permitted to do this. Sneyd-Kynnersley witnessed what the boy had done through a window and as soon as the parents had gone the boy was flogged (p.72).

'Nothing was more strange at this school,' writes Baring, 'than the sudden way in which either a treat or a punishment descended on the school' (p.76). One day, the 'first division' were suddenly all taken away to London for a matinée and didn't return for 24 hours. Another day a boy was 'suddenly flogged for cutting off a piece of his hair and keeping it in his drawer 'We lived in a constant atmosphere on uncertainty. We never knew if a harmless action would be construed into a mortal offence' (p.77). One afternoon, Baring and some friends – Broadwood and Bell - got bored watching the school cricket team play another school, so they wandered off to have some fun. They were eventually noticed by a master, presumably Macdonald, who was angry and told the head. The Head was livid. After tea, he summoned the entire school and berated the three boys for being guilty of:

'. . . want of patriotism, bad manners, inattention and vulgarity. He was disgusted, he said, with the behaviour of the school before strangers. We were especially guilty but the whole school had shown want of attention and gross callousness and indifference to the cricket match (which was all too true), and consequently had tarnished the honour of the school. There was to be no expedition to the New Forest next week' (p.79).

However, there was also to be no birching for these offences, which had clearly particularly infuriated the head. The birching would instead be reserved for really serious crimes, such as operating a light switch (though this was direct disobedience of an established and specific rule) or cutting off a piece of your hair and keeping it in a drawer. Although, as we will see later, this latter piece of individualism may be regarded as precisely the form of behaviour which the public school system was designed to obliterate in the upper class, in its attempt to, in effect, create an army. There may also have been more to this, such as the boy initially lying when challenged about it. 'Broadwood' and 'Bell' were Ivo Arthur Broadwood (1874-1899), a

Lieutenant who died suddenly in London of a heart attack aged 25 (*The Army and Navy Gazette*, 21st October 1899) and was the son of a Brigadier-General, and Lt Col. Eustace Morrison Bell (1874-1947), whose older brother was at the school during the 1881 census and who was the son of a Sussex land owner, Justice of the Peace and Deputy Lieutenant. Baring probably wouldn't even have known the Christian names of most of his friends. In the novel of prep and public school life, *David Blaize* the narrator explains that, '. . . Christian names at Helmsworth were hidden secrets; if you liked a boy very much you might tell him what your Christian name was, but to have it publically shouted out so that everyone knew was quite horrible' (Benson, 1916, p.82).

Behaving 'Foolishly'

The degree to which Sneyd-Kynnersley attempted to inculcate his pupils to support the Conservative Party is almost amusing. Baring remembers that on Guy Fawkes Night they would burn Liberal Prime Minister William Gladstone in effigy. In August 2018, handwritten correspondence between Gladstone and Sneyd-Kynnersley actually came to light; the letters being up for auction. Former Liberal Party MP Sir Arthur Hamilton-Gordon (1829-1912), who had until 1882 governed New Zealand, was about to move to Ceylon to become its governor and wanted to spend some time with his son, a pupil at St George's, before he left, which would be during term time. Hamilton-Gordon had obviously asked Sneyd-Kynnersley to allow his son to leave school a week early in order to facilitate this and had been refused. So on 21st September 1883, Gladstone personally wrote to Sneyd-Kynnersley to ask if he might do him the favour of allowing Gordon's son an extra week off school. Sneyd-Kynnersley wrote back the next day, flatly refusing the request, doubtless enjoying turning down a man he so implacably despised (Robertson, 22nd August 2018). Years before Baring was at St George's, Roger Fry recalls them burning an effigy of the Emir of Afghanistan — Ayub Khan (1857-1914) — Britain being at war with Afghanistan at the time (Brendon, 2009, p.68).

Intriguingly, Maurice Baring remembers that a boy once sent the fanatical Conservative headmaster a Liberal Party campaign leaflet for a joke. The Head duly sent it back, in a different envelope, without a stamp, but with some copper coins enclosed, so that the boy had to pay the postman 8d to receive the letter (pp.77-78). Of course, the fact that the boy would play this joke on the headmaster implies that, for that boy at least, Sneyd-Kynnersley was not some monster who instilled nothing more than fear in his charges. He must have had a sense of humour and the boy was presumably confident that his prank would not cause some terrible reaction . . . and it didn't. Sneyd-Kynnersley engaged in an equally witty jape by forcing the boy to pay to receive his own Liberal leaflet, with the boy obviously not knowing that the contents of the envelope were simply his Liberal leaflet being returned. One day there was a parliamentary by-election in Ascot, so Sneyd-Kynnersley organised a school trip into town so that the boys — all wearing Tory rosettes — could campaign for the Conservative candidate. The 7 boys who had previously made it clear that they were Liberals had to stay behind and work! On another Bonfire Night, the pupils burnt Liberal politician Joseph Chamberlain (1836-1914) in effigy, because the Head regarded him as a radical (Baring, p.78).

One particular incident seems to best sum up the childish aspect of the character of Sneyd-Kynnersley. One day, the Head sent for Baring and told him:

> "'You have been especially invited to a children's garden party at Marlborough House by the Princess of Wales and you are to go up to London at once. Are you,' said the Head ironically, "a special friend of the Princess of Wales?'" (p.80).

The Princess of Wales was Alexandra of Denmark (1844-1925), wife of the future King Edward VII (1841-1910). Baring attended what he describes as the very enjoyable party. However, he managed to miss the train back to Ascot. As the next train wouldn't leave for Ascot until gone midnight, Baring's mother felt it was best that he should stay the night and return to school the following day. She telegrammed Sneyd-Kynnersley to tell him that this is what would happen. Incredibly, the Head replied that 'if I did not come back tonight I was not to come back at all.' The Head's telegram left everyone distraught, with Baring's 'incensed' mother saying that if his father — who was in Devon on a trip — was there then he wouldn't let him go back. Eventually it was decided that Baring would be escorted back on the 12.30am train, which pleased Baring because, 'I wanted to go back, on the whole' (p.80). This would, of course, imply that, overall, Baring was happy at St George's. He earlier remarks, 'The boys were happy - in any case, they thought that was happiness, as they knew no better' (p.74). Baring was surprised, in the days after his return to school, that the Head didn't mention anything about the telegram incident. However, it turned out that Baring's father had complained to the headmaster of Eton, Dr Edmond Warre (1837-1920), who had written to Sneyd-Kynnersley to tell him how 'foolishly' he'd behaved, instructing him to 'make amends.' Sneyd-Kynnersley did this by giving Baring time off to go to London to see the dentist (p.81).

Maurice Baring

Baring felt that he 'never seemed to be able to do right either in the eyes of the headmaster or the second division master' (p.81). However, the following term it came to light that the other two masters – the two 'friendly' ones – were thinking of leaving to set up their own school, St Vincent's School, Eastbourne. In that Robert Estcourt Macdonald did not leave St George's, the two 'friendly' masters were H. Martin Cooke, whom we met earlier, and the Rev. Sherard Montagu Statham (1859-1947). Statham was one of seven children of the Rev. Francis Freeman Statham (1814-1884), a rector in the East End of London, and Jane Kington (1816-1892) (Statham, 1925, p.71). Statham studied at St Paul's School in London and Queen's College, Cambridge, and in 1903 he was awarded an LLD by Trinity College Dublin (Venn, 1911). In 1880, he had married Clara Bull (1854-1933), the daughter of a Cambridgeshire 'boot closer' (a worker who stitches the upper part of a shoe). Statham's family life was tragic.

His first son, Sherard Francis Kington, was born and died in 1881. A daughter, Violet Clara Kington Statham (1882-1970) born in 1882 in Birmingham, was married to a Lancashire vicar by her father (*Bicester Herald*, 16th August 1912, p.3). Statham became a priest in 1883 and ministered in Birmingham from 1882 to 1884, in which year it seems he began working at St George's. This was the same year in which his second son, Freeman Sherard, was born and died. Nevertheless, Statham was 'friendly.'

The Rev. Sherard Statham

Baring wrote to his parents, asking if he, and his younger brother Hugo, might go to this new school. Maurice had assumed that his parents would answer that the idea of changing schools was ridiculous, so he wrote the letter merely as a 'flight of fancy.' To his surprise, they did not answer at all. Soon, however, one of the departing masters approached Baring to discuss the issue and it turned out that Lady Baring had been corresponding with him. When it came to light that the brothers were leaving the two remaining masters – Sneyd-Kynnersley and Macdonald would occasionally 'scowl' at them. The following term, which commenced in January 1886, Baring and his brother began at the Eastbourne school. Sneyd-Kynnersley wrote to Baring's father to ask what he should tell parents who enquired as to why the Baring brothers had left. Baring's father replied with an unusually lengthy letter, refusing to reveal the contents. 'I knew what the man wanted to know and I told him' Baring's father told his son. Sneyd-Kynnersley wrote back to say he was 'entirely satisfied' with the reasons (Baring, 1922, p.82).

Maurice and Hugo arrived in Eastbourne to find that another St George's boy — Broadwood — had also transferred. Statham was the school's headmaster and H. Martin Cooke his assistant. After Sneyd-Kynnersley's death, 'several more' boys left St George's for St Vincent's, Eastbourne. The school quickly filled up and within about a year there were 40 boys, about the same size as St George's. Interestingly, the boys at Ascot were not allowed to correspond with those who had left for Eastbourne (p.82). At St Vincent's, 'a new life began. There was more amusement than work about it and everything was different.' The boys were even allowed to put on a theatrical performance lampooning the teachers at St George's, with one scene where:

> 'the Ascot headmaster discovered his wife kissing her brother, another of the Ascot masters, the villain, and she sang a song composed by Broadwood and myself, of which the refrain was "What would Herbert say – dear? What would Herbert say?' . . . Herbert then broke onto the scene and gave way to paroxysms of jealous rage' (p.82).

Note Macdonald is the 'villain' *not* Sneyd-Kynnersley. Baring last saw Sneyd-Kynnersley in the summer holidays – not yet begun at Ascot – of 1886, when he passed through Slough railway station on his way to London. This would date it to July 1886, probably around 20th July, as this is when term ended at St George's in 1883 according to a Churchill school report. Baring's former headmaster was on the platform, leading a first division expedition. Baring's mother suggested that Maurice put his head out of the window to say 'How do you do?', but Baring refused to (p.84).[41]

The Decline of St George's, Ascot

Macdonald became headmaster of St George's in 1886, when Sneyd-Kynnersley died (*Crockford's*, 1908, p.1626). In 1887 he was made a deacon (*Reading Mercury*, 26th February 1887) and in 1888 he was ordained a priest (*Reading Mercury*, 2nd June 1888). Harry Kessler's American biographer Laird Easton has speculated that the decline of St George's occurred because of rumours about the severity of Sneyd-Kynnersley's floggings. Easton (2002, p.25) writes:

> 'In wooing the parents of prospective pupils, Sneyd-Kynnersley naturally made no mention of this aspect of his instruction, and boys did not directly mention it in their letters home. Nevertheless, word of this dark side of St George's eventually got out, and many parents withdrew their children. It may be that such behaviour eventually led to the decline of the school and the relatively early death of the headmaster.'

However, this is not consistent with the evidence. We know that Roger Fry mentioned the floggings in his letters to his mother. Baring left St George's just under a year before Sneyd-Kynnersley died, and it had 40 boys at the time, just as it had when Churchill was there. Baring saw Sneyd-Kynnersley with what he knew to be the First Division on the platform of Slough Railway Station just four months before the headmaster's death. Considering the level of detail that Baring provides with regard to his time at St George's, if he had noticed that the First Division was much diminished in size, with many faces he knew absent, we can reasonably assume he would

---

[41] Baring's autobiography also provides us with a number of names of fellow pupils who were his friends. These include the New Yorker Hamilton Fish, III (1873-1898) who Baring remembers was killed fighting in Cuba (McCain & Salter, 2014, p.121), Basil Temple Blackwood (1870-1917), a peer, lawyer and book illustrator who was killed in World War I; and Niall Campbell (1872-1949), later an historian and Duke of Argyle, as well as Campbell's younger brother.

have mentioned this. He also notes that it was only *after* Sneyd-Kynnersley's death that boys started to migrate to Eastbourne. Only 3 months prior to his death, the Head installed an expensive new organ in the school's chapel, implying that all was well financially (*Windsor and Eton Express,* 3rd July 1886). So, if there was a decline it was nothing to do with Sneyd-Kynnersley.

If there was a decline, it may have been Macdonald's fault. Certainly, Sir Edmund Backhouse implies that Macdonald was childish, threatening an errant pupil, in a schoolboy-like manner, to 'tell the Head' and this tallies with Baring's descriptions of Macdonald's infantile behaviour. But years after Sneyd-Kynnersley's death, with MacDonald as headmaster, there does not appear to have been a serious numbers problem. In June 1888, St George's held a successful sports day which was reported as having been extremely well attended (*Reading Mercury,* 30th June 1888). Macdonald married Agnes Gwyn Elger (1866-1905) in August 1891 at All Souls Church, Ascot (*Guardian,* 19th August 1891, p.13). She was the daughter of barrister George Gwyn Elger (1830-1874). The seismographer and lunar observer Thomas Gwyn Elger (1836-1897), after whom the Moon's Elger Crater is named, was a distant cousin. In other words, Macdonald had married into a wealthy family in August 1891 and we would suspect that such a family would be very conscious of the financial situation of any spouse, implying that the school was not in financial difficulty. Similarly, in February 1892, Agnes Macdonald was advertising for a new cook, implying the same (*The Morning Post,* 24th February 1892).

In June 1892, St George's was revealing that it had space for 'a limited number of' pupils on the front page of *The Morning Post* (2nd June 1892). However, by 8th December (*The Morning Post,* 8th December 1892) and then again a week later it was proclaiming something very different: 'The Rev. R. E. Macdonald, MA' was leaving St George's at the end of the year to 'join' headmaster 'Mr. R. F. Johns' in running a prep school called Winton House, in Winchester (*The Morning Post,* 15th December 1892), an ancient cathedral city. Specifically, the two headmasters amalgamated their two schools and Macdonald presumably took many of his pupils with him to Winchester (*The Morning Post,* 26th May 1893). If Macdonald had managed to run a very successful prep school into the ground, then it is quite likely that rumour of this would have got round which would probably have dissuaded Johns from contracting a financial partnership with Macdonald. At the end of the year, St George's Gymnastics Club hosted a farewell party for their leading member (*West Middlesex Herald,* 2nd January 1893) and by 18th January 1893, St George's had been auctioned off (*The Morning Post,* 18th January 1893, p.12). It was purchased by 'Mr Blair and Mr Gordon Shackle' who were assistant masters at Fretherne House School in London. Blair, coincidentally, was also originally from Uttoxeter. They took their boarders to St George's and re-established the school. It was under *these* masters that the school declined. Charles Gordon Shackle (1866-1902) died at the end of 1902 (*Windsor and Eton Express,* 13th December 1902) and Edward Blair (1848-1923) had gone bankrupt by September 1904 (*Windsor and Eton Express,* 24th September 1904). The school was auctioned off again (*Windsor and Eton Express,* 31st December 1904) and by April 1905 it was being advertised as 'a high class school for girls' (*Windsor and Eton Express,* 15th April 1905). So, St George's did not significantly decline at all in its first incarnation, and certainly did not have some problem with its reputation.

It was while co-running Winton House that Macdonald ran into a serious problem. By 1900, Macdonald had left not only Winton House but England. Macdonald was living at Meinhard Strasse 10 in Innsbruck in Austria. As an engineer, Thomas Gwyn Elger had directed railway construction in Austrian-occupied Holstein prior to the 1866 Austro-Prussian War (*Monthly Notices of the Royal Astronomical Society,* 1897, p.210), which may explain why a relative had property in Innsbruck, which would have transferred to Macdonald upon his marriage to Elger's relative. In 1900, Macdonald was appointed British Vice-Consul for Innsbruck (*Almanach de Gotha,* 1900). Having had a German-speaking governess, he presumably spoke the language fluently. But why was Macdonald in Austria? While there, he contributed an article on skating in Austria and Germany to the book *Sports of the World* (Macdonald, 1905) and played in Badminton competitions (Watson, Jan-June 1901, p.458). He would have needed to keep himself occupied because his wife wasn't in Austria with him.

By 1901, and thus presumably by 1900, Macdonald and his wife, who never had any children, were clearly estranged, indeed they were apparently estranged by 1899. In 1901, Agnes was 'living on own means' as head of a household in Leamington Priors in Warwickshire. Her three brothers were all living with her. In August 1905, she was staying with her brother, Ronald Haydon Elger (1870-1929), at The Grange in Melford in Buckinghamshire. One Saturday afternoon, 12th August, Ronald and Agnes were in a pony and trap, with Ronald driving, when the pony bolted and threw them both to the ground. Ronald was relatively unscathed but Agnes was badly hurt. She was taken to a hospital in London, where she died of her injuries (*Derby Daily Telegraph*, 25th August 1905). According to Agnes' 1899 will, her husband was left a lifetime annuity of £200 or a third of her estate, whichever was less. In 1906, Macdonald exchanged Agnes' property portfolio with her brothers in return for this lifetime annuity (Bedfordshire Archive, X 877/3). The 1899 will suggests that the marriage had broken down before 1899, because, by law, a spouse had to bequeath a third of their property to their spouse. Without a will, all of Agnes' inheritance would simply have gone to Macdonald. Macdonald returned to England in 1909, because this is the last year in which he was recorded as being the British Vice-Consul in Innsbruck (*Shipping World Yearbook*, 1909, p.239).

His second marriage provides us with a further clue as to why he left the country. Macdonald married again — to Dorothy Norah Hutton (1878-1926) of Charleville Forest, Tullamore, Ireland — in Tullamore, in 1909 (*The Globe*, 29th March 1909). Dorothy was the daughter of Col. Edmund Bacon Hutton (1841-1904) and Lady Katherine Bury (1851-1917). Lady Katherine was the daughter of Charles Bury, 3rd Earl of Charleville (1822-1859) (*Debrett's Peerage*, 1879, p.122). The peerage became extinct with this man's brother, the 5th Earl of Charleville (1829-1875), leaving behind his widow, Emily Frances Bury, neé Wood, (1851-1911), who employed Dorothy Hutton as her servant. Dorothy was 24 years Macdonald's junior. By the time of the 1911 census, it seems that the marriage had already broken down. Robert Estcourt Macdonald was lodging with a grocer's widow and her daughter in Braunton in Devon, and can be found on the electoral roll (England and Wales Electoral Registers, 1832-1932). Dorothy cannot be found on the census at all, because she was in Ireland and census records do not survive. In 1917, Dorothy successfully sued Macdonald to annul the marriage, something which would have been scandalous at the time. A *decree nisi* was issued on 12th November 1917, on the grounds of Macdonald's 'incapability . . . to consummate the marriage' (The National Archives, J 77/1294/9528).[42]

So, Macdonald's first marriage had clearly collapsed by 1899, with the couple presumably wanting to avoid the public scandal, as it would have been at the time, of a divorce. But then Macdonald left the country and remained abroad for almost a decade. We also find that, once widowed, Macdonald married yet another wealthy woman but the marriage fell apart within two years and was annulled because he could not consummate it. Something appears to have been covered up and a little detective work reveals precisely what that was. Gerald Brenan, CBE (1894-1987) was a British writer, from a wealthy Anglo-Irish military family, who spent much of his life in Spain. By about 1902, he was a pupil at Winton House under its headmaster Edward F. Johns (1861-1948), whose father had founded the school. In many ways, this headmaster – known as 'Jumbo' – sounds rather like Sneyd-Kynnersley and was seemingly a non-practising pederast. According to Brenan, Jumbo's sexuality

'made the school the centre of his life. That was why for those of us who were over twelve or thirteen (he did not interest himself in the younger ones) he was such a good school master . . . He was a pasha all over, unpredictable in his moods, now flushing with anger, now gentle, but most often relaxing into a pun . . . On Saturdays, he swished one – he was very fond of caning – and on Sundays he read aloud Sherlock Holmes and distributed sweets. The same offence on different days would lead either to a tweak of the ear and a pun or to a thunderous brow and five strokes of

---

[42] In June 1918, Dorothy married a US army major, Lionel Asher Stuart Corkins (1888-1926) of the French Medical Corps, who was ten years her junior. They both died in Paris in 1926.

the cane. However, this was what we liked about him (Brennan, 1979, p.58).

But Brennan also recalls that:

'Some years before I arrived at the school there had been a scandal. Mr Johns's partner, Mr X, and been discovered in a compromising situation with a boy and had had to leave. This was something which it took a good deal of social manner to live down, for although I am certain that Mr Johns was always more careful in his actions and indefinite in his feelings, it was only too obvious that his tastes lay in the same direction' (p.57).

Mr Johns' 'partner' 'some years before' Brenan arrived at the school was, of course, Robert Estcourt Macdonald, with their two schools having amalgamated. Consistent with Macdonald being a pederast, Macdonald's first marriage had broken down by 1899 and he had left the country. Macdonald's second marriage could not be consummated – 'Mr X' was Robert Estcourt Macdonald. Such scandals were seen as so grotesque that they had to be covered-up, as happened in the case of Harrow headmaster Charles Vaughan being caught engaging in homosexual activity with a pupil. Subject to blackmail from a boy's father, he had to leave Harrow and could not accept a teaching or senior church position until this father had died (Gathorne-Hardy, 1978, pp.80-83). Perhaps Macdonald was forced to leave the country for these kinds of reasons, only able to return once his blackmailer had passed away. When Robert Estcourt Macdonald died, in 1923, he was living in Clevedon in Somerset, the village in which his brother also lived. Childless, he left his entire estate to his widowed sister, Flora Sneyd-Kynnersley who was buried alongside him.

The Decline of St Vincent's, Eastbourne

On 27th July 1889, Statham and Cooke dissolved their partnership and Statham left, leaving Cooke in charge of the school (*London*

Gazette, 30th July 1889). Thereafter, Statham was rector of Elsworthy in Somerset, before being appointed a vicar in Kent while at the same time being the military prison chaplain in Dover. In 1911, he was appointed a vicar in Oxfordshire, continuing in this position until his death. Statham also became an accomplished writer. He authored at least twelve books, including the novel *Hephzibah* (Statham, 1922) and the philosophical works *Immorality* (Statham, 1938) and *The Wisdom of the Serpent* (Statham, 1930).

At the 1904 St Vincent's school prize giving, Cooke, by then a long-time headmaster, presented a prize to Sydney Maxwell Innes-Cross (1894-1914), (*Loris*, 1973, p.58), son of the widowed Sarah Innes-Cross (1857-1911), only daughter of the late Col. William Cross of Dromantine, County Down. Cooke married his pupil's mother in 1907. Cooke appended 'Cross' to his surname in 1908 (*Walford's County Families*, 1913, p.624), and was granted the right to use his wife's coat of arms (National Library of Ireland, MS 111, pp.218-219). This was because his wife was an armigerous heiress. Her father's will had stipulated that any future husbands of his daughter were to change their surname if they wanted to take control of her inheritance. Sarah's first husband had also appended 'Cross' to his surname (National Library of Ireland, MS 153, pp.605-610). Cooke-Cross, now part of the landed gentry, promptly moved to Dromantine and was church warden at Donaghmore from 1909 to 1911, when his wife died (Cowan, 1914, p.258). The couple had no children. Cooke-Cross returned to England, living out his days in Maida Vale in London. Shortly after Cooke-Cross's departure to Ireland, St Vincent's was amalgamated with another Eastbourne prep school, Ascham School, to become Ascham St Vincent's (Molonet, 2015). Cooke-Cross died in Cambridge in July 1931 with an estate valued at only £378.

Count Harry Kessler's Inspiration

The Red Count, Henry Kessler, was at St George's from 1880 to 1882. His account is so positive that we must keep in mind the well known 'Rosie retrospection effect' whereby we tend to see the past through rose-tinted spectacles. That said, however, we will see that Aubrey Jay's memories of St George's were very similar. Kessler was writing more than 50 years after the events he described. The Red Count also mentions the many exciting school trips, such as to London and to Royal Ascot, where he was introduced to Queen Victoria in July 1881. He explains how it was compulsory to learn to swim and that the pupils were taught boxing and fencing (Kessler, 1935, p.104). Having read Churchill's *My Early Life,* Kessler also makes a point of highlighting Churchill's implication that Sneyd-Kynnersley was a sadist, insisting that although the floggings were severe the headmaster was applying 'an ancient formula for turning barbarous young English into gentlemen' (Kessler, 1935, pp.118-119). In his memoir (Kessler, 1935), Kessler even stressed the systematic and apparently reasonable nature of Sneyd-Kynnersley's beatings:

'The school was called after England's patron saint and first Christian knight, 'Saint George's School' and emphasized . . . the virtues of chivalrous conduct and truthfulness. Whoever lied or else offended against these supreme commandments whose observance constituted a gentleman was punished . . . according to an old English custom with bare bottom over a wooden block and personally beaten with a rod by Mr Kynnersley until he bled.'

However, flogging, he stresses, was far from the only method employed, with the Head using a system of rewards as well. But, more importantly, for Kessler, the headmaster 'sought to provide what put us in a boyish state of nature, stimulated our imaginations, involved adventures' (Kessler, 1935). Like Roger Fry, however, Kessler was never actually flogged himself (Trevor-Roper, 1977, p.17, citing Kessler, 1935, pp.127-160). Sneyd-Kynnersley was, for Kessler, a superb teacher who 'played like an artist with a keyboard' upon young minds.

'For myself I must admit of all my educators Mr Kynnersley is the only one whose personality truly influenced me. Despite his methods of punishment, which he inherited, he was . . . an adventurer in the field of the formation of young modern individuals, guided and driven by empathy for the souls of young boys which in his own case, as with many great educators since Plato, may well have been erotic in origin (Easton, 2002, p.25, citing Kessler, 1988).

Kessler suspected that the Head may well have been sexually attracted to (older) children, though he was not aware that this was acted upon in terms of sodomising any of them. Sneyd-Kynnersley — who was 'tall and long-legged with sandy mutton chops' — also enthusiastically joined in with school sports. He'd lead them, like a 'hare' pursued by hounds, on cross-country runs looking 'cunning, and dashing as a boy.' During these runs, he'd play tricks on the boys by taking them off the path into the undergrowth and then escaping and appearing somewhere else. When he managed this, 'They saw his eyes behind his gold-rimmed spectacles sparkle.' His involvement in this aspect of school life, according to Kessler, meant that, 'a comradeship was fashioned between younger and older members of an officer corps, a code of conduct that was scarcely violated' (Kessler, 1935). It would be enlightening to be able to pursue Kessler as to what constituted one of these very 'scarce' violations.

Kessler (1935) certainly provides evidence that Sneyd-Kynnersley had feelings for some of the boys and had some form of arrested development. He describes how the headmaster's favourites, including Kessler himself, would be invited to the headmaster's drawing room for tea and cakes. There Kessler met 'Mrs Kynnersley' who was:

'a childless, somewhat dim and temperamental woman; sandy-haired with a set of horse-teeth; like her husband she was more at home with 8 to 10 year olds. She was jealous of the older boys, who Mr Kynnersley preferred – this led to scenes which were tragic or tragi-comic and were for us, in this restrained English way, full of tension.'

We can only speculate on the kinds of tensions beneath such a marriage but one way of reading it is that the couple were unable to have children — possibly because of Sneyd-Kynnersley's predilection for young boys — and so the sight of her husband being so happy with these boys, while she had no boy of her own, was infuriating for Flora Sneyd-Kynnersley.

Aubrey Jay's 'Extremely Good Teacher'

In his autobiography, Douglas Jay (1907-1990), a Labour cabinet minister (President of the Board of Trade) in the 1960s, tells us that his father, the barrister Aubrey Jay (1869-1950), was at St George's with Churchill (Jay, 1980, p.15). In many ways, Aubrey Jay, who was the son of a land owner from Malvern, is the most reliable source because he kept a diary throughout his time at St George's and drew upon this when he penned his memoirs in 1947 (Jay, 1947, p.13). Jay's recollections are very similar to those of Kessler. Indeed, he specifically refers to Fry's summary of 'the Head' as 'much too negative' (p.10), insisting that Kessler's memoirs, of which he had been given a translation, were the most accurate of all those 'Old Boys' who had written about Sneyd-Kynnersley, and that the Head was not as childish as Fry implied. Jay assumed that 'Mr Kynnersley was not dependent on the school for a living' because he 'spent his money so lavishly' (p.7), presumably on prizes and trips for the boys. In his diary, on 1st August 1881, Jay could hardly contain his excitement at receiving one of Sneyd-Kynnersley's end-of-term prizes:

> 'As [*Sneyd-Kynnersley*] said "We now come to the most important prizes of all," the prizes for general school work I thought I should go mad, especially as he waited a second after he had said, "Second division prize" but I was very much relieved when I heard him say JAY. When the prizes had been given, the Head said that he needn't detain us any longer except to wish us very happy holidays and this was followed by a tremendous clapping. And so the great final reading over came to an end.'

There is, however, a subtle hint in Jay's memoirs, congruous with Kessler, that the Head was attracted to the older pupils:

'I am sure he was devoted to the boys but it was not until we reached a certain age that we really felt we were appreciated. But with the first division he was like a schoolboy, although he could be strict enough and even awe-inspiring when occasion demanded' (p.7).

Jay also concurs with regard to the reasonable yet harsh nature of the corporal punishment:

'Winston Churchill, who came to the school before his eighth birthday (I was then thirteen), was not amenable to discipline and was constantly in disgrace. In any case I do not think Mr Kynnersley ("The Head" as we always called him) had much patience with boys of that age. Consequently, Winston was continually being beaten for various misdemeanours' (p.8).

'As a result of his somewhat brutal treatment (*Churchill*) has written in his autobiography a scathing account of the school, under the thinly veiled title of "St James's School". When this was published I received an appealing letter from Mrs Kynnersley, who was still alive but had been a widow for many years. I could only assure her that the Old Boys had very different feelings about "The Head." There could be no doubt, however, that he did use the birch too freely, although not without discrimination, and that the "executions" were too much in the nature of solemn ceremonies. In my own case, he knew that I was an only child and had lost my father at the age of three, and I doubt that anything but the most heinous offence would have induced him to resort to corporal punishment' (p.9).

Thus, according to Jay, the general feeling among the boys was that although Sneyd-Kynnersley was too severe and ritualistic in his birchings, he was consistent and fair. Jay concurs with Fry that the 'Reading Over' took place every Monday. However, in contrast to Fry, and in line with other Old Boys, Jay is clear that this ritual only involved 'agonising suspense for those who had a reason to expect a really bad report' (p.9). In other words, breaking the rules and very bad behaviour, *not* minor misdemeanours, resulted in a flogging.

Aubrey Jay, OBE

Like Kessler, Jay is extremely positive about Sneyd-Kynnersley. When 'Sis,' the school's favourite rabbit, who'd had many different families, died, the Head accorded her 'an imposing funeral, her numerous relatives following her in a procession of wheel barrows to her final resting place' (p.11). The Head enthusiastically threw himself into inspiring his charges: 'I doubt whether any other headmaster of a preparatory school has ever taken his boys for so many interesting expeditions' (p.12). On Bonfire Night 1882, the Head provided lots of expensive fireworks and secreted half a pound of gunpowder in the head of the Guy — an effigy of Arabi Pasha (1841-1911) who had overthrown the Anglo-French administration of Egypt — so that Pasha dramatically exploded (pp.14-15). Sneyd-Kynnersley managed to get his boys into the best public schools, personally taking Schuster, Bonham Carter and Jay to Winchester to sit that school's entrance exam, which they all passed because, 'we were thoroughly well taught.' They all began at Winchester in autumn 1883 (Wainewright, 1907, pp.419-424). Jay had already accepted a place at Wellington but Winchester was more prestigious and Sneyd-Kynnersley was clearly very ambitious for his pupils (p.16). Indeed, he was 'an extremely good teacher, because he made things live and so never failed to interest us' (p.12), something Kessler also recalled. 'Mrs Kynnersley' cared for the younger pupils, bought them presents, and took them on her own expeditions. Jay's 'affection and regard for both Mr and Mrs Kynnersley was sincere and lasting' (p.18).

Brief Recollections: Arthur Bonham Carter & Claude Schuster

Arthur Bonham Carter (1869-1916) was at the school until 1883. In a letter to his father, an MP, written in 1883, he explained that Mr

Kynnersley is 'awfully angry because I have got into 17 Bramstons House and he does not know if the other two boys have got in at all, he's going to write to the Times and do an awfull [*sic.*] amount of rot' (Hampshire Archives and Local Studies, 70M88/59). This seems to be consistent with the childishness highlighted by Baring and Fry and the proneness to anger recalled by Baring and Backhouse, but also with the genuine care for his pupils remembered by Kessler and Fry. Bramston's House was one of the houses at Winchester College, so Sneyd-Kynnersley was clearly extremely anxious to know whether or not his school's applicants had been accepted. There may have been a mercenary aspect to this — the more boys from his school that got into Winchester the better for its reputation — but it may also imply that he deeply cared about what would happen to them.

Arthur Bonham Carter

We have already seen that Claude Schuster only mentioned Sneyd-Kynnersley's 'sumptuous prizes.' As historian Howard Pedraza (1916-2008) (Pedraza, 1986, p.7) has summarised, 'the headmaster was undoubtedly severe but Churchill's naughtiness was outstanding and gained him no sympathy from his schoolmates.' So, having explored all of the known sources with regard to life at St George's, Ascot, under Sneyd-Kynnersley we are left with a simple question: How reliable are they?

Chapter Five

How Reliable are Sneyd-Kynnersley's
Former Pupils?

Backhouse the Fantasist

HAVING EXPLORED ALL of the sources we must now assess
their reliability. It is reasonable to have very little trust in
Sir Edmund Backhouse. It can easily be proven, as we
have already explored, that many of his assertions about Sneyd-
Kynnersley are simply untrue. Sneyd-Kynnersley did not die while
flogging a pupil in July 1886. Indeed, Backhouse was a proven forger
and fabricator of history (Trevor-Roper, 1977).

Who's Afraid of Virginia Woolf?

Of the more reliable sources, the one who is the most negative
towards Sneyd-Kynnersley, with regard to the harshness of the
headmaster's floggings, is Roger Fry. But how reliable is he? The first
problem is that although we have Fry's recollections they have been
presented by Virginia Woolf, who appears to have her own biases
against Sneyd-Kynnersley. Most obviously, we have already seen that

Fry wrote: 'When my parents told me that there were no punishments
. . .' (Woolf, 1940, p.32). He then tells us about the birchings, and
cannot understand how his parents 'who were extremely scrupulous
about verbal inaccuracy reconciled it to their consciences to omit'
the fact that the headmaster used the birch, something they must
have known 'or else they would have expressed more surprise than
they did when later I revealed the horrid fact to them' (pp.32-33).
Woolf earlier paraphrased this as 'Mr Sneyd-Kynnersley had assured
the Frys there would be no punishments' (p.31). But this was *not* Fry's
recollection at all. It was his *parents* who gave him this assurance and
his parents may have been lying. Certainly, Fry's mother, Mariabella
Hodgkin (1833-1930), seems to have been a very strange woman. She
instilled in Fry the dogmas that Nature was sacred and should never
be interfered with and, also, that he must always obey her. When
Fry was 7, she told him to take a cutting from his '*adored* poppy
plant,' which he had grown himself and which she knew he would be
devastated to have to cut. Fry did as she commanded and she then
'reproved' him for his interference with Nature. It had all been some
kind of perverse test (Woolf, 1940, p.16).

Woolf's misleading summary has been embellished by literature
scholar Louise DeSalvo (1942-2018) who writes that:

> 'Roger was sent to Sunninghill House, chosen in part because
> the parents were assured by the headmaster, Sneyd-Kynnersley,
> that corporal punishment, which would be an infringement of
> Quaker principles, was not permitted' (DeSalvo, 1990. p.194).

This implies that Sneyd-Kynnersley lied to Fry's parents, something
for which there is no evidence whatsoever.

How Reliable is Roger Fry?

Turning to Fry himself, we have already observed that Fry is
prone to exaggerate. He states that Sneyd-Kynnersley's intellectual
achievements were limited, when this was evidently not the case,
something Fry must have known. He refers to masters who were

widely respected and highly intellectually accomplished as, by implication, 'imbeciles', as they have replaced earlier teachers, with Sneyd-Kynnersley always replacing 'masters of intelligence' with 'imbeciles.' This description is simply incongruous with the evidence. While Fry was still at the school, an obviously highly intelligent teacher was replaced by somebody who would be difficult to describe as an imbecile. One 'Mr Holmes', who was clearly very intelligent, was replaced by Mr Scudamore, who was likewise. Fry refers to a 'Mr Holmes' being involved in the flogging of Algernon Ferguson. I can find no evidence either in *Alumni Cantabrigienses* (Venn, 1911) – which provides detailed biographies of graduates' work lives in a way that *Alumni Oxonienses* (Foster, 1891) does not, or in extant copies of the *School Masters' Directory* that anyone called Holmes was working at Sunninghill House in the period that Fry was there. Of course, it is possible that 'Mr Holmes' did not attend university or attended some other university. But, if this was so, there should be a schoolmaster on the 1881 census called Holmes who could plausibly have been at Sunninghill just a few years earlier. There was a Birmingham teacher, who had been to teacher training college, called George Holmes, but it's most unlikely that he was at Sunninghill in the late 1870s because his address in both 1871 and 1881 was exactly the same. Accordingly, the only schoolmaster, by a process of elimination, whom Mr Holmes could be is Harry Arthur Holmes (1855-1917). Harry Holmes matriculated at St Catherine's College, Cambridge, in 1874 as *sizar*, a kind of scholarship where he received financial help from the college in return for performing menial duties. He graduated in 1878 but did not begin his job as assistant master at Haverfordwest Grammar School in Pembrokeshire (West Wales) until autumn 1879. As such, he may have taught at Sunninghill House in the school year 1878-1879, when Fry was a pupil there. Unfortunately, I have not been able to access Fry's letter about the flogging of Ferguson in order to confirm when exactly it was written, but this candidate would be a strong probability. Harry Holmes had gone to King Edward's School, Birmingham (Venn, 1911) which was a public school (Tyerman, 2000, p.221) of which Sneyd-Kynnersley's father was one of the governors in 1880 (*The Biograph and Review*, 1880, p.112). According to the 1871 census, Holmes' father was a plasterer, originally from Derbyshire.

Perhaps this clever plasterer's son — with his scholarship to a public school — had somehow managed to connect with Sneyd-Kynnersley through the headmaster's father or Cambridge University contacts. His rise from the Birmingham working class to public school and Cambridge would imply that he was one of the 'master(s) of intelligence' which Fry claims that Sneyd-Kynnersley 'took care' to get rid of and replace with 'imbeciles.' His replacement was almost certainly Cyril Scudamore (1856-1945), who graduated from St John's College, Oxford in 1879 and who was teaching at St George's, Ascot according to the 1881 census. Scudamore went on to be a noted historian and travel writer, producing such volumes as *Scenes from the War in La Vendée* (Scudamore, 1888), *Belgium and the Belgians* (Scudamore, 1901), *Normandy* (Scudamore, 1906), *Heroic Lives of the Nineteenth Century* (Scudamore, 1912) and *English Officers of the Nineteenth Century* (Scudamore, 1913). His travel books were updated with third and fourth editions respectively in 1924 and 1928. Scudamore is most unlikely to have been an imbecile. As we have seen, the second assistant master at St George's in 1881 was Herbert Martin Cooke. I cannot find the third assistant master on the 1881 census, but there must have been one because the school's 1883 entry in *Our Schools and Colleges* (1883, p.69) was clear that there were '3 resident masters and 1 non-resident.' According to Aubrey Jay's diary entry for 1st August 1881, 'The Head got up and read the reports of the 4th division and 3rd set, who had not been examined by Mr Macdonald,' meaning Robert Estcourt Macdonald was the other master.

By 1883, Scudamore had left and Sneyd-Kynnersley had appointed the Rev. Thomas Cooke Sanders alongside Herbert Martin Cooke and Robert Estcourt Macdonald. These, then, were the masters that Churchill would have known. In addition to these assistant masters, there was yet another music (specifically violin) teacher, Richard Blagrove (1826-1895), organist George Francis (1851-1937), and gym and fencing master Sgt (William) Henry Tollerton (1855-1895) of the 4th Hussars, who was garrisoned in Aldershot in 1881 but, by 1883, was an army pensioner. These appointments provide an interesting insight into Sneyd-Kynnersley's character.

Snobbery and Intellectual Inferiority

Fry portrays Sneyd-Kynnersley as a snob. However, there is a great deal of evidence which implies he was no such thing. Sneyd-Kynnersley's employment of Sgt Tollerton, who was the son of a photographer and dyer from Grantham in Lincolnshire, is hardly consistent with his being a snob. Sgt Tollerton was supporting his wife and seven children on an army pension, aged just 28 — presumably due to illness or injury — and responded to an advert placed in *The Naval and Military Gazette* (22nd August 1883). Also inconsistent with the accusation that Sneyd-Kynnersley was a snob was his appointment of plasterer's son Harry Holmes as assistant master. The headmaster's employment of George Francis mounts the most serious challenge of all to Sneyd-Kynnersley's supposed snobbery.

George Francis was working as a footman in Burbage, Leicestershire, 10 years prior to being appointed an organist at St George's, presumably attending musical academy in the 1870s, as he subsequently obtained the positions not just of 'teacher of music' but also, by 1891, of Organist's Secretary. Francis was raised in Carlton in Bedfordshire, the son of an agricultural labourer who had migrated from Norfolk. Francis likely had a noticeable country accent and rustic manners, even if he attempted to hide them. Yet Sneyd-Kynnersley employed him as organist, strongly challenging the blanket view that he was stuck up. Having married a local woman, after the closure of the school, Francis remained in Sunninghill, working as a tax collector.

The appointment of Richard Blagrove (1826-1895), if nothing else, gives the lie to the assertion that Sneyd-Kynnersley wanted to avoid being around intelligent adults supposedly because of his own intellectual inferiority complex. He must have heard of Blagrove — who was described in *The Illustrated Sporting and Dramatic News* (3rd February 1877, p.458) in 1877 as 'the well known concertina player' — and probably appointed him in part for this reason. Blagrove, who had studied at the Royal Academy of Music (Schaarwächter, 2015, p.564), was one of the first teachers of and composers of music for the concertina (Meyerbeer, 1999, p.138, note 226), published the

Concertina Journal, composed fantasias for concertina and piano, and was Professor of the Viola at the Royal Academy of Music (Boden & Hedley, 2017, p.85), a position he held in 1881, prior to moving his wife and children to Ascot. Blagrove was also viola player for the London Philharmonic Orchestra (*The Strad*, 1896, p.197). He was a famous, eminent and innovative musician, the appointment of whom is hardly consistent with a headmaster who shuns intelligent adults.

Richard Blagrove

Blagrove wasn't the only obviously intellectually gifted man whom Sneyd-Kynnersley appointed. Thomas Cooke Sanders was an expert chess player, sufficiently prominent to be discussed in the *Oxford Companion to Chess,* and he had published in *The Chess Player's Chronicle* in 1871 (Hooper & Whyld, 1996, p.353). Chess ability has been found to be an excellent measure of general intelligence (Frydman & Lynn, 1992). Indeed, Sanders' replacement — the Rev. Sherard Montagu Statham — was, similarly, evidently a highly intellectual man, as we have already seen.

Fry's Fondness for Hyperbole

Put simply, Roger Fry is prone to hyperbole, half-truth, and perhaps even wilful falsehood. The hyperbole can be seen even in very small details, such as how often the headmaster read books by Charles Dickens to the school. It can even be observed in Fry's description of Sneyd-Kynnersley's appearance. For Fry (Woolf, 1940, p.32), the headmaster had a 'pair of floating red Dundreary whiskers which waved on each side of his flaccid cheeks like bat's wings.' In other words, Sneyd-Kynnersley was exceptionally skinny, had ginger hair, and had comically long sideboards. Neither Churchill nor Baring regard this apparently risible appearance as worth mentioning and even Backhouse refers only to the Head being 'thin as a whipping post' with 'droopy whiskers,' that is whiskers that hang down. He does not mention red hair, though he does mention this — 'russet' — with reference to Sneyd-Kynnersley's wife. Kessler refers merely to 'sandy mutton chops'; that is relatively long sideboards. So, it is likely that Fry is exaggerating both in terms of whisker length and rareness of hair colour.

There is also reason to suspect that Fry, if only due to failings of memory by the age of 64, may be exaggerating. This is especially likely due to his clear trauma as a consequence of witnessing the headmaster's beatings, which he actually goes so far as to term 'executions,' another example of Fry's penchant for dramatic hyperbole. It must be borne in mind that a recollection becomes inherently less reliable with time. This is due not only to forgetfulness but because of our need for a satisfactory life narrative, sense of identity, and thus sense of self. Maintaining a stable and positive sense of self is imperative because, without it, little makes sense, leading to intolerable levels of anxiety and depression. The nature of this sense of self evolves over time. We select and augment memories which are congruous with it at any given point and have the capacity to forget memories which are not (Bluck, 2003; Conway & Pleydell-Pearce, 2000). We are also prone to 'false memories,' whereby something that we imagine, could plausibly have happened, and which neatly fits with our current sense of self is selected to be a 'memory' (Brainerd & Reyna, 2005).

In addition, those who, like Fry, have undergone trauma tend to have particularly exaggerated or distorted memories of events (Gilbert, 2014, p.298). When a memory is traumatic, it is, in fact, *more* susceptible to disruption each time it is recalled than is a normal memory (Alberini & Le Doux, 2013). With regard to Fry's recollections of St George's relatively late in life, it is most improbable that the beatings would have involved such a high number of strokes as Fry recalls that they did, let alone with a relatively young man's 'full strength.' If that was what happened, we would expect Fry to also report pupils passing out, having to be carried out of the Head's study, or limping for a good while afterwards. Also when Fry gives the example of the beating of the boy who 'let fly,' he adds that the headmaster continued with 'increased fury.' This means that Sneyd-Kynnersley wasn't using his 'full strength' in the first place.

Fry claims that after a flogging the victim's bottom was 'a mass of blood.' Churchill and Kessler concur that the beating continued until the child 'bled freely' or merely 'bled.' But neither talk of 'a mass of blood.' Insomuch as the boys would have proudly shown off the results of their floggings, rightly believing that it made them more popular (Gathorne-Hardy, 1978, p.112), it is probable that if they had been as savage as Fry suggests then this would have been more widely remarked upon by people like Churchill and especially Baring as he subsequently attended Eton, which birched its pupils. Sir Edmund Backhouse, who evidently despised Sneyd-Kynnersley, does not mention the floggings being extraordinarily severe, an omission which is important following the criterion of embarrassment. 'A mass of blood' is likely an exaggeration as well. The children would have been effectively hospitalised if the beatings were that brutal. Fry claims that after three strokes of the birch 'spots of blood began to develop everywhere.' 'Everywhere' presumably implies on the walls, ceiling and furniture, but, Fry tells us, Sneyd-Kynnersley would continue until he had administered between 15 and 20 strokes. If this were so, surely his entire study would be awash with blood. Yet, apparently, he was only 'ashamed' enough to clear up the mess himself when 'the ceiling and walls of his study were spattered with' excrement. When they were, at least once a week, inundated with children's gore he was happy to let the maids do it; the same kind of maids who went to the police when they found blood on Thomas Hopley's sheets in 1860.

As for Fry's specific allegation of the headmaster continuing to beat a boy — seemingly Algernon Ferguson — after he 'let fly,' this needs to be carefully examined. There would have been at least three other witnesses — the deputy head boy, Harry Arthur Holmes and Ferguson himself — and the incident is so revolting that it is rather improbable that rumours would not have got round, as they did about Churchill's behaviour, as we will see later. It should also be borne in mind that Fry didn't mention the excrement element when writing home about what appears to be exactly the same incident at the time. So, this is probably another example of Fry's proneness to exaggerate, with distortion especially heightened by trauma, and Fry was apparently traumatised by what he witnessed as is clear from how he describes his feelings about it and the fact, as we will see below, that it sexually aroused him. The 'letting fly' incident, therefore, may well not have happened. Nauseating as it is to even contemplate, examples of this happening during the flogging of school boys, at the hands of different headmasters, have been recorded (Gay, 1993, p.559, endnote 40). And, as we will see below, the Hopi tribe of Arizona would routinely beat children to the point of defecation as part of their coming of age ritual. Moreover, Maurice Baring (1922, p.74) was friends with a 'new boy' called Ferguson, this would have been Algernon's younger brother, who was born in 1874. This signifies that Algernon's St George's experience wasn't bad enough to deter his parents from sending his younger brother to the same school.

Perhaps a reasonable conclusion is simply that the floggings were relatively severe by the standards of the time. But, at that time, almost all prep schools and public schools beat boys (though increasingly with a cane) and, in addition, it was almost always on the bare buttocks and until they bled. By the end of prep school, a boy would be 'thoroughly broken into the beating system' of public school (Gibson, 1978, p.70) where 'boys were flogged till they ran with blood for a mistake in their Latin verses' (Orwell, 1955, p.431). By the late nineteenth century, only Eton continued to birch — other public schools caned — but many prep schools imitated Eton because it was regarded as the best public school: 'we know that there were many prep schools where the Eton treatment was imitated, with differences only of frequency or ferocity' (de Symons Honey, 1977, p.198). In his introduction to the first volume of *The Letters of Roger Fry* (Sutton, 1972, p.4), the art critic Denys Sutton (1917-1991) writes that for Fry:

'the headmaster the Rev. W. H. Sneyd-Kynnersley [*sic.*] was a sadist and, secondly, the school itself was a terrible place. It is true that from his very first term, when the school opened, Fry as head boy was exposed to the harsh experience of being present when his companions were flogged; but punishment of this sort was customary at that time.'

John Lord (1970, p.68) explains that savage floggings at prep schools were 'not uncommon.' At a nineteenth century Winchester prep school, 'floggings abounded . . . "The blood ran through my shirt into my breeches." Sometimes the violence got completely out of hand' (Walvin, 1982, p.48). There is evidence that beatings were more pitiless and more likely to happen at prep school than at public school. A witness to a prisoner being bloodily flogged in early twentieth century colonial Kenya — district officer Henry Seaton (1887-1979) — was specifically put in mind of his own prep school canings (Ocobock, 2017, citing Seaton, 1963). Indeed, as De Salvo (1990, p.195) has pointed out, Fry wrote to his mother about the birchings, but despite her being a Quaker, and thus generally opposed to corporal punishment, she never acted to withdraw him from the school. De Salvo notes that this was presumably because what her son was describing to her was normal and accepted at such schools. Certainly, many prep schools used the birch in the late nineteenth century, such as Mulgrave Castle in Whitby in Yorkshire (Gronn, 1999, p.50) and, according to Gathorne-Hardy (1977, p.112), 'The beatings and violence I have described was administered as much, if not more, to small boys as to big ones. They were beaten continually at prep schools.'

Flogging to the Point of Bleeding

In fact, caning on the bare bottom to the point of bleeding is remarked upon by Roald Dahl in *Boy* (1984) when he recalls an incident, sometime between 1929 and 1932, of a boy being caned at Repton by the headmaster, Dr Geoffrey Fisher (1887-1972), who was later Archbishop of Canterbury.

> 'I was given a vivid description of one of these ceremonies by my best friend at Repton, whose name was Michael. Michael was ordered to take down his trousers and kneel on the Headmaster's sofa with the top of his body hanging over one end of the sofa . . . This slow and fearsome process went on until ten terrible strokes had been delivered . . . At the end of it all, a basin, a sponge and a small clean towel were produced by the Headmaster and the victim was told to wash away the blood before pulling up his trousers.'

Caning across the bare buttocks — under the headmaster Anthony Chenevix-Trench (1919-1979) (see Peel, 1996) — continued at Eton until at least 1970 (Onyeama, 1972). But this was very much a public school and prep school tradition. In 1906, a housemaster at Manchester Grammar School caused outrage when it was discovered that he had caned a boy on his bare bottom (Rose, 2002).

Clothed, canings continued until the point of bleeding at prep and public schools well after 1970. Canon Giles Fraser (5th February 2017) has written of his own thrashings at his prep school — Hollingbury Court in Sussex — up until 1977. He would regularly be beaten 'several times a week . . . Often we would go to bed with our underpants drenched in blood.' Accordingly, there is nothing unique about the system that was operated by Sneyd-Kynnersley, though it may have been slightly stricter than was the norm. Even with that conceded, this has to be balanced against evidence that, in all other respects, St George's lacked the privations associated with the public school system. There was clearly severe corporal punishment but, on the other hand, the food was excellent and the school had electricity and other modern conveniences. It is as if Sneyd-Kynnersley focused the Spartan element into just one aspect of school life. But, the key conclusion must be that Roger Fry exaggerates and lies, even if not on a Sir Edmund Backhouse scale. He is not a reliable source.

How Reliable is Winston Churchill?

Churchill can also hardly be regarded as a reliable source. Evidently, he maintained a lifelong bitterness against Sneyd-Kynnersley and would have had every motive to paint him in a particularly unfavourable light. As we will see later, Churchill, in general, was a thoroughly dishonest and manipulative individual. He also suffered from depression (Storr, 1989), which would imply that he was high in Neuroticism, a personality trait which is defined by experiencing negative feelings intensely (Nettle, 2007). Those who are high in Neuroticism are particularly prone to remembering negative events — and forgetting positive ones — and to creating negative false memories (Norris et al., 2018). So, we would expect Churchill to be prone to exaggeration and false memory in a negative direction. Consistent with this, not only are all his surviving letters home from St George's quite positive, but he even noted — in a letter to his father on 3rd December 1882 — that for his birthday 'Mrs Kynnersley gave me a little bracket' (Churchill, 1966). In another letter, he tells of how Mrs Sneyd-Kynnersley had been to Birmingham and that everyone was discussing Randolph's election campaign (Sandys, 1994, p.58). This is hardly consistent with a cold, heartless environment.

Winston Churchill

Churchill's statement that the floggings were more severe than those at reform schools or at Eton or Harrow is misleading because, as we have seen, floggings tended to be harsher at prep schools than at public schools, so Churchill is not comparing like with like. His statement is also simply untrue, something he must have known as a former Home Secretary.[43] Fry, who seems to generally exaggerate, claims that Sneyd-Kynnersley's standard flogging with the birch was '15 or 20 strokes.' In 1886, at Manchester Assizes, a 14-year-old boy was found guilty of 'improper conduct' with a 7-year-old girl. He was sentenced to fifteen strokes of the birch (*Manchester Guardian*, 17th May 1886). In 1913, a Home Office report stated that the maximum number of birch strokes inflicted on a boy at an industrial school (a school for juvenile delinquents) should be 12 and at a reform school it should be 18, implying that it was often higher prior to this instruction (Griffith, 1913, p.27). Consistent with this suspicion, on 24th November 1875, a 12-year-old boy was sentenced to go to a reform school and receive 'twenty strokes of the birch' (*Punch Magazine*, 18th December 1875, p.251), which would have been to the bare buttocks (Gibson, 1978, p.167). In 1872, 'twenty strokes of the birch' was described as 'little more than a Harrow boy used to get for playing truant' (*Public Opinion*, 20th April 1872, p.489). In 1896, eighteen strokes of the birch was described as 'not being anything of a punishment' for a strong, healthy boy and, certainly, commensurate with the punishments meted out at Eton (Humphries, 1983, p.224).[44] In his 1930 autobiography, Churchill was simply exaggerating

---

[43] Interior Minister.

[44] Corporal punishment was generally less harsh at girls' private schools. In 1937, a 17-year-old girl at a girls' boarding school in Dublin was given 17 strokes of the birch on her bare bottom by the headmistress for smuggling supposedly inappropriate literature into the school. A friend, who refused to reveal the smuggler's name to the headmistress, was given fourteen strokes of the strap in the same way. Birching was the norm at that school for serious misbehaviour, with the strap used for almost any misbehaviour. When the father of the latter girl discovered this he withdrew her from the school and complained to a newspaper (Ryley Scott, 1968, p.90). Such treatment of boarding school girls was more common around 1870, but it seems that while periodicals would happily discuss such treatment of boys, they found it improper to detail bare bottom birchings when it came to girls: 'The young ladies are birched . . . but the story is too abominable to repeat' (*Appleton's Journal*, 1870, p.499).

in order to make the headmaster he loathed appear particularly unpleasant.

What Do the Reliable Sources Tell Us?

We are then left with Baring, Jay, Kessler, Bonham Carter and Schuster. Kessler is very positive about Sneyd-Kynnersley. But, on the other hand, he does acknowledge that the floggings were to the point of bleeding (though stresses that they were not capricious) and he cautiously asserts that Sneyd-Kynnersley was motivated by pederasty. Thus, despite an overall positive appraisal of the headmaster, Kessler does look at negative aspects of Sneyd-Kynnersley and, indeed, of the school, such as the fact that he was at first badly bullied. Kessler is ostensibly not a man prone to rewriting his past in order to make it appear rosier. He openly admits, for example, in his memoirs that he was so mercilessly bullied at the beginning of his time at St George's that he tried to commit suicide by taking chloroform which he obtained from the school chemist (Easton, 2011, p.2). So he is likely reliable. Indeed, as he was likely a depressive, we might expect him to exaggerate negative memories, of which the suicide attempt might be an example. Jay, as we have noted, is particularly reliable by virtue of having kept a diary. He very much corroborates Kessler: the floggings were severe but they only happened as a punishment for extreme misbehaviour or blatant rule-breaking. There is a single error in his account, though it does not relate to his schooldays. Jay recalls that 'Mrs Kynnersley, who was still alive but had been a widow for many years' wrote to him when Churchill's *My Early Life* was published; in 1930 (p.9). This recollection must be wrong because Flora Sneyd-Kynnersley had died in 1925. It may be that it was Herbert's widowed sister-in-law Margaret Ethel Sneyd-Kynnersley (1856-1939) who wrote to Aubrey Jay, with Aubrey, aged 78 in 1947, somehow becoming confused.

From these reliable sources, it can be concluded that Sneyd-Kynnersley administered severe thrashings, though evidently not as severe as many of those explored in Chapter One. That said, Baring is understood to have been extremely high in Neuroticism, meaning he would have exaggerated and perhaps even unconsciously concocted negative memories (Powell, 21st September 1991). But the fact that almost all the sources mention the harsh beatings means that by the criterion of multiple attestation we can be very sure that these occurred, though probably not to the extent suggested by the more unreliable sources. The politician and historian Roy Jenkins (1920-2003) writes that St George's, Ascot 'appears from the disparately independent testimonies of Churchill himself and the art critic Roger Fry to have been a place of appalling brutality, even by the flogging standards of the age' (Jenkins, 2001, p.9). But Jenkins ignores the fact that Fry goes further than Churchill, so the testimonies are inconsistent, and that three testimonies — Kessler, Baring and Jay — regard the floggings as severe but for clear violations of the rules or of accepted standards of behaviour and, to some extent, deserved. Jenkins also ignores Baring's recollections of serious misbehaviour that was not punished by flogging. Schuster, as we will see later, was aghast at Churchill's behaviour, for which, in the instance recalled, he wasn't even flogged. In reality, it appears

Harry Kessler

that Sneyd-Kynnersley was far fairer and less inclined to administer corporal punishment than many headmasters of the time. You were not beaten for minor faults, such as mistakes in your Latin homework or talking during class, as happened at Repton in the 1930s. You were beaten, albeit ferociously, if you specifically broke the rules, behaved in a supposedly un-gentlemanly way or did something really odd. If you were a relatively 'good boy' — like Fry, Baring, Jay or Kessler — then you could get through your time at prep school without being beaten at all.

With regard to Sneyd-Kynnersley's being a 'sadist,' this is, again, only averred by the more unreliable sources, prone to exaggeration and, in two cases, clearly embittered: Churchill, Roger Fry and Sir Edmund Backhouse, who refers to the headmaster's 'sadistic smile.' Kessler is adamant that Sneyd-Kynnersley was not a sadist while Baring doesn't seem to be of this view, and he provides the most detailed account. Baring doesn't seem to particularly like Sneyd-Kynnersley so, following the criterion of embarrassment, it is noteworthy that he does not accuse him of sadism. By the same criterion, it is significant that Kessler *does* take the view that Sneyd-Kynnersley was attracted to boys, as does 'Arbuthnot' (paraphrased in Leslie, 1966, p.21, see below) and Backhouse. However, Fry is certain that this was not so; that Sneyd-Kynnersley was not an 'unconscious Sodomite.' We can, therefore, say that a reliable and pro-Sneyd-Kynnersley source — Kessler — is of the view that the headmaster was a non-active pederast but not a sadist. The pederast idea is backed-up, in a stronger form, by a much less reliable source (Backhouse) and a third source, albeit reported second hand – 'Arbuthnot' who claimed Sneyd-Kynnersley was attracted to boys. Jay has great admiration for Sneyd-Kynnersley and does all he can to defend him, so presumably did not think he was a sadist, though he does seem to imply that the Head preferred the older boys. So, we should, at least, take seriously that the headmaster was a non-practicing pederast. We will explore this issue in more detail below. The only source which asserts he was an *active* pederast is Backhouse and, as we have seen, he clearly exaggerates and lies with regard to the headmaster he so obviously reviles.

Deciding whether or not Sneyd-Kynnersley was a 'sadist' is more complicated and we will examine this possibility in more detail in the next chapter. But it would seem reasonable to conclude that Sneyd-Kynnersley's floggings were nowhere near as frequent, severe, or unusual in their severity as is commonly believed. In addition, we have no reason to doubt the reliability of Claude Schuster or Arthur Bonham Carter, especially as his letter is a contemporary source. Thus, Sneyd-Kynnersley was prone to tantrums but he also cared about, doted on and entertained his pupils and we have multiple attestation in this regard. With the sources explored, let us turn to the nature of personality, an understanding of which is necessary to see whether or not Sneyd-Kynnersley was arrested in his development or a sadist.

Chapter Six

The Psychology of Herbert

Sneyd-Kynnersley

The Big 5

PERSONALITY IS DEFINED as 'the combination of characteristics or qualities that form an individual's distinctive character.' Thus, personality can be seen as a series of variable traits (McAdams & Pals, 2006, p.212). In general, in psychology, discussion of personality differences is focused through the prism of the so-called Big Five personality traits, all of which have been estimated, from twin studies, to be somewhere in the region of at least 50% heritable (see Nettle, 2007) and possibly up to around 66% heritable (Lynn, 2011). The Big 5 have been developed because various personality traits — such as 'warmth' or 'depression' — have been found to correlate positively or negatively with each other, but to have no correlation, or only a very weak correlation, with other personality traits. As such, five has been widely accepted as the number of separate personality variables, and these variables are regarded as substantially independent of intelligence. The Big Five are:

1. *Extraversion*: Those who are outgoing, enthusiastic and active, seek novelty and excitement, and who experience positive emotions strongly. Those who score low on this express Introversion and are aloof, quiet, independent, cautious, and enjoy being alone.

2. *Neuroticism*: Those who are prone to stress, worry, and negative emotions and who require order. The opposite is those who are Emotionally Stable and who are better at taking risks.

3. *Conscientiousness*: Organized, directed, hardworking, but controlling. The opposite types are spontaneous, careless, and prone to addiction.

4. *Agreeableness*: Trusting, cooperative, altruistic, and slow to anger. This is contrasted with those who are uncooperative and hostile. There are two key aspects to Agreeableness: altruism and empathy (theory of mind; the ability to intuit what others are thinking). These positively correlate but they are not the same thing.

5. Those who are creative, imaginative, aesthetic, artistic, and open to new ideas (this latter aspect being the 'intellect' dimension) (Nettle, 2007). This is contrasted with those who are practical, conventional, and less open to new ideas. The traits which compose Openness such as 'unusual thought patterns,' 'impulsive non-conformity,' or 'aestheticism,' are often only weakly correlated. This has led some researchers to suggest that Openness-Intellect is, essentially, a combination of intelligence (intellectual curiosity), low Conscientiousness and low Agreeableness, and should simply be abandoned (e.g. Dutton & Charlton, 2015)

In each case, the traits are conceived of as a spectrum and are named after one extreme on the spectrum. They are considered useful because variation in the Big Five allows successful Life History predictions to be made. For example, the Termites were a cohort of 1,500 Americans of above average intelligence first surveyed in 1921 and then finally in 1991. Drawing upon them, it was found that extraversion, independent of any other factor, was a predictor of early death, increasing the risk threefold, probably because Extraversion encourages you to take risks in pursuit of the high positive emotional reward (Friedman et al., 1993). Low Agreeableness predicts criminality and divorce. High Conscientiousness predicts doing well in the worlds of education and work, while low Conscientiousness predicts criminality, low socioeconomic status, and addiction. High Neuroticism predicts depression, anxiety, marital breakdown and aspects of creativity (Nettle, 2007). It is also associated with being a religious seeker and having periodic phases of religious fervour (Hills et al., 2004) as well as, very specifically, with heart disease (Cukic & Bates, 2015), which was the cause of Sneyd-Kynnersley's premature death, at a time when there was no reliable medication for anxiety. An optimally high level of Openness is associated with artistic success. (Nettle, 2007). These personality characteristics also predict the kind of subjects that will interest you. Science types tend to be high in Conscientiousness, Agreeableness and Intellect, and low in Neuroticism and Openness. In Humanities types this is reversed (e.g. De Fruyt & Mervielde, 1996).

Personality and Sexual Disorders

A personality disorder is characterized by maladaptive patterns of behavior and inner experience which cause the sufferer to differ sufficiently from the norms of their own culture so as to be regarded as pathological. The symptoms tend to cluster together, meaning that psychologists have been able to identify a number of distinct personality disorders. Some people are more pronounced or clearer exemplars of these disorders than others. Equally, many disorders involve extremes of personality, meaning we can conceive of a spectrum, with 'normal' in the middle. For example, Autism is characterized in part by poor theory of mind; that is an inability to 'mentalize' and so imagine the feelings of others or read mental states from environmental cues. An autistic will not understand how someone feels from subtle facial expressions or mild verbal indications. In this sense, Autism sits at one end of a spectrum. At the other end of the spectrum is schizophrenia. This is characterized by over-mentalizing (Badcock, 2003). Schizophrenics are obsessed with other people's minds, they read far too much into cues, and this makes them paranoid or simply wrong. Thus, a subtle cue indicating that someone is slightly annoyed or upset may be understood by a schizophrenic to mean that the person is dangerously angry and wants to kill them. By contrast, the typical autistic will likely read nothing into it at all.

There are a number of more specific disorders which it would be useful to explore before examining Sneyd-Kynnersley. Borderline Personality Disorder involves a markedly disturbed sense of identity, such that sufferers aren't really sure what they believe or what their goals are. They suffer from strong negative reactions, especially to the possibility of abandonment; extreme black and white thinking, inexplicably impulsive behaviour, intense emotional reactions that are disproportionate to the situation, unstable interpersonal relationships, a distorted self-image, frequent anxiety or rage, and dissociation. Dissociation is any form of detachment from reality. Daydreaming is mild dissociation whereas psychosis — such as is suffered by paranoid schizophrenics who believe aliens are controlling their minds — would be extreme dissociation (see Gunderson, 2009).

A further pronounced example of dissociation is Dissociative Identity Disorder (DID), something which used to be called Multiple Personality Disorder. This tends to manifest itself as the presence, in one person, of two or more highly distinct personalities. Everybody can be described as having different sides to their character, but in cases of DID these differences are so conspicuous that it is as if there are two (or more) quite separate people inhabiting one body. The personalities will have separate memories as well. This disorder is often a response to childhood trauma. A sufferer finds certain memories too agonizing to cope with, so he or she dissociates from them via a kind of amnesia. However, when these memories are unconsciously triggered, such as under stress, an alternative self (who does remember being abused) will manifest. This other self may be the kind of person you might predict would have been abused as a child in some way: aggressive and angry (see Ringrose, 2018).

These two disorders can sometimes cross-over with simple arrested development. If a child is physically or sexually abused, or otherwise suffers some significant loss of attachment or trauma at a very young age, then it can damage the development of the part of the brain that controls the regulation of emotion and even the development of moral reasoning (e.g. Carson et al., 2013). As a consequence, the individual can become psychologically 'stuck' at a stage of emotional development that significantly lags behind that of his or her physical development. This is commonly termed 'arrested development.' Those who suffer from it may well have far lower impulse control or emotional maturity than others of their age: they will come across as childish or childlike (Pfeifer & Allen, 2012).

We have already looked at suggestions that Sneyd-Kynnersley may have been a sadist, an 'unconscious Sodomite,' and so an unconscious pederast if we consider the age of the pupils involved, and literally a pederast, who was sexually attracted to some of his pupils and who was sexually aroused by flogging the bare buttocks of his pupils. These kinds of sexual disorders are known as paraphilia. These are defined as any intense and persistent sexual arousal via means other than genital stimulation and fondling from phenotypically normal sexually mature, consenting adult partners, with it having been previously stressed by psychologists that these consenting adults must be of the opposite sex (Balon, 2016a). 'Sadism,' though broadly a paraphilia, is slightly distinct. To be diagnosed as a 'sadist,' a person must be sexually excited by the psychological or physical suffering of the victim, where this suffering includes humiliation (Marshall et al., 1999, p.255). It follows that if Sneyd-Kynnersley was turned on by flogging his pupils it may not have been because of their pain — if that were so, he could have electrocuted them — but because he had a fetish.

A fetish normally begins when a person reaches puberty or is in their teenage years. They are predominantly sexually aroused by a particular object or activity. An example of this would be spanking fetishism. There is much debate over the causes of fetishes. In understanding the causes, it is highly relevant that a significant

155

aspect of sexual arousal is conditioning. Just as Pavlov's dogs were conditioned to associate the sound of a bell with food (causing them to salivate upon hearing the bell), humans have a tendency to associate certain conditional stimuli. A particular song may be impossible to listen to for a long time after a traumatic break-up, because the spurned partner associates it with his longed-for ex. The same process can occur with sexual arousal, meaning that people can become aroused by the associated stimuli itself (Akins, 2004). A particularly attractive female might wear a certain perfume, leading to this perfume — for a period of time, at least — being arousing for a certain male.

With regard to spanking fetishism, one possibility is that a child develops an association between being spanked and being sexually aroused, due, for example, to the stimulation of the anus and the nerve endings in the buttocks. Another possibility may be a childhood experience of being somehow traumatized either by being spanked or by witnessing a spanking or by both, leading to an intense memory. Later, upon being sexually aroused by buttocks — as they are a sexual characteristic — the repressed traumatic memory may be recalled, leading to an association between buttocks, sexual arousal and spanking (e.g. Colarusso, 2010, p.100). In *Psychopathia Sexualis,* for example, Austro-German psychiatrist Richard Krafft-Ebing (1840-1902) reported the case of a 22-year-old Frenchman who, aged 7, in about 1884, had witnessed his governess 'chastise' his 14-year-old sister on the (presumably bare) buttocks. This traumatised him. He would, thereafter, seek out fellow children to play spanking games with (Krafft-Ebing, 1998, p.78), because those who are traumatized often allay anxiety through 'repetition compulsion' (Levy, 2000). One day, he played a game where he was 'father' with two girls as his 'daughters.' He smacked a 'lean' girl on her clothed bottom. However, the 10 year-old 'plump' girl let him smack her bare bottom and from this he obtained an erection. Thus began his 'Sadism-Fetishism' (Krafft-Ebing, 1998, p.78).

Something like this may have happened to Sneyd-Kynnersley. He may have witnessed bare bottom birchings or himself have been birched at Rugby and later been sexually aroused by buttocks, leading to the association. It has been found that those who have a paraphilia are motivated by a desire to allay anxiety, achieve feelings of power, and recreate or take control of a childhood experience. Around 30% of male paraphilia sufferers were physically abused as children. They may also cope via projection: so a person who was traumatized by being spanked or aroused by it as a child will perform that act on others and so become aroused themselves. For arousal to be achieved, the recreation would need to be relatively precise, helping to explain, possibly, why Sneyd-Kynnersley insisted on using the birch rather than the cane, which was more common by the late Victorian period.

Paraphilia is often comorbid with high levels of anxiety —helping to explain the significance of trauma — as well as with a weak sense of self and arrested development, consistent with problems at critical developmental periods more generally (for a review see Seligman & Hardenberg, 2000). Equally, there is some evidence of a genetic dimension to paraphilia (see Balon, 2016b), meaning that the brain has developed in a suboptimal fashion, due to mutant genes. Consistent with this, it has been shown that some paraphilia — such as paedophilia — are comorbid with a number of accepted markers of high mutational load, such as left-handedness, which is in turn associated with many neurological problems. Paraphilia themselves also tend to be comorbid with each other, potentially implying an underlying cause, which may be genetic (Labelle et al., 2012). It should be noted, with regard to left-handedness, that we are evolved to be symmetrical and only when the brain is asymmetrical, overusing its right side, does someone tend to become left-handed. Accordingly, left-handedness is a marker of 'developmental instability' (something having gone wrong in early development), mutation or of both (Woodley of Menie et al., 2018a).

The Nature of Mr Sneyd-Kynnersley

Based on our sources, we can now begin to better piece together the psychology of Mr Sneyd-Kynnersley. Firstly, as we have already observed, he was evidently a highly intelligent man, as betokened by his having been awarded a LLD from Cambridge towards the end of his life. High intelligence is positively associated with a number of characteristics including high theory of mind, high levels of altruism, a rejection of political extremes, not being conservative, low levels of authoritarianism, low dogmatism, low criminality, high honesty, low religiousness, and high levels of trust (see Jensen, 1998).

There are many correlates of intelligence and highly intelligent people will vary in terms of the extent to which they conform to the stereotype, usually due to the strength of personality traits, which will also influence their behaviour. However, the fact that Sneyd-Kynnersley's life indicates such low intelligence on so many intelligence correlates — high authoritarianism, politically extreme and dogmatic, high religiousness even by the standards of the time — means that he was probably quite extreme on various personality spectrums. Indeed, this is what we are going to find. There seems to be quite a convincing case that Sneyd-Kynnersley suffered from some kind of Borderline Personality disorder. But before turning to this, let us look at him in terms of the Big 5.

The subject which fascinated Sneyd-Kynnersley, despite his legal qualifications, was Classics. Fascination with such a subject is predicted — compared to those who might teach Maths — by relatively low Agreeableness, relatively low Conscientiousness, relatively high Neuroticism, and relatively high Openness. Consistent with relatively high Openness, the headmaster seems to have been a highly creative man, constantly organising stimulating school trips. The school itself also reflected a high level of Openness. It had electric lights, top quality facilities, high standard food (where school food tended to be notoriously awful even at very expensive schools), and he employed innovative pedagogies, such as when teaching Shakespeare plays. His pupils also recall how much they enjoyed his story time. An important aspect of Openness, as well as of Neuroticism, is the ability to dissociate. Actors and artists are high in Openness (Nettle, 2007). This helps them to become the people whom they portray or to immerse themselves in the world that they are portraying, so rendering it all the more hypnotically realistic. Roger Fry refers to Sneyd-Kynnersley as a 'dandy'; though this may well be an exaggeration. At that time, this meant a man who was particularly interested in dressing in a fashionable and stylish manner. This is predicted both by aestheticism, from whence derives the stylishness, and also plain Openness, which predicts the interest in novelty (Feyn et al., 2015). Equally consistent with the headmaster's high Openness was his interest in aesthetically pleasing things. Baring (1922, p.68) remarks that the headmaster's study was full of 'a great many knick-knacks.' In his will, Sneyd-Kynnersley didn't seem to care much about bequeathing people money. Instead, he assumed they wanted 'my old gold watch chain . . . my silver headed sticks,' 'pictures to be selected for him by my wife and my leather dispatch box' or 'my gold studs and solitaires and two pieces of china.' Sneyd-Kynnersley was evidently an aesthete, aestheticism being an Openness trait.

The fact that Sneyd-Kynnersley was very adept at organizing popular 'expeditions' for his pupils would imply that he had a certain degree of empathy for them. He was able to get inside their minds and imagine, correctly, how they might think. The headmaster put a great deal of effort into these expeditions, read exciting stories to the pupils, participated in school games, invited pupils for tea at his house (Easton, 2002, p.25) and distributed 'sumptuous prizes' at his own expense. Cross-referencing Sneyd-Kynnersley's 1880 will with the 1881 census (which took place during term time) reveals it to be mainly populated by current school pupils. He left them — 17 pupils receive bequests with one directly referred to as 'my friend and pupil' — various books, pictures, ornaments and articles of expensive jewellery. The 'friend and pupil,' as we have already discussed, was George Hubert Olliver who was 12 years old when Sneyd-Kynnersley wrote his will. In October 1883, Sneyd-Kynnersley announced that, as he had quite a large house in a rural area, other priests could come and stay if they needed a period of prayer and contemplation. On that occasion, 24 clergymen took up his generous offer (*Reading Mercury*, 6th October 1883). This was not a selfish man by any stretch of the imagination. The fact that he was able to organize and run a successful school would also tend to imply that he was not especially low in Conscientiousness. One incident, however, is recorded of his taking financial advantage of someone. He paid a policeman 10 shillings for a stray dog, who was a valuable pedigree, with the policeman not realising this. Sneyd-Kynnersley also billed Churchill's mother for the entire autumn term of 1882, despite Churchill only having started in the November, something about which she complained to her husband (Churchill, 1966). However, it appears that it was standard practice in some nineteenth century educational institutions to charge latecomers for the entire term, if not those who had arrived quite as late as Winston had (e.g. Northwestern University, 1864, p.97). Moreover, the school's prospectus was crystal clear that 'Terms . . . are strictly inclusive' (*Ours Schools and Colleges*, 1883, p.69).

There is, also, evidence of high Neuroticism. Insomuch as Sneyd-Kynnersley was, it appears, high in Openness — which predicts liberal attitudes politically and religiously — his profound religious and political conservatism would seem to be indicative of high Neuroticism. He is more complex than the Big 5 model permits. It has to be remembered that these personality factors are composed of traits which themselves inter-correlate. Most people who score highly on one trait of Openness score highly on all of them. But this is only an average. Some people, seemingly people like Sneyd-Kynnersley, would score extremely high on some traits of a Big 5 factor but extremely low on others. The same would likely be true of his Agreeableness and Conscientiousness. Sneyd-Kynnersley's conservative religious fervour and political traditionalism would be consistent with low Openness on certain traits and also with high Neuroticism, leading to an intense dislike of certain kinds of change. In addition, we know he suffered from low blood pressure, which itself has been shown to predict elevated levels of Neuroticism (Davies, 1970).

Sneyd-Kynnersley's Personality Disorders

However, it may be possible to make sense of these contradictions via diagnosis with a personality disorder. There is certainly evidence, in Sneyd-Kynnersley, of some form of arrested development. This can be observed in Roger Fry's recollection that the headmaster was, to some degree, a show-off, who would boast of how well he did as part of the Dickens Society at Cambridge. It can be found in his will, in which he was still stressing, aged 32, that certain books which he was bequeathing were prizes given to him at Rugby when he was a teenager, presumably for writing the best essay. Roger Fry recalled Sneyd-Kynnersley explaining about how elevated he was because he was a priest, which would also be a form of childish bragging, though also consistent with his Tractarian views. Similarly, the headmaster's rather simplistic sense of humour can be seen in Kessler's recollection of 'Mr Kynnersley' leading his pupils off the main path on a cross-country run, managing to quickly disappear back onto the path, and then clearly feeling proud of himself for having successfully orchestrated such an hilarious jape on his charges.

Sneyd-Kynnesley was also very impressed by the rich and famous, to the extent that he would collect their autographs either by writing to them in the hope of a response or, presumably, through purchasing or obtaining them from others. For example, he possessed, in addition to a bulging autograph album, a three-page letter written by the Duke of Wellington (1769-1852) on 4th December 1832. It began 'Dear Sir' but later stated that 'you are a minister in the word of God in the Church of England' (Unpublished Primary Sources: Duke of Wellington, Autograph Letter), giving us a clue as to how Sneyd-Kynnersley might have obtained it. Sneyd-Kynnersley amassed a collection of around 200 such autographs over his life time, which he carefully kept in a book. He even kept the letter he'd received from William Gladstone, whom he obviously hated. His collection included the signatures of various obscure European Royals, Queen Victoria, Cardinal John Henry Newman (1801-1890), Prime Minister Sir Robert Peel (1788-1850), Prime Minister Benjamin Disraeli (1804-1881), politician William Wilberforce (1759-1833), novelist Sir Walter Scott (1771-1832) and the composer Sir Arthur Sullivan (1842-1900) (Unpublished Primary Sources: Autograph Album), who wrote the music for the Gilbert and Sullivan operettas. In other words, as the Lord High Executioner sings in *The Mikado*, Sneyd-Kynnersley was one of 'those pestilential nuisances/ Who write for autographs.'

Similarly, we have seen many examples of the headmaster imposing unnecessary, arbitrary rules and then becoming overwhelmingly upset when they are broken. We have also observed him sulking when disobeyed or otherwise slighted, going into a rage, or both. This exemplifies infantile behaviour patterns (see Hill, 1952). Sneyd-Kynnersley insisted that his pupils not eat any of the Spanish chestnuts, brooded over this when he realised that they had disobeyed him and then had a sudden fit of pique at tea that evening. He thrashed pupils for disobedience of *his* arbitrary rules — such as about touching the light switches — but was far more lenient when it came to breaking more general rules, which everybody would accept, such as with regard to cheating or bullying. Sneyd-Kynnersley organized a presumably quite fun trip into town to campaign for the Conservative candidate in the by-election, but made the boys who had previously made their support for the Liberal Party clear stay at school: 'You're not a Tory – so boo sucks to you!' Only his favourites would be invited to tea at his house (Easton, 2002, p.25) and the best Rugby players could wear a blue cap on Sunday but so could his favourites (Baring, 1922, p.74). Sneyd-Kynnersley divided the school into four 'divisions' who experienced a descending order of expedition quality, with the division *he* taught receiving the best expeditions. When the pupils weren't sufficiently enamoured by the cricket match he became profoundly upset and sulkily cancelled their trip to the New Forest. His treatment of Maurice Baring's mother was clearly infantile. Likely jealous that Baring had got to meet the Princess of Wales, he threatened to expel her son from the school if she didn't send him back that night, on an unreasonably late train. Sneyd-Kynnersley's fits of impulsivity are also congruous with arrested development, as is the way that expeditions or punishments would suddenly descend on the school. Males tend to become lower in Neuroticism with age and higher in impulse control (Soto et al., 2011), but the headmaster evidently lagged behind, making him a slightly unpredictable character. This might help to explain such events as suddenly taking a class to London for 24 hours without warning or suddenly flogging a boy for cutting off a piece of his hair and keeping it in a drawer, though, as already suggested, there may be more to this, for example the boy may have lied about how the hair got there.

As we have seen, Roger Fry commented that Sneyd-Kynnersley suffered from some form of arrested development and that this was why he enjoyed the company of children, even possessing a similar kind of sense of humour to theirs. This appears to be not uncommon among the kind of men who become primary school teachers. Similarly, as the psychiatrists Anthony Stevens and John Price (2000, p.206), explain, not all 'paedophiles' rape children. Many are celibate but go into professions, such as primary school teaching, gaining some sexual satisfaction from so doing:

> 'The great majority of paedophiles are male and they vary in the degree to which they can sublimate or feel compelled to act out their desires. Some, possibly a majority, are able to find a measure of fulfilment in committing themselves to a mentoring role such as school teacher, sports coach, scout master or child care worker, while successfully inhibiting physical expression of their erotic desires; others may limit their amorous propensities to touching or fondling children, occasionally sharing sexual innuendos or erotic jokes with them . . . The course of the condition is usually chronic, especially in those attracted to boys.'

It is certainly worth noting, in this regard, that of the eight men whom we know were masters at St George's, Ascot, while Sneyd-Kynnersley was headmaster — Sneyd-Kynnersley himself, Thornber, Holmes, Cooke, Sanders, Macdonald, Scudamore, and Statham — only one (Statham) actually married and had children. Three (Cooke, Macdonald and Sneyd-Kynnersley) contracted childless marriages, ending in estrangement and annulment for failure to consummate in Macdonald's case, and, according to censuses, four (Holmes, Sanders, Scudamore and Thornber) never married at all. They remained bachelors despite there existing, as we have seen, a 'spinster crisis' among the upper and upper-middle class at the time.

When I was at junior school, we all liked our headmaster. He was one of only two male teachers at the school for most of my time there, and he was a bachelor, probably in his late-fifties. He played with us at playtime, made us laugh, told us hilarious stories, hugged kids, and had them sitting on his knee if they were upset, was excellent at sorting out arguments between kids, played the guitar, kept a python who lived at the school, and always seemed very fair. When I didn't want to go to my class swimming lessons, he offered to drop whatever work he was doing and accompany me. However, on the occasion he personally took my group swimming, as part of a school trip. he changed with us boys in the communal changing room set aside for school parties rather than in a cubicle. He also made no effort to cover himself up while he did so or to change quickly. One afternoon he told me off for being especially mean to a particular girl. The following afternoon he came and found me, took me to his office, put me on his knee, and read me a comical book which he said he'd found, which he thought I'd like. He would always check on children in the sick bay, holding their foreheads to test for temperature, or putting on plasters. In retrospect, his motives for doing so were possibly less than entirely innocent, but that wasn't clear to anyone at the time. I could never understand why everybody's parents, including my own, thought he was weird. The probable answer is that he suffered from arrested development and this is why he got on so well with children aged 7 to 11 but not with their parents. In many key respects, he was probably quite a similar character to Sneyd-Kynnersley. With the exception of 'unstable personal relationships,' Sneyd-Kynnersley appears to have had all of the components of Borderline Personality Disorder, as we have already outlined it. It is even possible that he had some very mild form of DID and could be triggered into an otherwise uncharacteristic rage by certain forms of relatively innocuous behaviour, although this seems less likely. All of the personality disorders which can be feasibly applied to the headmaster are generally underpinned, in part, by childhood trauma.

Corporal Punishment, History and Sexuality

As we have seen, it has been widely argued that Sneyd-Kynnersley had some kind of sexual disorder. It is suggested he was a sadist, a flogging fetishist and even a pederast. But before we assess Sneyd-Kynnersley it may be revealing to try to understand why humans strike each other on the buttocks at all and doing so will also reduce the extent to which Sneyd-Kynnersley might be regarded as somehow 'perverted.' With regard to his floggings, the fact that they were administered to the bare buttocks means very little in itself. This is because, as I have already noted, this is essentially the only way such punishments were administered at such schools at the time (see Gibson, 1978) and, indeed, for much of European history, meaning there may even be evolutionary reasons for this.

Children were beaten on the bare buttocks in ancient Pompeii (Beard, 2010, p.77). Medieval European images of schooling depict boys being birched on their bare bottoms as punishment in front of the entire class (Willemsen, 2008, p.183) and beating children, wives, and servants in this way seems to have been quite common (Orme, 2006, p.146), often continued to the point of bleeding (McCoy & Keen, 2013, p.5). A Middle English poem aimed at children includes the line, 'And but thou do, thou that fare the worse/And thereto be beat on the bare arse' (Furnivall, 1868, p.401). The Medieval English poem *Piers Plowman*, written in about 1370, refers to the commonness of this practice by school teachers (Bowen, 1975, p.324) and we have already seen that it continued at Eton until the 1970s.

Spanking children on their bare bottoms seems to be relatively socially acceptable in the USA (see Buck, 12th September 2011) and it was in the UK a generation ago. In 1993, in England, a woman was successfully prosecuted for slippering her 9-year-old daughter on her bare bottom for stealing sweets. The conviction was overturned on appeal with the judge declaring that 'If a parent cannot slipper a child the world is going potty' (Barton & Douglas, 1995, p.130; Taylor, 2004). When I was a postgraduate at Aberdeen University, I conducted participant observation anthropological fieldwork with fundamentalist Christian students at British universities, born circa 1980, and I also knew many such students when I was an undergraduate (Dutton, 2008). The issue of childhood punishment came up in conversation a number of times. One girl had been regularly slippered on her bare bottom by her father until she was 8; another girl had been caned on her bare bottom by her mother until she was 9, and a boy had been smacked in this way by his mother until he was 10. Indeed, spanking children on their clothed bottoms was accepted in schools, especially public schools. When I was an undergraduate at Durham University, I got to know many students who had attended public schools, in which corporal punishment was legal until 1998. One student, who had been to Harrow, told me, 'I was beaten with a table tennis racket on my first day at prep school for "general attitude". One public school girl informed me of how her brother had been given stroke after stroke of the belt on his (clothed, by that time) bottom until he agreed to do whatever the master was demanding of him. He endured fifteen strokes before finally 'breaking', though he may have exaggerated the number.

Indeed, there may inherently be an unconscious sexual element to spanking. English zoologist Desmond Morris (1969) suggests that the origins of spanking may lie in chimpanzee behaviour. Chimpanzees have sexual intercourse, at least for most of the process, 'from behind': The female presents her posterior to the male, who then mounts her. Morris (1969) observes that if a subordinate male gets into conflict with a dominant chimp then the subordinate will present his posterior to the dominant chimp. The dominant chimp will briefly mount or even enter him, which defuses the situation. Spanking is likely to have evolved from these primordial beginnings. So, spanking is adaptive because it increases the fitness of the lower status individual. Many mammals — with dogs offering their necks or being mounted by same-sex superiors as the obvious example — perform acts of submissiveness, humiliation, and ritualised violence in substitution for real violence (see Abrantes, 1997). Likewise, mimicking femininity may function to obviate violence by changing the role of the adversary from a male to be competed with into a female to be mated with if one wishes.

Also, voluntarily presenting the posterior whilst not being able to see it is associated with a range of psychological changes related to defeat, because this position prevents fight and defence and it also involves total exposure to the whims of the dominant agent. Exposing a private part of the body will likely heighten this, in cultures where such an area is rarely exposed. Serotonin levels follow the individual's position in the social hierarchy, rendering the dominant partner pacified and the dominated partner submissive for a substantial period of time (e.g. Ziomkiewicz-Wichary, 2016). So, the dominant agent — typically the teacher or parent — can therefore avoid inflicting serious injury, which would have been detrimental both to the individual and to his or her relation or group member. In the process, the child is taught to associate the negative behaviour with pain and humiliation, to cooperate with authority, to gain self-control, and to cope with pain. By also being highly ritualised, it constitutes stability in a time of disorder and allows those involved to 'move on.' Simply striking an errant child would potentially teach it that life is unpredictable and dangerous. However, forcing the child to undergo a marked ritual — which involves submissiveness, degradation, pain, but also control and predictability — teaches it that life is harsh yet also highly predictable (Dutton & Madison, 2019). It can be argued that the sexual element to it may, on some unconscious level, be inescapable, which may explain the relative commonality of spanking fetishism.

Sneyd-Kynnersley's Sexual Disorder

So, the question is, 'Was there a sexual element to Sneyd-Kynnersley's floggings beyond that which may be inherent in such activity? Was he, even by the standards of his time, a flagellant? And, further, was he a sadist?'

That he was sexually aroused by the pain of other people seems rather unlikely. It is clear that he relished the happiness of his pupils. He liked giving them 'sumptuous' prizes, organizing exhilarating school trips for them, entertaining them with lively stories, hosting them at his own house, and, in his will, giving them expensive gifts without any possibility — as he would be dead — of receiving anything in return. Indeed, Algernon Ferguson — a boy whom Sneyd-Kynnersley certainly flogged — was one of his 17 favourites, bequeathed to in his will. This is hardly consistent with a man who was motivated by causing other people pain, though he may have been aroused by so-doing only in a very specific set of circumstances. According to Ian Gibson (1978, p.69) 'Dr Anthony Storr has not hesitated to diagnose [*Sneyd-Kynnersley*] as a sadist.' Anthony Storr (1920-2001) was a psychiatrist, but, even so, there should always be some hesitation when it comes to diagnosis, especially if you haven't met the patient. However, I have checked Gibson's source for this assertion, as well as the other Storr book which he cites just in case he has confused two sources (Storr, 1965; 1969, 1972, 1991, I have only been able to check the later editions). I can find no evidence that Storr ever made such a diagnosis. Further, if Sneyd-Kynnersley was a sadist, then there would not need to be the strongly ritualistic or controlled aspect to his violence. You would expect reports of his bullying pupils, publically humiliating them and conceiving of elaborate means of really hurting them (such as by electrocution). None of this appears to be the case, meaning that he was probably not a sadist or, at least, no more sadistic than any headmaster who was prepared to flog his pupils.

What about the idea that Sneyd-Kynnersley's sadism was part of a fetish? Was he aroused by flogging the bare bottoms of pupils, possibly as part of some kind of sublimated paedophilia or pederasty? This, I would suggest, may be correct. He was specifically sexually aroused by flogging boys and, independently of that, sexually aroused by certain boys, though he does not seem to have unfairly flogged those boys as he never flogged Roger Fry and Fry was evidently one of his favourites. It also seems that Sneyd-Kynnersley was more generally disinclined to flog because he wanted the boys to like him. Consistent with the homosexual flogging fetishism idea is the severity of his floggings (far worse than those at Winchester, for example), the fact that he alone was allowed to flog pupils, and the very specific and antiquated nature of his floggings. It can be argued that there was a sadistic element to his floggings — he had a flogging fetish and floggings are inherently excruciating — but there is a clear difference between this and being an archetypal sadist who is simply aroused by hurting people. Consistent with the pederasty hypothesis — a reflection of arrested development — is Sneyd-Kynnersley's obvious favourites, his childlike nature, the fact that his marriage was childless, his restraint with regard to the frequency of floggings (because he also wanted the children to like him), and the fact that such an educated and wealthy man should go into prep school teaching at all; a point we will discuss below.

With regard to his restraint, Sneyd-Kynnersley — even when confronted with behaviour which by most headmasters' standards even 50 years later would merit a beating (such as cheating) — would often not administer a flogging at all. Kessler (1935) recalls tell of an incident in which Churchill jumped up on the desk during class and began singing a rude stable song to everybody. Sneyd-Kynnersley merely 'threatened' to birch him if he didn't stop. Fry reports that some weeks, there were no Monday-morning floggings, because no excuse could be found in the reports. This reticence would be congruous with the headmaster balancing his fetish with other desires, possibly implying that though he may have been aroused by flogging he was likely also aroused by the boys themselves. It seems probable — especially considering evidence of Sneyd-Kynnersley's non-practicing pederasty — that there must have been some arousal, at least when birching the older boys. However, his reticence would imply that he did not administer the punishment purely for sexual reasons and, as stated, there is no evidence that he, by the standards of the time, sexually abused the children. Accordingly, I would suggest that Sneyd-Kynnersley was a homosexual flogging fetishist and non-active pederast who, in part, sublimated his homosexuality through flogging, which it can be argued involves an inherently sexual element.

In this respect, he was no different from many prep school or public school headmasters. Indeed, his activities were, if anything, less egregious than those of many of them. Anthony Chenevix-Trench was the headmaster of Eton. This, usually drunken, man would give ten pats to boys' bare buttocks before and after beating them. In that this had nothing to do with punishment, it was simple unwanted fondling: it was sexual abuse even by the standards of the time. During one such beating, Chenevix-Trench actually asked one victim if the victim thought that his headmaster was a 'pederast.' He would tell the victims that he loved them during such thrashings. In 1964, Chenevix-Trench offered the future journalist Nick Fraser (who was 18) the choice between a bare bottom beating or expulsion; and he was an 'arch-flogger' who used bare bottom beatings for pretty much every offence. While patting Fraser's buttocks and whipping him, Chenevix-Trench 'wept profusely' and told Fraser how much he 'hated himself' (see Saunders, 2018; Fraser, 2012). The Rev. Dr Leopold Bernays (1820-1882), headmaster of the prep school Elstree, a feeder school for Harrow, between 1847 and 1860, would froth at the mouth as he flogged little boys, presumably because he was having an orgasm and he would flog boys at every opportunity (Leinster-Mackay, 2012, p.60).

Also, it is worth noting, with regard to Sneyd-Kynnersley, that Roger Fry was evidently a neurotic individual. His biographer, Frances Spalding (1980, p.13) observes that he was constantly overwhelmed by feelings of anxiety, guilt and melancholy. If anything, he was even more unhappy at his public school, Clifton in Bristol, than he was at Sunninghill House, despising the entire public school system. And Fry *was* aroused by the floggings at Ascot. In a passage censored from his memoir by Virginia Woolf (1940) he recalls that when he returned to his room, after witnessing a particular flogging, he experienced his first erection. Fry actually wrote that his own conflation of sex, cruelty and pain was 'revealed to me one day, when I went back to my room after assisting at an execution, by my having an erection . . . the first I had ever had. I had not even the faintest idea of the function of the organ whose behaviour so surprised me' (quoted in Briggs, 2007). So, perhaps Fry — though he is likely right that the floggings aroused the flogger — is also engaging in the common psychological defence of projectionism. Perhaps he was specifically aroused not by the flogging but by the idea of the agony of the victims. Spalding (1980. p.13) paints Fry as having been unnaturally close to and strongly dominated by his mother, to whom he would write from Ascot begging forgiveness for his having felt grumpy one morning when he got up early to read the Bible. There is evidence that those who become sexually deviant tend to have mothers of this kind (Stevens, 2015). It may, however, be that Fry was aroused by the possibility of being flogged, as it has been found that masochist males tend to have strong bonds with their mothers, in contrast to sadist males, where the bond tends to be insecure (Sandnabba et al., 2002).

Attracted to (Ginger Haired) Boys

As an aside, as we are discussing fetishes, a peculiar element is added to Churchill's experience by his biographer Squadron Leader

Norman Rose (1916-2006) (Rose, 2009, p.10) who wrote in *Churchill: An Unruly Life* that according to a pupil of Sneyd-Kynnersley's the headmaster was 'sexually excited by any boy with red hair.' Churchill had red hair, and Rose, therefore, asserts that this 'adds another dimension to poor Winston's beatings.' As already discussed, the headmaster flogged Algernon Ferguson, who also very probably had red hair. According to Sir Edmund Backhouse (2017), Sneyd-Kynnersley's wife had 'russet' hair: dark ginger or auburn. Rose gives no source for his quote. However, the exact same words can be found in the American magazine, *The Commonweal* (Fremantle, 27th October 1967, p.127), where they are not in quotation marks. They are part of a review of the autobiography of Winston's maternal cousin Sir Shane Leslie, *Long Shadows* (Leslie, 1966). Leslie (1966, p.21) writes that:

'Virginia Woolf's *Life of Roger Fry* gives a nauseous account of these floggings, which in Winston's case a fellow pupil, Arbuthnot, attributed to the headmaster being incited sexually by any boy with red hair.'

So, Leslie was indeed the source of the quote. However, Rose, also did not report the fact that the allegation was specifically made about Winston's floggings and he quotes the words in the *Commonweal* review, which differ from those in the book. So, clearly, Rose read the review of *Long Shadows* but not *Long Shadows* itself.

But once more, let us examine the reliability of the sources. We know from Maurice Baring (1922, p.68) that Arbuthnot started at the school in autumn 1884, on the same day that Baring did. This was after Churchill had left, so Arbuthnot could only have heard rumours, if even those. However, it is probable that Leslie knew Arbuthnot personally. Based on Arbuthnot's likely age when he started prep school and probable social class, it is fairly certain that he was Andrew Carmichael Arbuthnot (1877-1953), son of Lt. Col. William Reierson Arbuthnot (1826-1913) of Plaw Hatch, East Grinstead, Sussex, the director of an insurance company and sometime member of the Madras Legislative Council. Andrew Arbuthnot went to Charterhouse and then joined the 3rd Seaforth

Highlanders, rising to the rank of Captain, receiving the Queen's Medal, and serving in the South African War of 1902 (Crisp, 1919, pp.78-82). By the time of the 1911 census, he was a company director, living in London. His brother, William (1866-1938) was married to Mabel Slade, daughter of Francis Slade of New York, whom he had married at Madison Square Presbyterian Church, New York, in 1907 (Crisp, 1919, p.80). Sir Shane Leslie was the son of New Yorker Leonie Jerome (1859-1943), sister of Jennie Jerome, Churchill's mother. So we can see how, through these connections between families of wealthy socialites, Leslie and Arbuthnot could have met.

Sneyd-Kynnersley may well have been attracted to ginger hair. However, his recorded hesitance with regard to thrashing Churchill makes it most unlikely that his floggings of Churchill were motivated by his fancying him. It is, it would seem, rather more likely that Sneyd-Kynnersley was simply attracted to young boys. As we have seen, Kessler suggests that there was a homoerotic element to Sneyd-Kynnersley's interest in boys. This would be congruous with his failure to have children, his wife's intense jealousy of his close friendships with certain older pupils, his reference in his will to a then current pupil also being his 'friend,' the fact that he made bequests to his pupils, the fact that he had obvious favourites whom he would treat and have round for tea, and the fact that he would unnecessarily heavily involve himself in physical education and school trips when he could easily have delegated this to an assistant master.

In addition, it is fascinating that in his will Sneyd-Kynnersley bequeathed 'my Rugby prize copy of Tennyson's poems in four volumes' to his brother Edmund McKenzie Sneyd-Kynnersley, 'but not my copy of Tennyson's "In Memoriam" which is hereinafter bequeathed.' Herbert left *In Memoriam,* along with 'my old gold watch and one of my silver-headed sticks,' to 'Leslie Smith of 11 Grafton Street, Piccadilly.' Smith's bequest is surrounded by those of pupils, so this is almost certainly what he was, though he had left Ascot by 1881 and cannot be found on that year's census.[45] Tennyson's

---

45   It has not been possible to discover with certainty who Leslie Smith was. However, he may have been Australian Leslie Shepherd Smith (1868-1938) who went to Trinity Hall, Cambridge, and became a barrister. Leslie Shepherd Smith

'In Memoriam' is about the extremely close friendship between Alfred, Lord Tennyson (1809-1892) and the poet Arthur Hallam (1811-1833). It is widely accepted that the poem reflects two men having been profoundly in love, albeit a love that was probably never consummated. Thus, it is about deep homosexual desire (Barton, 2012; Dellamora, 1990). Consistent with this, Hallam's father burned all of Tennyson's letters to Arthur, and Tennyson's son, Hallam, Lord Tennyson (1852-1928), destroyed all of his own father's letters from Arthur Hallam (Kleinberg, 2002, p.518). This bequest potentially implies that Sneyd-Kynnersley had sexual feelings for Smith.

There is a body of evidence, it should also be noted, that homosexuality itself — not just paedophilia — is often associated with mental instability and thus the kind of neuroticism which might underlie experiencing trauma and so aberrations in psychological development, such as arrested development (see Blanchard, 2008) of the kind which it appears impacted Sneyd-Kynnersley. Around 60% of the variation in male sexual orientation is due to environmental factors (Långstrom et al., 2010) and up to 40% of male paedophiles are exclusively homosexual in their paedophilia (Blanchard, 2000).

Male Primary School Teachers and Paedophilia

There is, then, a circumstantial case that Sneyd-Kynnersley was a non-practicing pederast (able to suppress his impulses via the sexual dimension to flogging) and, as Stevens and Price (2000) have indicated, this is, anecdotally at least, far from uncommon among the kinds of men that go into primary school teaching. People often seem to have difficulty discussing this issue, perhaps because of their belief that 'paedophiles are evil,' especially when confronted with the empirical reality that many paedophiles go into teaching and do not break the law. Similarly, they experience difficulties when their belief in sexual equality is confronted with the reality that women, though

---

was the son of Shepherd Smith (1835-1886) a County Durham-born Australian banker and High Churchman (Holder, 1976, *The Sydney Morning Herald*, 29th January 1868 and 31st January 1938).

not so much men, may go into teaching simply because they enjoy nurturing children (Baron-Cohen, 2002).

This conflict creates cognitive dissonance (Festinger, 1957) and, thus, an emotional reaction. This was epitomised, in the UK, in 2011 when a supply teacher was sentenced at Reading Crown Court, in Berkshire, for having downloaded 4,500 indecent images of children. Judge Mary Jane Mowat told the 63-year-old offender that, 'I don't criticise you for being attracted to children. Many teachers are, but they keep their urges under control, both when it comes to children and when it comes to images of children.' Her comments were met with precisely the kind of reaction American psychologist Leon Festinger (1919-1989) (Festinger, 1957) would predict when a person experiences dissonance with regard to something they, deep down, know to be true, but which conflicts with what they desire to be true. The head of a children's charity emoted that it was 'outrageous for this judge to say that teachers are attracted to children.' The general secretary of a teachers' trade union dogmatically asserted that 'Teachers are professionals whose interest is in ensuring that children . . . achieve their educational potential. To suggest their interest in children could understandably be anything else is totally unacceptable.' In another appeal to emotion, a lawyer from another union, told a newspaper that teachers 'would be appalled by the suggestion that they're in any way attracted to children' (Wardrop, 29th July 2011). These kinds of reactions are simply textbook cognitive dissonance. It is difficult to conduct surveys on this topic, as few paedophile teachers are going to admit to their proclivities, even in anonymous surveys. However, a survey in the USA found that 10% of high school pupils had experienced, among other things, 'lewd comments, exposure to pornography, peeping in the locker room, and sexual touching or grabbing' from teachers (Palmer, 8th February 2012). As we have already observed, a culture of sexual abuse was so endemic at many prep and public schools, until at least the 1970s, that it is manifestly ludicrous to argue that a significant minority of male teachers were not sexually attracted to children at such institutions.

In many ways, the question of pederasty among male primary school teachers should be turned on its head. Males tend to be high in systematizing, meaning that they are attracted to analytical or machine-based professions, such as engineering or construction (Baron-Cohen, 2002). They also tend to be strongly status-seeking (Buss, 1989). Females tend to be high in empathy, causing them to be attracted to caring professions, such as nursing and primary school teaching (Baron-Cohen, 2002). Accordingly, we would expect that a male primary school teacher would be a relatively feminized male, something which is true of homosexual males (Miller, 2000), and we would expect a female engineer to be a masculinized female, and there is clear empirical evidence for this (see Baron-Cohen, 2002). If the male primary school teacher was not homosexual (in the sense of being attracted to adult males), then there would have to be some motivation for him to pursue a profession which we would expect to be anathema to the average male due to its lack of systematizing and its relatively low social status. That the male was child-like or sexually attracted to children or both, due to paedophilia being, in part, a manifestation of arrested development, would be a reasonable default hypothesis.

Quite what caused Sneyd-Kynnersley's personality disorder and probable sexual disorder is unclear, because insufficient evidence exists about his early childhood. However, two issues do protrude in the available primary sources. On the 1851 census, the two year-old Herbert Sneyd-Kynnersley and his one-year-old brother, Charles Walter, were not with their mother. They were staying with their maternal grandfather in Taplow in Buckinghamshire while their parents, and their 11-year-old older brother, were staying at the house of their paternal grandmother in the countryside outside Uttoxeter. This may be because the family were in crisis, with their eldest son, John, having died the previous month. Nevertheless, it is quite surprising that Sneyd-Kynnersley's mother would leave such young children with others over night, especially the baby Charles. It may imply that Charles had a wet nurse and so did, therefore, his older brother. This would limit the degree to which mother and baby would bond (Coles, 2015, p.41). Accordingly, the mother may have treated Herbert in a cold, unloving fashion, subjecting him to harsh physical punishment without the concomitant strong love which has been shown to create the most well adapted children. Parents of well adapted children are, in general, harsh yet loving, as opposed to lax yet loving or harsh and unloving (see Wilson & Herrnstein, 1985). There is also evidence that Sneyd-Kynnersley very much rebelled against his maternal grandfather, which may also imply his having spent relatively little time with his parents. If this kind of parenting was combined with Herbert being genetically high in anxiety anyway, then we can start to understand why things may have gone wrong with the future headmaster in terms of his psychological and sexual development.

The second issue of note is that when Herbert was 3 years old his oldest brother died. When he was 12 years old his mother and maternal grandfather both died. And the following year, when Herbert was 13, Archdeacon William Macdonald — to whom he may have been close — also died. These are formative periods and there is evidence that grief, especially in adolescence, and parental separation at a young age, increases the likelihood of suffering from mood disorders in adulthood, such as depression or anxiety (e.g. Tyrka et al., 2008). So, having established, to some extent, Sneyd-Kynnersley's psychology, let us turn to why he employed the educational methods which he did.

Chapter Seven

The Spartans of Ascot

Ritualised Child Abuse?

I T IS TEMPTING to dismiss Sneyd-Kynnersley — and the entire public school system of the time — as little more than the ritualised abuse of children, in part for the pleasure of the sexual predators who comprised at least some of the teaching staff. But if we understand the purpose of the system more clearly, then we can perhaps begin to assess Sneyd-Kynnersley in a less unfavourable light.

The older public schools were dominated by Latin and Greek. As testimony to this, a statue of Perseus the King (212-166 BC), successor to Alexander the Great, is prominently placed at Eton College. All Classical scholars had heard of the Spartans; whose sometime queen was Helen of Troy. The infamously harsh city-state was as dominant as it was because of the way in which it turned all upper class boys into a warrior caste. Under a system known as *agoge*, upper class Spartans left home aged 7 to commence military training. They lived in communal messes, were given only just sufficient (bland) food, were exposed to privation which they had to survive, were intensively educated in reading, writing, and even music and dancing, and were subject to merciless beatings and, according to some sources, pederasty (see Cartledge, 2003). If such a system had made Sparta great, it would surely do the same for Britain.

Creating a Warrior Class

The Scottish anthropologist Victor Turner (1920-1983) conducted lengthy fieldwork on the rites of passage undergone by the teenage boys of the Ndembu, a tribe in what is now Zambia (Turner, 1969). The system Turner documented has also been found in many other tribes that are settled and are in a frequent state of warfare (Bloch, 1992). Teenage boys are removed from the community, via a rite of separation, and remain separate from it for an extended period of time, during which they are initiated into the higher status of warriors and of men. They undergo 'segregation, marginalization, and aggregation.' The purpose of the system is to render them 'passive and humble' so that they may be 'ground down, to be refashioned anew' (Turner, 1969, p.94). In what Turner calls a 'liminal' ('transitional') phase, they are neither children nor adults. They are in a nebulous 'state of transition' in which they lack a specific 'cultural space' (p.94). According to Turner, these 'neophytes,' in this state, are trained to be warriors and inculcated with the secrets and myths of the tribe. They are entirely subject to the whims of the adepts, who act as their teachers. The neophytes are exposed to agonizing arbitrary punishment, including ferocious flogging (Mason, 1962, p.43), scarification, and other physical mutilations in order to showcase their warrior identity. They must obey the instructions of the adepts without question, and they must follow arbitrary rules. Among the Hopi of Arizona, for example, young boys underwent a rite of being ritually flogged, often until they urinated and defecated through pain and fear (Dozier, 1954, p.327; Goldfrank, 1945). In addition, a sense of *communitas* — a weakening of social structure — is created by making the neophytes all the same, such as by stripping them all naked (summarized in Dutton, 2008, Ch. 1). Also, there is evidence that people can become, to some extent, inured to pain (e.g. Davies, 2004), so the agonizing aspects of the rite would make the neophytes braver and more successful warriors.

In some tribes, there is a clear homosexual element to the rite of passage, as has been documented by Dutch-German anthropologist Arnold Van Gennep (1873-1957) (Van Gennep, 2013, p.171). It is believed that the warrior or manly power of the initiated is somehow transferred to the neophytes via some form of sexual congress with the adepts, such as by anal sex (Van Gennep, 2013, p.171). Among the Samba of Papua New Guinea, neophytes — aged between about 7 and 10 — daily fellate initiates and swallow their semen, because it is believed that only through this process can the neophytes obtain their own semen and so become men (Soble, 1997, p.124). We can only speculate on how this homosexual element to the rite of passage might be adaptive. If it is traumatic and forced, then it may compel the initiate to maintain a sense of humility well into adult life. If it is consensual, then it might be regarded as a means of bonding the neophytes to the values and system represented by the adept. In that sense, it parallels the way in which many New Religious Movements will love-bomb religious seekers. Through this technique, a bond is created with the proselytiser and by extension with the religious institution and its values (see Galanter, 1998). A prominent example of this is the way in which the Mormons' central evangelizing program involves sending out same-sex pairs of young, and thus attractive, missionaries, who will invariably be extremely friendly to those whom they attempt to convert.

The neophytes also strongly bond with each other, often through a phase of homosexual activity, which does not continue once they become warriors (Van Gennep, 2013, p.171). At the end of the rite of passage, neophytes must pass a test of their physical prowess, which acts as a rite of incorporation, after which they are returned to society as fully-fledged warriors, eligible to marry and have children. According to Turner, Van Gennep and other anthropologists, these rites of passage have the effect of breaking the boy's bond with his family and with his sense of place, so rendering him psychologically helpless and thus receptive to indoctrination and the imposition of a new identity. The ritual process means that he is receptive to being turned into a warrior, and it will likely ensure that he creates strong bonds with other neophytes, making him more likely to take risks in battle.

Public Schools and Tribal Rites of Passage

In many ways, the English public school system, including its feeder prep schools, was specifically modelled on Sparta and the teachings of Plato (see below). In the early nineteenth century, what were to become known as 'prep schools' were simply private schools for younger pupils, run for profit. The 'public schools' were either upheld through philanthropy ('endowed schools') or they were based around some religious interest. However, all three kinds of school gradually coalesced so that by the 1880s they were a definite integrated system of education for upper middle and upper class boys (Leinster Mackay, 2012, pp.58-59). At the same time, with the Indian Mutiny of 1857, the abolition of the East India Company, and a rise in colonial expansion; the British became increasingly conscious that they weren't a country; they were an empire. This consciousness only increased with the imperialistic policies pursued by (non-public school educated) Prime Minister Benjamin Disraeli (1804-1881), who had Queen Victoria made Empress of India (Leinster-Mackay, 2012, p.59). The entire public school system, including the prep schools, became oriented towards empire, and the Classicists who ran the system knew exactly how empires, or world-leading states, worked. As historian and sometime member of the Indian Civil Service Philip Mason (1906-1999) has put it in *The Men Who Ruled India* (Woodruff, 1971, p.16):

> 'Plato taught that the guardians of the state should not know their parents. The English did not go as far as that, but when they were eight years old the children from whom the rulers were to be chosen were taken away from home for three-quarters of the year, taught not to mention their mother or their own Christian names, brought up in the traditions of Sparta which Plato admired. And the children grew up to be the true guardians; no other people in history can equal this record of disinterested guardianship' (quoted in Leinster-Mackay, 2012, p.60).

As Victorian life became less harsh, the public school system was a kind of time warp; deliberately brutal, just like Sparta or a tribal rite of passage. However, with a much larger and more differentiated society than there is among the Ndembu of Zambia, the 'warrior class' was limited to the upper class and the uppermost ranks of the professional classes, who could afford to send their children to public schools and to the prep schools — such as St George's, Ascot — which prepared them for these public schools. From there, such pupils would become army officers or go into some other high status profession, where they would assist in running the British 'tribe.'

The traits promoted by both tribal initiations and the public school system, it should be noted, are part of a syndrome of psychological and physical traits known as a Slow Life History Strategy (LHS) which tend to develop in harsh yet predictable environments. The opposite is a fast LHS. This develops in an easy but unstable ecology, in which you must respond to sudden, unpredictable challenges by being extremely aggressive. A fast LHS is called an r-strategy, while a slow LHS is known as a K-strategy (see Woodley, 2011). Those who are r-strategists 'live for the now'. They live fast and die young, because they could be wiped out at any moment. They tend to be born after less gestation but more developed, they reach childhood developmental milestones more quickly, enter puberty earlier, begin their sex life younger, engage in promiscuous and frequent sex in order to procreate as much and as quickly as possible, invest little in their partners or offspring, and they tend to die relatively young, as they age more quickly. They create weak social bonds – 'What's the point of bonding? The other person may be suddenly killed so they'll never be a pay off.' The ecology is so favourable that basic needs are pretty much met. But they have poor impulse control and low altruism; allowing them to respond with massive aggression to very sudden dangers.

An extreme slow LHS occurs in a harsh yet stable environment, because this means that the carrying capacity of the ecology for a particular species is reached. Accordingly, its members start to compete much more strongly with each other. They do this via an arms race of adapting to the environment. They begin to invest less energy in procreation and more energy in growth, adaptation, and, crucially, the *nurture* of their offspring. In such an ecology, somebody could have numerous children but they might all die of cold and starvation. By contrast, the competitor who invested in nurture would ensure that his fewer offspring would grow up to be adapted to and to understand the harsh yet predictable environment, so his offspring would survive. The result is that life slows down, so people can learn about their complex but predictable ecology. Puberty comes later, as does the beginning of a person's sex life. The slow LH strategist has fewer sex partners, has less sex with them, and invests more resources in them. This selects for higher altruism, as there is competition for mates and you're more likely to survive if you can get along with people; and higher impulse control, allowing you to plan for the future. Also, in such an ecology, there is more likely to be a payback for cooperation. In harsh ecologies, people who are part of cooperative groups are much more likely to survive, as are cooperative groups in general, further elevating these personality qualities, leading to people who create very strong social bonds. These groups impose strict norms and are highly conformist (see Dutton et al., 2016). At the level of environmental influence on personality, a cooperative personality can only be developed if children's tendencies to be selfish and impulsive are removed; in other words, the spirit of impulsive non-co-operators has to be 'broken.'

As the group becomes more *K*, its niche becomes more specific, because the harsher and more predictable the ecology is the more specifically adapted you must be to survive. In an easy ecology you can forage for food all year round, in a harsh one you must specialize, innovating very specific techniques and systems to catch the (relatively rare) sources of food. This means that the different components of *K* end up being less strongly inter-correlated, because selection favours the highly environmentally *specific*. Paradoxically, an extremely high *K* group can be quite r-selected in certain specific ways precisely because its ecology is so harsh and predictable (Woodley, 2011). For example, Japanese psychologist Kenya Kura and his team have shown that the Japanese are, in essence, extremely *K*-selected and so very high in conformism and social anxiety, concerned about what others think of them (Kura et al., 2015). However, they are concomitantly highly r-selected in the sense that they can be very aggressive and hostile towards foreigners

(Dutton et al., 2016) and those whom they regard as impure, leading to very low levels of adoption, despite adoption being — from an evolutionary perspective — nurture for the sake of it and thus a *K* trait (Dutton & Madison, 2018).

Public School and Slow Life History Strategy

Overall, the public school system elevates *K*-strategy, but it is so high in this that it also adopts aspects of r-strategy. It involves taking people whose environment is very easy and artificially creating a harsh environment through deprivation, ruthless and humiliating physical punishment and home-sickness. It also imposes a clear system of rules and order, with agonizing punishment for disobeying the rules. These rules are fairly clear: you obey the arbitrary rules of the school, you behave in the manner expected of a gentleman, and you conform to the group's norms. This, of course, means not doing anything weird or individualistic. In a strongly cooperative group — the creation of which allows you to better survive a harsh ecology — individualism must be ruthlessly supressed. The system also reduces differences between pupils and forces them to share space; compelling them to foster strong bonds and to learn to cooperate. Indeed, the nature of the punishment — in the form of bare bottom flogging — is going to reduce testosterone, impose complete dominance on the child, and strongly inculcate it with the idea that authority must be obeyed and feared. It will also help to inure it to pain, vital in training a warrior caste, many of whom will go on to be army officers.

However, the system adapts the child to a very specific niche, so it is not an archetypal *K*-strategy. Fearing violent punishment all the time, the child will suffer from anxiety about the future, something generally true of *K*-strategists, because a harsh yet predictable ecology forces you to conceive of a winter's day in the midst of a summer's one. In such an environment people are more open to indoctrination as people tend to become more religious during times of stress (see Norenzayan & Shariff, 2008). Accordingly, the public school system creates the optimum conditions in which children can be inculcated with a form of religiosity which promotes in-group cooperation but out-group hostility, in other words high positive and negative ethnocentrism: valuing the in-group and despising the out-group. It has been demonstrated through computer-modelling that, all else being equal, groups which are the highest in these two traits tend to dominate and wipe out other groups (see Hartshorn et al., 2013). Religiousness and nationalism, which is exactly what these pupils were inculcated with, very strongly elevate these two traits. When primed to be religious, people become more positively and negatively ethnocentric (Shariff, 2015). In addition, children can be taught to direct their suppressed emotions in an adaptive fashion. This system appears to be the optimum way of creating societies which come to dominate other societies, and the Hebrews in the Old Testament managed to do so by very precisely following it. However, there is clearly a balance between creating Agreeable, Conscientious, internally cooperative people who are also aggressive, selfish people — though only to outsiders — which has to be accomplished for the group to be the most successful. Put simply, a broadly *K*-strategy society is created, but it is concomitantly imbued with certain adaptive r-strategy traits, such that it is aggressive to outsiders in times of war. There is an extent to which school teachers were perfectly aware of this 'rite of passage' dimension to flogging in particular. One exploration of the subject quotes a number of different male teachers: 'Caning is a personal relationship. A boy places himself in the position of a son to his father . . . by bending over, a boy shows he can stand up to his punishment and take it. It's tribal. Of course it is,' says one (Mercurio, 1975).

Pederasty, Flagellation and Evolution

It could even be argued — although this is rather speculative — that Sneyd-Kynnersley's possible sexual deviance, as well as that of other male school masters, would actually be important to maintaining this system, and even the tribal rites of passage. There are many theories that have attempted to understand why — from an evolutionary perspective — homosexuality remains in tribal populations, despite having no obvious adaptive benefit. Proposals include 'gay uncle theory' – that a gay uncle will be childless, invest in his kin and thus ensure that they are more likely to survive. But there is no empirical evidence that homosexuals do invest significantly in their kin. Another idea is that females are most attracted to males with some feminine qualities — because these men will be caring — meaning that, by genetic chance, some males end up being extremely feminized, even being attracted to other males (Miller, 2000).

Another possibility is that homosexuality, and other sexual deviations, are useful in terms of what is called 'group selection'. There are a number of types of selection in addition to the widely known individual selection, where an individual's beneficial mutation is selected for and spreads through the population. *Sexual selection* involves one sex selecting for certain qualities in the other sex, such as markers of health or fertility. A peahen selects for a peacock with a large and colourful tail because his tail is an 'honesty signal' of genetic fitness. A peacock with lots of unhealthy mutations would have to expend proportionately more of his energy fighting off disease, leading to a small, asymmetrical and dull tail. There is also *kin selection*. People indirectly pass on their genes by aiding their kin, such as their cousins, as they share 12.5% more of their genes with a cousin than they do with a random member of their society. This is why a spinster auntie might spoil rotten her nephew or niece; in so doing she is indirectly passing on her genes (see Salter, 2006).

American biologists David S. Wilson and Elliot Sober (1994) have drawn upon this to advocate the 'Multi-Level Selection Theory'. They argue that once cooperative groups develop within a species then selection will act to promote those groups which possess the optimum level of certain qualities which permit them to out-compete other groups. Thus, selection will still operate on individuals within a group but can also be seen to operate on groups themselves, as collections of individuals, and, in some circumstances, can shift away from individual and towards group selection. This model helps to explain, for example, the development of altruistic tendencies. People are more altruistic to people, in general, the more genetically similar they are to self and helping a coethnic is indirectly promoting your own genes more than assisting a foreigner is (see Rushton, 2005). Kin selection involves making sacrifices for your kin and group selection is a logical extension of this, as ethnic groups are extended genetic kinship groups (Salter, 2006). Groups tend to be selected, under conditions of intergroup conflict, if they are internally cooperative but externally hostile, as has been shown in computer models (Hammond & Axelrod, 2006). In addition, the more genetically endogamous they are, the more successful in group selection they tend to be, as the enemy group is thus more genetically different from them, and members of their own group are more similar to them, providing a stronger reason for a group member to, for example, lay down his life to protect his group. In doing so, he will help to indirectly pass on more of his genes than he would do if he laid down his life for a less endogamous group (see Salter, 2006).

'Group selection' has been criticised in depth by American psychologist Steven Pinker (18th June 2012). His key criticisms are that (1) 'group selection' deviates from the 'random mutation' model inherent in evolution (2) We are clearly not going to be selected to damage our individual interests, as group selection implies and (3) Human altruism is self-interested and does not involve the kind of self-sacrifice engaged in by sterile bees. Each of these points can be answered. Firstly, if the group selection model is building on the individual selection model then it is bound to present a slightly different metaphor. To dismiss it on these grounds seems to betoken a fervent attachment to the original idea. Secondly, the group selection model merely suggests that a group will be more successful if there is genetic diversity, meaning that an optimum percentage of its members are inclined to sacrifice themselves for their group. Thirdly, it is clearly the case that a small percentage, in many groups, is indeed prepared to sacrifice itself for the group. So, it seems to me that it is reasonable to accept multi-level selection.

With this in mind, it may be that many forms of sexual deviance remain in populations because they are useful at the level of the group. Priests and shamans — the generally unmarried and supposedly celibate (Winkelman, 2010, p.143) priest-figures in tribal societies (Lewis, 2003) — are useful in terms of group selection because they promote the society's religiousness, in particular through their own charisma, religious experiences, and perceived miraculous powers, underpinned by their relationship with the spirit-world (Lewis, 2003). This religiosity will tend to alleviate people's fears, provide them with a sense of hope and order, and cast the society as uniquely special, looked after by the gods or spirits, with outsiders as something 'other.' Accordingly, religiousness helps to promote ethnocentric behaviour, with ethnocentric groups tending to win the battle for group selection. More generally, religiousness tends to promote evolutionary imperatives as the will of the gods or spirits: It is God's will that you 'Go forth and multiply,' for example (Sela et al., 2015). So, if priests and shamans were more likely to be sexually deviant we can begin to understand how sexual deviance might stay in the population.

It has been found that, cross-culturally, celibate priest figures tend to be homosexual. For example, many anthropological studies have found shamans tend also to be transvestites, non-practicing homosexuals, or actually practicing homosexuals and pederasts. This has been found among the Ojibway Indians (Grim, 1987, p.25), in Siberia (Vitebsky, 2001, p.93), in Burma (Spiro, 2017) and in the Far East in general (Neill, 2011, p.252). A large minority of Catholic priests in the USA are homosexual (Benes, 20th April 2017). Indeed, homosexual men, in general, are more religious than heterosexual men (Sherkat, 2002). One way of making sense of this is that homosexuals shun family life and become shamans, investing most of their time in healing and sacrificial rituals which have a placebo effect on the tribe. This form of religion unites the tribe, promotes its evolutionary imperatives as divinely ordained, and the shaman helps to inculcate the tribe with this religion. This provides the tribe with an evolutionary advantage and the shaman would be less able to invest his energy in these activities if he had children. This is especially the case if societal abhorrence at homosexuality forces the priest to be celibate, meaning he directs all his energies towards religious devotion. In addition, deviant sexuality is associated with mental illnesses such as schizophrenia and forms of depression (Bouchard, 2008). These are, in turn, associated with intense religiosity (Koenig, 2012) and the obvious mental instability of shamans has been widely remarked upon, such as in the research examined already. So this may help to explain why these sexual activities remain in the population. They are indirectly associated with intense religiousness, which is useful at the level of group selection. This idea has been termed the 'Gay Shaman Theory' and it would explain high levels of homosexuality and pederasty among religious devotees, such as the Catholic clergy (see Dutton, 2019).

The pederasty associated with public schools — which inculcate the upper class with the society's religious and warrior values — may operate in a similar way, especially as they were mainly run by clergymen. These clergymen were highly religious, as products of group selection, and thus attracted to boys due to the association between religiousness and homosexuality (Sherkat, 2002). Indeed, it could be argued that the pederasty associated with many tribal rites of passage is the anthropological foundation of the public school system. As we have already seen, we would not expect men to particularly wish to look after young boys. But if they were homosexual or pederasts then they would have the incentive to organize this important aspect of group selection, meaning we would expect some inclination towards homosexuality, and pederasty, to stay in populations. Accordingly, we can understand the strong crossover between clergy and school teaching. As an extension of 'Gay Shaman Theory,' we might call it 'Pederast Teacher Theory.'

'If you're going through Hell, keep going'

In light of this theoretical background, St. George's, Ascot, under Sneyd-Kynnersley, can simply be regarded as a very extreme manifestation of the public school system. No matter how distasteful or even horrific we may find this now, such a system — as Harry Kessler (Easton, 2002, p.25) stated — merely applied an 'ancient English formula' for turning barbarous young men into 'gentlemen,' by which he implicitly meant gentlemen who were prepared to lay down their lives to defend the British Empire. No matter what sexual gratification Sneyd-Kynnersley obtained from his regime and no matter how mentally unstable he may have been, his school was very much in line with a long established and evidently successful system of training England's ruling class to be loyal warriors for their tribe. As Canadian historian Michael Antony (2009, pp.11-12) has put it:

'It may be true, however, that the general harshness of public school life was a good preparation for the conditions of war (when it did not break the boys entirely). The brutality, the pitilessness, the physical misery and discomfort, the endless bullying, violence and persecution that prevailed at public schools was excellent training for military life. This was a world without women, where there were no shoulders for small boys to cry on. The first lesson was never to show emotion or weakness. There was no one it was safe to show it to. They must get used to swallowing injuries, insults, beatings, degradation, humiliation, injustice, pain and betrayal without blenching . . . This is the sense in which "the playing fields of Eton" were the training ground for Britain's military successes – the psychological toughening of boys to endure to the end a world without pity.'

Selfishness, disobedience and impulsivity needed to be eliminated at the in-group level and focused purely towards the out-group; authority, even if capricious, had to be obeyed, because in a battle situation there is no time for argument. Indeed, for this reason, there is evidence that we are strongly evolved to obey even arbitrary demands from those who seem to be in authority (see Boyer, 2001).

It could even be argued that the Sneyd-Kynnersley regime was particularly successful, if measured by the relatively large number of people who passed through it who went on to achieve eminence. Despite there only being a maximum of 40 boys at the school at any one time, it produced Roger Fry, Maurice Baring, Basil Blackwood, Claude Schuster and, albeit in spite of the school, Winston Churchill. Of course a strong aspect of this may be that St George's was a particularly exclusive prep school, educating the children of particularly high SES parents. Parental SES robustly correlates with an individual's intelligence, which itself robustly predicts an individual's SES (Jensen, 1998). It has been found, it is worth noting, that the studies which conclude that corporal punishment causes poor life outcomes are heavily genetically confounded. Poor life outcomes are strongly genetic and predicted by poor impulse control (Nettle, 2007), which also predicts being violent to your children. However, when this violence is ritualistic, structured, controlled and administered by a parent who is otherwise loving — with factors such as socioeconomic status controlled for — then use of corporal punishment (specifically to the buttocks), as long as it is not overly severe and is administered by a predictable parent or guardian, is associated with positive life outcomes (Larzelere, 2000). Indeed, when the children are from groups which tend to have poor impulse control and low Agreeableness — in other words, people like Churchill — the outcome was positive even if the corporal punishment was extremely severe, as long as it was structured and predictable (Lansford et al., 2009). When imposing genetic controls, corporal punishment only led to poor life outcomes if comprised of random violence, such as punching and kicking (Lynch et al., 2006). This is unsurprising, as unpredictable danger is precisely what pushes people towards a fast Life History Strategy.

In his book *Latin Prose Composition* (Sneyd-Kynnersley, 1886, p.113), which he completed in March 1886, Sneyd-Kynnersley provided his school boy readers with 'A List of Idiomatic Phrases in English and Latin.' Second on the list of 100 phrases was '*Barbaros suae ditonis fecit*': 'He reduced the barbarians to subjugation.' This, according to Harry Kessler, who remembers him the most fondly, was the purpose of the headmaster's floggings. Once subjugated, fathers would see signs of phrase 11 on the list – '*Filium docendum curavit*': 'His son got taught.' The school's motto was '*Vincent Qui Se Vincunt*' – 'They will conquer who conquer themselves.'

Chapter Eight

A 'Very Disgraceful' Boy

Churchill Arrives at St George's

CHURCHILL BEGAN AT St George's, Ascot on 3rd November 1882, five weeks after the beginning of term and just before he turned 8 (Churchill, 1966, Ch. 3).1882 was the year that a Scottish madman attempted to shoot Queen Victoria with a pistol at Windsor, the year that the British crushed a nationalist uprising in Egypt, and the year that the football team Tottenham Hotspur was founded, as was the Society for Psychical Research, reflecting the late Victorian fascination with the supernatural. Gilbert and Sullivan's operetta *Iolanthe* opened at the Savoy Theatre, also in November 1882. It told the story of how Iolanthe had been banished from Fairyland. Suddenly removed from his nursery full of toy soldiers, Churchill might have empathized.

Churchill got off to a bad start at St George's. As we have seen already, this clearly intelligent boy had absolutely no problem learning the declension of 'Mensa,' something which likely delighted Robert Estcourt Macdonald. Macdonald may even have been impressed by Churchill's inquisitive nature, when he pressed him on when you would use the form, 'O, table' – to address a table. However, the boy's flippant, 'But I never do!' was clearly a warning of what was to come, even if Macdonald over-reacted to it. Winston was going so far as to, albeit by insinuation, mock what he was being taught. He'd also failed to address the form master as 'Sir.' Even at my own school, this resulted in the teacher, at least if he was insecure, barking, 'Pardon?' until the answer was repeated, but with the word 'Sir' on the end of it.

This did not portend – Macdonald must have, on some level, realised – good things. It signified a wilful, difficult, insensitive, rude, overconfident little boy. And there is an extent to which he would grow-up into just such a man. As we have discussed, intelligence is about 80% genetic in adults[46] and personality may be as much as 70% genetic, so there is space, though not a large space, for environmental factors to make a difference. For this reason, there is a large body of evidence that personality is relatively stable across the lifespan. Even personality in early childhood correlates with adult personality at about 0.3 (Tasman et al., 2015, Ch. 8).

'Very Bad' School Reports

Winston's school reports — presented in his son's biography of him — demonstrate that Macdonald's likely intuition about Churchill was devastatingly accurate. This is all the more worrying because conduct disorder in childhood tends to be associated with an adult who is high on the psychopathic personality spectrum. This is characterised by the inability to sustain consistent work behavior, by non-conformity, irritability and aggressiveness, failure to honour financial obligations, frequent lying, failure to plan ahead, and impulsivity, including addiction-proneness, reckless behavior, inability to function as a responsible parent, failure to maintain long-term monogamous relationships, lack of remorse and conduct disorder in childhood (American Psychiatric Association, 2013). We

---

[46] In children it is less so, because they are subject to an environment that reflects the intelligence of their parents. Only as they break free of this, creating an environment which reflects their own innate intelligence, does the heritability rise to 80%.

will see later that almost all of these traits apply to Churchill. But we will concentrate on his childhood behaviour for the time being.

Churchill's reports and letters written at the time provide every indication of the low Conscientiousness and low Agreeableness, combined with high intelligence, which marks out the high functioning psychopath; precisely the kind of person which the public school system was developed to tame. A letter from Churchill's mother to his father written on Boxing Day 1882 states that Churchill is 'slangy and loud' and 'teases the baby.' His brother Jack Churchill apparently remarked to his father's colleague, Conservative MP Sir Henry Drummond Wolff (1830-1908), that 'brother is teaching me to be naughty.' That summer term, Churchill managed to be late for class 19 times and his report stated that he 'Does not understand the meaning of hard work.' In autumn 1883, H. Martin Cooke wrote on Churchill's report card that Churchill 'began well but latterly has been *very* naughty.'

There was a slight improvement in the first half term of 1884, when it became clear that Churchill was very good at Mathematics and other subjects which interested him. However, the headmaster remarked, 'He is rather greedy at meals.' In the second half term of 1884, Cooke wrote on Churchill's report, under 'Diligence': 'Conduct has been exceedingly bad. He is not to be trusted to do any one thing. He has however notwithstanding made decided progress.' He had been late 20 times with Cooke noting it was 'Very disgraceful' and the headmaster interjecting to add 'Very bad.' Under 'General Conduct,' for some reason filled in by Sneyd-Kynnersley (as is clear from the handwriting), most of the diligence remarks have been repeated verbatim, with Sneyd-Kynnersley having added that Churchill is 'a constant trouble to somebody and is always in some scrape or other.' Under headmaster's remarks, he has written: 'He cannot be trusted to behave himself anywhere. He has very good abilities.' By the summer term, things had slightly improved, his conduct being 'Fair on the whole but he still gives a great deal of trouble,' according to Sneyd-Kynnersley. There were subjects which he evidently excelled in, such as History and Geography, but overall he was stated to not be very hard working; he seems to have lacked the impulse control and future orientation to bother with subjects that didn't interest him. Churchill was withdrawn from the school at the end of the Summer term of 1884.

Even former pupils recall what a problem child Churchill was. Harry Kessler (1988) described Churchill as a 'quarrelsome' 'play-actor' and 'red haired dwarf' whose attitude 'got on everyone's nerves,' presumably based on what contemporaries of Churchill later told him as Churchill arrived the term after Kessler left (Easton, 2002, p.415, note 3). In later life, Churchill told his doctor how he had been bullied by other boys at the school. 'They beat him, ridiculed him and pelted him with cricket balls' (Manchester, 2015). In other words, his defiant behavior towards the teachers did indeed get on everyone's nerves. It likely resulted in 'treats' being cancelled for everyone in Churchill's division, just as the New Forest treat was later cancelled for the whole school, in part due to the 'want of patriotism' of three boys. The Rev. Christopher Turner (Interview, 7th July 2018), the grandson of Claude Schuster, told me that:

'Winston Churchill arrived at the school 3 or 4 years after my grandfather. He regarded Churchill not quite with contempt, but he said his language was appalling . . . "It was straight out of the stables of Blenheim Palace" . . . He found Churchill fairly objectionable.'

This aspect of Churchill — which would have been deeply shocking at the time — was also remarked upon by Kessler (1935) who suggested Churchill had been 'under the influence of the stable lads or his game keeper and had learned their words' and 'spicy means of expression.' Churchill would even 'leap on the desk and recite a stable song to the boys' leading 'Mr. Kynnersley' to 'threaten to use the birch.' As noted above, Kessler had left the school before Churchill arrived, so he must have picked this information up from another old boy. Perhaps he discovered it from Claude Schuster, as the wording is so strikingly similar and the two were close friends at the school, founding its newspaper *St George's Gazette* together, along with Roger Fry (Easton, 2002, p.26).

Claude Schuster

Moreover, Churchill's school reports cannot be put down to some unreasonable school master. Churchill's division tutor was H. Martin Cooke, whom we met earlier, according to Churchill's school reports. Although Maurice Baring does not refer to him by name, this master was one of the two 'friendly masters' that left St George's to establish St Vincent's, Eastbourne in 1886. This means that Churchill, whose division master was H. Martin Cooke, mainly had a 'friendly' teacher, sufficiently friendly to induce some St George's boys to abandon their school for his new one. Yet Churchill still behaved atrociously. This 'friendly' master may even have played down the extent of Churchill's delinquency in the reports that had to be read out in front of the whole school every few weeks. Referring to Churchill as 'Very truthful but a regular "pickle" in many ways' (Churchill, 1966), he comes across as a sympathetic character. But Cooke presumably needed to balance this with enough honesty not to be unfair to the well-behaved children, meaning that Churchill was still sometimes a guest in Sneyd-Kynnersley's study.

Dreadful Legends . . .

Regarding Churchill's naughtiness — as well as Sneyd-Kynnersley's sadism — there is a clear tendency for legends to develop. Maurice Baring joined the school in autumn 1884. He recalls (Baring, 1922, p.71) that:

'Dreadful legends were told about Churchill, who had been taken away from the school. His naughtiness seemed to surpass anything. He had been flogged for taking sugar from the pantry and so, far from being penitent, he had taken the Headmaster's sacred straw hat from where it hung over the door and kicked it to pieces. His sojourn at the school had been one long feud with authority. The boys did not seem to sympathize with him. Their point of view was conventional and priggish.'

The clue is in the word 'legend.' One can easily imagine how reality becomes exaggerated, especially among boys as young as 8, and when the boy in question is the son of a household name. There is no first hand evidence that this incident happened. To destroy a member of staff's property would have been so egregious as to merit correspondence with the parents or even expulsion. It is also inconsistent with the report for the summer term being reasonably fair, as one assumes that a straw hat implies that it was summer. However, Churchill's report for the Summer term of 1884 is quite positive by Churchill's standards. So, the incident would have to have occurred in the summer of 1883. But, if that were so, would it be so fresh in everyone's memories when Baring started at the school, over a year later? A reasonable conclusion is that this 'legend' is indeed a 'legend,' though there might be some kernel of truth to it. Maybe Churchill – who was 'greedy at meals' - was punished for smuggling sugar out of high tea and took revenge by knocking the headmaster's hat off the door and running away.

It is surprising that nobody has questioned this piece of St George's lore. But, as we have seen, much about St George's, Ascot, is not questioned. Most obviously, the 'sadistic' Sneyd-Kynnersley, described by Randolph Churchill and Roger Fry and portrayed in *Young Winston,* only appears to get more evil with time, just as Churchill becomes ever more heroic. Churchill's second cousin once removed and daughter of Sir Shane Leslie, Anita Leslie (1914-1985) (Leslie, 1969, p.97), states, of St George's, Ascot, that, '. . . the perverted sadist who ran it died of a heart attack – none too soon.' She provides no reference for this piece of information. Anita Leslie's remarks are a good example of the striking lack of objectivity that can be found in many biographies of Churchill, especially as they relate to St George's. They seem to assume that the reader will share this lack of neutrality. Like Anita Leslie, the authors frequently make unreferenced statements, as if author and readership are part of some trusting community of Churchill enthusiasts, with nobody being so cynical as to actually ask for historical proof.

The most extreme example of this mythology can be found in a June 2018 presentation at the Chalke Valley Festival in Wiltshire, entitled 'Churchill: The Origins of Greatness' given by the English novelist Michael Dobbs. According to a report on this in the *Daily Telegraph* (Bird, 1st July 2018), Dobbs claimed that Churchill was 'abused physically, emotionally and probably sexually too' by his headmaster, 'at the age of eight he was stripped naked and repeatedly thrashed.' He was 'physically' scarred. Apparently, Dobbs stated that:

'Winston was one day found to have stolen a packet of sugar. For that crime he was taken to the headmaster's study and thrashed. He had to be broken.' Dobbs adds, 'He was stripped, held down over a beating block, and thrashed and thrashed again until the blood was coming from the wounds. And, it was only after this appalling treatment was discovered by his nanny that his parents eventually took him from this school . . . But, Winston wasn't like the rest of us. After he recovered from that thrashing he found an opportunity to sneak back into that headmaster's study and stole the headmaster's straw boater, that he used for official occasions. He took that straw boater - the sign of authority - to the woods and for one glorious afternoon kicked the crap out of it. Not bad for an eight-year-old boy who had just been so cruelly abused.'

The inaccuracies in this are numerous and yet this was subsequently reported worldwide (e.g. Giuliani, 5th July 2018). Sneyd-Kynnersley did not strip anybody naked to thrash them. They had to lower their trousers, as was the case at most prep schools at the time. There is no evidence whatsoever that Sneyd-Kynnersley sexually abused anyone. If what he did is defined as sexual abuse, then we must accept that most English people — as well as most people from many other countries — were sexually abused as children until relatively recently. Only Sir Edmund Backhouse, the most extreme anti-Sneyd-Kynnersley source, mentions anything of sexual abuse (in the conventional sense of the term), and he was more than happy to make things up about his former headmaster. As I have noted, Churchill's final report was okay, so it is most unlikely that this straw hat incident — which was only ever a 'legend' but which surely took place in the summer — happened in summer 1884. The mortar board, *not* the straw hat, was the symbol of the Head's authority. Also, even if the straw hat incident did occur, Dobbs has got Churchill's age wrong. He would have been 9 rather than 8. As I have said, it could have taken place in summer 1883, but Churchill wasn't withdrawn from the school until a year after that. Michael Dobbs has also written *Never Surrender – A Novel of Winston Churchill* (Dobbs, 2004), the first chapter of which focuses on Churchill being beaten by Sneyd-Kynnersley. The chapter's inaccuracies and speculations include that boys with ginger hair were more likely to be caned, that anybody was ever caned (Sneyd-Kynnersley, as we know, used the birch), that Sneyd-Kynnersley was alone with boys when he caned them, and, of course, that Churchill stole sugar and kicked the Head's straw hat to pieces.

For some salacious reason, Sneyd-Kynnersley's actions are ripe for exaggeration. In a biography of Churchill's mother, British journalist Anna Sebba seems to take Fry's recollection of Algernon Ferguson 'letting fly' during his flogging — an isolated and likely embroidered or even imagined incident — and turn it into a regular occurrence, also abandoning all historical objectivity:

> ' . . . the headmaster, the Rev. H.W. Sneyd-Kynnersley, was a particularly revolting sadist who not only enjoyed inflicting a cruel flogging on the children in his care, but then took pleasure afterwards in clearing up the explosions of excreta left on the walls by his terrified victims' (Sebba, 2012).

Evidently, this is nothing close to an accurate paraphrasing of what Fry wrote. It is an extreme misrepresentation, with the speculation that the headmaster 'enjoyed' cleaning away Ferguson's diarrhea thrown in for good measure. Sneyd-Kynnersley is not merely a 'sadist,' as Roger Fry suggested. He is now a coprophiliac as well. In Mary S. Lovell's (2011) book *The Churchills*, there is similar hyperbole, albeit not to the same extent as in Sebba's work. Lovell writes:

> 'According to the witness statement of a fellow pupil (forced by the demands of self-protection to assist the headmaster by holding down the terrified victims) Kynnersley took great pleasure in flogging small boys until they bled or even excreted in pain and fear. This punishment was administered for the slightest indiscretion – for being late or performing badly in an exam.'

If Sneyd-Kynnersley took pleasure in beating boys until they excreted 'through pain and fear,' why does Fry — present at so many beatings — only recall one incident of it? If he enjoyed cleaning up the 'explosions of excreta' then why would he get one of his 'favourites' to help him with the task? This would be far more consistent with Fry's interpretation, that Sneyd-Kynnersley was terribly ashamed of what he'd done and that he didn't want even the servants to find out about it. Regarding Lovell's comments, there is no evidence that the headmaster particularly liked beating 'small boys;' the recollections of Fry, Baring and Kessler concur that beatings were not administered for 'the slightest indiscretion,' and Fry had to assist with the floggings not out of 'self-protection' but by virtue of being head boy, something which was common practice at public schools.

In addition, Sebba suggests that Churchill didn't tell his mother about the flogging regime at St George's because he knew his letters home would likely be read by the headmaster and censored. Similarly, Churchill's granddaughter, Celia Sandys (1994, p.45), asserts that as Sneyd-Kynnersley was 'sadistic' it is 'most unlikely' that he 'would have allowed any correspondence to leave his school without personally checking it.' It is clear from Roger Fry's letters home that Fry didn't think the headmaster would read them and, even if he did, they evidently were not censored. In addition, Churchill had ample opportunity to tell his mother what happened to him at school during the school holidays. It seems clear that Churchill's parents were not particularly loving or even caring; too busy with politics and socializing to notice their children (see Churchill, 1966). This is to be expected because, as we have seen, personality traits such as altruism are strongly genetic. Exaggerating the same flogging, Carlo D'Este (2009, p.13) writes that 'One student was flogged so hard that he let fly with feces.' Evidently, this is not an accurate summary of Roger Fry's recollection. Moreover, Fry speculated on a number of possible reasons for the boy losing control of his bowels, only one of which was the intensity of the beating. D'Este also tells us that Churchill was 'verbally abused by the headmaster' (p.13). He provides no source for this assertion.

In *The Last Lion,* American historian William Manchester (1922-2004) similarly goes way beyond what the sources actually say (Manchester, 2015). He ascribes every negative comment on Churchill's reports to Sneyd-Kynnersley, when many of them were from the 'friendly' master, H. Martin Cooke. Manchester says that, based on the reports, Churchill's conduct was, according to Sneyd-Kynnersley, 'all down hill,' which is completely wrong. Churchill's final report was not that bad; implying that Sneyd-Kynnersley's regime was working. Manchester writes that:

'Winston, flayed beyond endurance, fled home to Mrs. Everest. Woomany [*this is how Churchill referred to his Nanny*] undressed him and recoiled when she saw his back and bottom criss-crossed with welts. She summoned Jennie and the sight of his wounds told her what he, in the mute, tortuous language of a child, had been trying to tell her for two years. She immediately removed him from St George's . . .'

In reality, Churchill was sent home because he was ill. He did not make his own way from Ascot to London. Servants did not 'summon' their mistresses. There is no evidence that Churchill was 'immediately' removed from St George's; he was simply removed from St George's. Biographer James Humes (2001, p.46) states that Churchill received 'almost daily floggings' and that:

'At one point Sneyd-Kynnersley forced Churchill to run in a circle around a chair at full tilt for hours, until he collapsed in dizziness. A visitor noting the red-haired youth asked, 'What on earth is that?' Sneyd-Kynnersley answered, 'Why that's young Churchill. It's the only way we can keep him restrained.'"

Humes also tells us that Sneyd-Kynnersley 'merged a bent for sodomy with sadism.' As we have discussed, there is no reliable evidence that Sneyd-Kynnersley sodomized anyone. There is no evidence that Churchill received 'almost daily floggings.' Following Churchill's own recollections, even if he was flogged at every single report reading — which is very unlikely and which he does not say — it wouldn't have been more than about twice or three times a month. Also, Humes provides no source for the 'making Churchill run round a chair' accusation. However, the source would seem to be American journalist Robert Lewis Taylor's (1912-1998). *Winston Churchill: An Informal Study of Greatness* (Lewis Taylor, 1952, p.53) where almost precisely the same quote is given; the word 'quiet' is used rather than 'restrained.' This is the only other book which includes a similar quote. No source is cited there, either. Unfortunately, Robert Lewis Taylor died in 1998, so I have not been able to enquire as to the nature of his own source.

In his book *Winston Churchill: Myth and Reality: What He Actually Did and Said,* Robert Langworth (2017, p.13) writes that Sneyd-Kynnersley was 'Described by one alumnus as "an Unconscious Sodomite" . . .' In reality, as we have seen, this alumnus, Roger Fry, stated that, in his view, Sneyd-Kynnersley was *not* an 'Unconscious Sodomite.' In *Stiff Upper Lip,* Alex Renton (2017) tells us, 'Other pupils of the time told tales of the sexualized sadism of the headmaster, the Reverend Henry [*sic.*] Sneyd-Kynnersley. He is said to have died, aged just 38, while flogging one of his charges.' The most basic historical research would reveal Backhouse's unreliability, that Sneyd-Kynnersley died near Birmingham, and that his Christian name was Herbert. However, the prize for Sneyd-Kynnersley hyperbole must surely go to Stella Margretson. In her book *Victorian High Society* (Margretson, 1980, p.146) she tells us that, 'the headmaster, Mr. Sneyd-Kynnersley, systematically flogged the boys until they were almost dead with pain.' If that were so, Roger Fry and others would have reported children passing out and being carried out of Sneyd-Kynnersley's study. They do not.

Churchill's Illnesses and Mrs. Everest's Intervention

A further legend is that Sneyd-Kynnersley's floggings led to Churchill being so unwell that he had to be sent home from school and that he was removed from the school due to these floggings. The historical evidence does not support either of these ideas.

Biographer David Cohen (2018) tells us that Churchill fell ill while he was at school and was sent home. The family doctor, Robson Roose (1848-1905), examined him, assuming the problem was something to do with his 'weak chest,' and noticed the marks from his floggings – the primary source is not given. Roose suggested to Churchill's mother that Winston enroll in Brunswick School in Hove, near Brighton, where Roose also had a practice. Carlo D'Este (2009, p.14) explains that Churchill was sent home from St George's because he was ill, though does not give a reason why. He draws upon Anita Leslie (1969) for this information, and we will examine this source below. Winston's nephew, Peregrine Churchill (1913-2002), said Winston's treatment was talked about in the family for years afterwards and that he had heard that the wounds from Churchill's floggings had 'festered,' meaning that it may have been this that was making him ill, as it implies that the wounds were infected (Lee & Lee, 2007, p.53). However, this is obviously hearsay from one source talking about an incident 30 years prior to his birth when he was, himself, an elderly man. Also, in terms of motivation, Peregrine Churchill sued an American publisher to stop an author alleging in a book that Winston's brother, Jack (Peregrine's father), was the result of an extra-marital affair (Langworth, 2017, p.224). Thus, Peregrine Churchill would seem to be particularly concerned about his family's reputation. Unconsciously exaggerating how much the family cared for Churchill, and even how abused the great yet resilient man may have been, are thus distinct possibilities.

It is generally taken for granted that it is correct that Mrs. Everest noticed the wounds from Churchill's floggings while Churchill was ill and, for this reason, persuaded his mother to withdraw him from the school. But in light of other evidence, this seems quite improbable. Victorian nannies regularly undressed and bathed their charges, thereby seeing them naked (Nelson, 2007, p.138), even if these boys were old enough to be at public school, as found above in the case of Marlborough boy Edward Lockwood, who was nine when the school opened in 1843 (Mangan, 2004, p.14). It follows that Mrs. Everest would have seen Churchill naked during every school holiday over the two years he was at St George's. She would have noticed the wounds and she probably would have regarded them as normal for a boy who was at such a school, even if she may have had misgivings about it, and she would have said nothing to Churchill's mother. Not even Churchill himself stated that he was withdrawn from the school due to the beatings.

Popular biographies of Churchill almost all concur that Churchill was sent home from school, seriously ill, in the summer term of 1884, and that, in nursing him, Mrs. Everest noticed the wounds and persuaded Jennie to send Churchill to a different school. But in that Mrs. Everest — periodically seeing Churchill naked — must have known that Churchill was being beaten, this series of events would only have occurred if Churchill was particularly severely beaten in that final term. As we have discussed, this is extremely unlikely, because his reports in that final term were relatively good – very good by Churchill's standards. It may be that the 'sugar stealing/ hat destroying incident' *did* actually occur during this term and that Churchill was thrashed twice in the same day, meaning that on this particular occasion his wounds were uniquely horrific. But one would have assumed that stealing not just sugar but also the headmaster's property, and then destroying it, would have been such an extraordinary breach of the rules as to merit the headmaster getting in touch with the parents about it, possibly with a view to expelling Churchill. In *The Private Lives of Winston Churchill,* John Pearson (1991, p.57) writes that Churchill was an 'uncontrollable, aggressive child who at nine had already been removed from his first school, St George's, Ascot, for his bad behavior.' However, there is no evidence that this happened – and this is a headmaster who was fully prepared to expel Maurice Baring for not returning to school on the evening that he was supposed to. That said, we should remember that the headmaster was a rather unpredictable character.

In the film *Young Winston,* a seething Mrs. Everest leads Jennie to the feverish, seriously ill, sleeping Churchill. 'How did this happen?' inquires the horrified mother. Hardly suppressing her rage, Mrs. Everest pulls back the sheets and lifts Churchill's nightshirt to reveal his welt-covered bottom. She then turns to Jennie and solemnly announces: "We shall be taking him out of that place, won't we, my lady." This scene almost certainly has no basis in reality. It is more likely that a number of factors converged — years of flogging, Churchill's illness, Churchill's intuited unhappiness — to induce Mrs. Everest to persuade her mistress to withdraw Churchill from St George's. Celia and John Lee (2007) dispute the involvement of Mrs. Everest in any way. They note that when Churchill was perilously ill, while a pupil at Brunswick School on 15th March 1886, Dr Roose wrote Lord Randolph Churchill a letter (printed in full in Churchill, 1966) in which he stated that in treating Churchill's double pneumonia that day he had 'used stimulants, both by the mouth and rectum.' Based on this, Lee and Lee speculate that Dr Roose would have followed the same course of action in 1884, noticed the 'festered' wounds on Churchill's buttocks, told his parents, and recommended Churchill go to the school near Brighton, also attended by Roose's son, with the added advantage that Roose had a practice in Brighton. As supposed proof of this conjecture, they add, without supporting evidence, that, 'The Nanny would have had no part in the undressing and putting to bed of a nine-year-old boy' (Lee & Lee, 2007, p.53). However, we have already discussed evidence that the Nanny very likely would have done, and, thus, would have seen Churchill naked. Actually, considering Churchill's notorious naughtiness, it seems highly probable that Mrs. Everest would have administered corporal punishment to him during the school holidays. It is, further, extremely probable that this would have been on the bare buttocks. It is clear from recollections that even the most loving Victorian nannies spanked their charges (Gathorne-Hardy, 1972, Ch. 7). Sometime Foreign Secretary and Viceroy of India Lord Curzon (1859-1925), for example, recalled that his Nanny, though she was not especially loving, 'spanked us with the sole of her slipper on the bare back [read 'bottom'], beat us with her brushes . . .' (quoted in Gibson, 1978, p.52). Lee and Lee's hypothesis is simply not credible.

The earliest reference to the idea that Mrs Everest intervened at all is in Randolph Churchill's (1966, Ch. 4) biography where he wrote:

'The exact causes which led Lord and Lady Randolph to take Winston away from St George's at the end of the summer term of 1884, and to send him in the middle of the following term to what was to prove for Winston a more agreeable school at Brighton, are not known. It is believed that Mrs Everest saw the wounds of his birchings and told his mother about it.'

So, even Randolph Churchill has merely heard some kind of rumour, and is not sure what happened. It may be that Mrs Everest mentioned the wounds to Jennie and that this was somehow later embellished, for example.

The only source that directly states the now accepted view as having been told to her, partly by Winston himself, is Anita Leslie in her biography *Lady Randolph Churchill* (1969, p.97):

'The child had now suffered nearly two years at this expensive boarding school where the small boys were ill-fed and beaten till they bled. When the good nurse showed the birch marks, Jennie determined to take her son away immediately to build up his health at the seaside.

The other little wretches lingered on at St George's until the perverted sadist who ran it died of a heart attack – none too soon. It was typical of English snobbery in the 'eighties that the aristocratic parents thought this a nice school because the headmaster's coat-of-arms hung outside the front door.

Many years later, when I took my eight-year-old son to spend a day with Winston, he described afresh the horror of those days. "If my mother hadn't listened to Mrs Everest and taken me away I would have been broken down completely. Can you imagine a child being *broken down*?" Then looking at my eight-year-old boy he said: "Well, he looks happy and mischievous too — that is how children should be — I can never forget that school. It was *horrible*."'

Anita's only son, Richard Tarka Bourke King, was born in 1949 (Perwick, 2018), which dates this incident to either 1957 or 1958. In 1957, Churchill was 83 and, according to historian Sir Michael Howard, many years earlier than this Churchill, having had a serious stroke, was 'trembling on the verge of senility. He was deaf, forgetful and repetitive' (Howard, 1996, p.184). Between 1951 and 1955, while still Prime Minister, Churchill was already suffering from dementia (Freemon, 2012, p.129). Accordingly, Churchill was not a reliable source even about his own life by 1957, meaning we are far better off believing what he wrote in 1930 (Churchill, 1930, p.13): that he was withdrawn from St George's because he was ill and the family doctor had a practice in Brighton, meaning Churchill could be 'under his constant care.' Moreover, in his 1930 memoir, where he praises Mrs Everest at various points, Churchill mentions nothing of any involvement by her in his withdrawal from the school which he so detested.

In addition, Anita Leslie is by no measure reliable either. It is obvious from the above quotation that she was far from objective and she seems to have felt negative feelings strongly. In other words, she was high in Neuroticism. Consistent with this, Anita suffered from depression (Perrick, 2018). As we have discussed, such people are prone to exaggeration in a negative direction. Some of her statements are manifestly untrue, such as that the children at St George's were 'ill-fed' or that the school shut down when Sneyd-Kynnersley died. Therefore, either Anita is not telling the truth or she has drawn upon others who do not tell the truth or she is prone to self-delusion. Thus, we must conclude that there is no reliable evidence that Mrs Everest intervened nor that Churchill's beatings played any direct part in his parents' decision to withdraw him from St George's. It appears that they withdrew him because of health problems, believing it was healthier for him to be in Brighton, where the family doctor lived.

If Churchill had not become ill then he would not have been withdrawn and Sneyd-Kynnersley could have, to a greater extent, broken him down into a more empathetic, group-oriented and rule-following individual, more suitable to run the Empire. It is possible that cuts from Churchill's birching wounds would have contributed to his becoming ill, through infection or just stress. Other punishments were imposed on Churchill at Ascot, such as being made to run around the playground until he had no breath left at all (Kiernan, 1942, p.15). Though the original source for this is also not given, this was published during Churchill's lifetime and was not challenged. It may be this punishment that somehow developed into having to run around a chair. However, it sounds more like the kind of punishment Robert Estcourt Macdonald - a keen sportsman who seems to have generally used punishments other than striking such as electrocution and 'the stool of penitence' (Baring, 1922, p.70) - rather than Sneyd-Kynnersley might have imposed. So, perhaps if more of these punishments had been employed Sneyd-Kynnersley would have been able to break Churchill. But, on the other hand, these punishments would also have been less painful and thus less of an incentive to behave, so it is a very difficult balance to strike.

Churchill came very close to death at his next prep school, a much softer regime, run by two spinsters, the Misses Thomson:[47] Brunswick School at 29 and 30 Brunswick Road, Hove; a large Georgian house (Brendon, 2009, p.67). While at Brunswick School, in March 1886, Churchill contracted double pneumonia and nearly died, to the extent that his Nanny, and even his parents, came to his sickbed at the school (Herman, 2010, p.46). In *Eisenhower and Churchill*, Humes (2001) writes that, 'Even with a less rigorous regimen, young Winston almost died from an attack of double pneumonia — possibly a delayed reaction to his abusive ordeal at St. George's.' This is speculation, but it is plausible — if Churchill had been physically and psychologically exhausted by Ascot as much as appears to be the case — then his body and mind would still be recovering from this a year and a half later, meaning that his treatment at St George's may have contributed to his inability to fight

---

[47] The headmistress was Charlotte Thomson (1843-1901) with her younger sister, and eventual headmistress, Catherine Amelia Thomson (1846-1906) as her assistant mistress. They were the daughters of a Marylebone pawnbroker.

off pneumonia until it was almost too late. Long term psychological stress can result in pneumonia, at least in mice (Klank et al., 2008).

So, it appears that if Sneyd-Kynnersley had treated Churchill very slightly differently — either less physically harshly or with more concern for his health — then there would have been no Churchill, or, at least, no Churchill as we know it. He'd have grown up to be a far more cooperative, altruistic character. And as we will now see, if that had been the case then there would likely have been no World War II as we know it, no bankrupting of Britain, no collapse of the British Empire, and no descent into many of the problems which Britain faces today.

Chapter Nine

Hero of the Empire?

Another Churchill Biography

WINSTON CHURCHILL HAS been built up to be Britain's national hero; the saviour of the country, the scourge of the wicked appeasers who were a very significant body of opinion before and even during, the first years of, World War II. To a lesser extent, he's also a hero in the USA and other Anglophone countries. Consequently, there is an insatiable thirst to read about Churchill, with biographies of him constantly being published. Most of them take a very positive view of him, too. Titles include *Hero of the Empire: The Making of Winston Churchill* (Millard, 2016); *Churchill: A Study in Greatness* (Best, 2001); *The Churchill Factor: How One Man Made Britain* (Johnson, 2014); and, for children, *Winston Churchill: Lion of Britain* (Epstein, 1971).

Some of these kinds of books allude to some of the less flattering aspects of Churchill's character. However, there is a great extent to which books of this ilk are hagiographies, often doing little more than putting a slightly new slant on evidence from earlier hagiographies. Frustratingly, if you read these kinds of books you will find that for many assertions no source is given and, if it is, it is yet another pro-Churchill biography which itself provides no source.

The Psychology of Churchill

We should be clear that Churchill undoubtedly had many positive qualities. He was highly charismatic; able to inspire people, make people laugh, and make a cold world seem warm again, as is true of the archetypal charismatic (Weber, 1991). He was extremely creative and must have had a deeply sensitive side, as evidenced in his penchant for painting and writing. Churchill possessed a great deal of charm when he wished to, as well. In June 1945, Churchill and his wife visited Crewe in Cheshire as part of Churchill's arduous nationwide General Election campaign tour (*Newcastle Evening Chronicle,* 26th June 1945). At Crewe railway station, they met Barbara Hovey (later Marke) (1921-2018) who was in the Auxiliary Territorial Service (ATS), the women's branch of the army during World War II. Marke recalled that Churchill spoke to her 'for about 20 minutes' while they were standing by his car. Churchill 'was very interested in what I was doing in the forces. He'd just had pneumonia and it was raining and his wife,' remembered Marke, 'told Churchill, "You must put something warm on. Put on a Mackintosh!" and Churchill said "No! I've got to be seen by the public!"' According to the former soldier, 'They stayed in a siding at Crewe Station. It must have been very uncomfortable . . . I was a great fan of his' (Interview: Marke, 7th October 2018).

Clearly, Churchill inspired many people. However, a few historians and other researchers have been daring enough to challenge this picture of the heroic Churchill which is so often presented in biographies. Anthony Storr paints a balanced and ultimately poignant picture of the kind of man Churchill was in his essay collection *Churchill's Black Dog* (Storr, 1989). Storr argues that manic depression ran in the Churchill family and that Winston hailed from a long line of depressives (p.15), likely including his own father. In Winston's case, however, unfortunate environmental factors conspired to make his proneness to depression particularly acute. He was born, in 1874, two months early, with preterm birth tending to negatively impact brain development and also interfere with the strength of the mother-child bond. Since Storr conducted his analysis of Churchill it has been shown that premature birth does indeed predict elevated levels of depression and anxiety (Kodjebachava & Sabo, 2015). In addition, mothers suffering from these mood disorders are more likely to give birth prematurely and have problems bonding with their baby (Committee on Understanding Premature Birth, 2007). Such mothers are also likely to genetically convey their depression-proneness to their baby (Nettle, 2007). Thus, Churchill's being born 2-months early augured very poorly for his future mental health. To make matters even worse, Storr shows that Winston's parents were emotionally distant and neglectful even by the standards of the Victorian nobility. Churchill was immediately farmed out to a wet nurse, and by 1875, his *de facto* single-mother was already Mrs Everest, as Jennie dedicated herself to socialising and his father to politics. Frequently away from home, his parents rarely wrote him letters and, generally, paid him very little attention at all.

Storr argues that what, unsurprisingly developed was a man prone to bouts of depression and self-doubt. However, though Storr does not concentrate on this, there is also evidence of psychopathic tendencies. Churchill displayed a tendency to expose himself to extreme danger, with Storr referring to Churchill's 'search for physical danger,' his 'reckless self-exposure' which would also 'put others in danger' (p.19) and 'his love of risk, of physical adventure' (p.22). At the age of 18, he nearly died when he was playing a game of chase with a cousin and he jumped over a bridge in order to escape him. This left Churchill unconscious for three days (p.20). Churchill graduated from Sandhurst in December 1894. After graduation, Churchill was sent to Aldershot, but he used his connections to get himself posted to the warzone of Cuba. Throughout his early military career, Churchill continuously ensured he was sent to unstable and dangerous areas, such as the Indian frontier and to Sudan. In 1899, anticipating a second war against the Boers, whose states were vying with the Empire for control of South Africa, Churchill went to South Africa as a journalist for *The Morning Post*. He was captured by the Boers, held in a POW camp (a converted school) and managed to escape, and join a South African regiment of the British army to lead the taking of Pretoria for the British (Storr, p.60).

Storr interprets most of this as being a consequence of depressive tendencies, arguing that Churchill was only happy if he was 'fully occupied, asleep or holding the floor' (p.62). In effect, Storr maintains, Churchill's low intrinsic self-worth meant that he had to be hunting for glory (and thus externally validated) and immersed in the action, because if he stopped then he would become profoundly melancholy. Storr also notes that Churchill boosted his self-esteem by perceiving himself as a special kind of person whose purpose was to fight and this was no truer than when he found Hitler (p.57). There was also a degree to which, argues Storr, Churchill identified with the underdog, because he had been the bullied underdog at school (p.57). But there are other aspects to Churchill's character which being a depressive does not so easily explain, and Storr actually looks at these. Churchill would put other people in danger, as a government minister he would demand that ideas were presented to him on half a sheet of paper, and he had trouble following complex arguments (p.26). Storr writes that Churchill was 'in many respects deficient in feeling. He had little appreciation of the feelings of others' (pp.26-27). Storr gives the example of Churchill promising Field Marshal Sir Alan Brooke (1883-1963) that he could lead the invasion of Europe during World War II, and then simply changing his mind, completely failing to understand how this might upset the Field Marshal (p.27). Most of Churchill's colleagues agreed that many of Winston's ideas were disastrous and he had to be kept on a tight leash (p.27).

Although it is clear from his bouts of low mood and self-doubt that Churchill was a depressive, there is a simpler model which makes sense of all, rather than some of, the above observations. This is that Churchill was a depressive as well as a highly intelligent psychopath. Consistent with this, he had a reckless disregard for his own safety and that of others, he was strongly impulsive, he had little patience, he was only happy as the centre of attention, he lacked empathy, and he simply didn't care about the feelings of others, meaning he enjoyed being in warzones, and he had something akin to a Messiah complex. Though some of these traits may be understood as markers of depression they are all markers of being high on the psychopathology spectrum. Churchill was an accomplished painter

(Singer, 2012). As we have discussed, it has been found that being good at Humanities subjects is predicted by low Agreeableness, low Conscientiousness and high Neuroticism (De Fruyt & Mervielde, 1996) – in other words by high psychopathology combined with mental instability. Being low in the traits associated with Agreeableness and Conscientiousness is particularly pronounced in artists (Feist, 1998) and they are also relatively mentally unstable (see Nettle, 2007).

Churchill Before the War

It is particularly informative to see how Churchill was regarded in his own lifetime, especially in the 1930s when he was out of government office — as he was from 1929 to 1939 — and generally understood to be in the twilight of his political career. Judgements at this time are likely to be far more accurate than during the stress of war or in the aftermath of victory. During the stress of war, the kind of charismatic, inspiring qualities which Churchill possessed — a sense of Messianic certainty (see Weber, 1991) — were just what many people wanted. In the aftermath of victory, there is a tendency to make sense of a devastated world by hero-worshipping the leader and also by finding some means of justifying all of the suffering, meaning that it was essential that the prosecutor of the war was beyond reproach. It has been found that the more people invest in something, the more they need to convince themselves that they have done the right thing; they need to avoid 'cognitive dissonance' and will find ways of achieving the desired 'cognitive consonance' (Festinger, 1957). This is why people can react in such an irrational way if it is demonstrated to them that someone whom they admire — who is central, to some degree, to the way in which they structure the world — is simply not who they thought they were. They cannot cope with the fact, in addition, that they have been duped. It leaves them feeling exposed.

For these reasons, we should see how Churchill was regarded in the 1930s and this is precisely what Brian Gardner (1968) did in *Churchill in His Time*. Many of the views of Churchill during this period are strikingly in line with the descriptions put forward by Anthony Storr. In 1931, a journalist opined that Churchill had 'no moderation or tact' and that he was 'rash, hot-headed and impulsive.' Gardner summarises that Churchill was widely considered to be 'unreliable. People were tired of him' (Gardner, 1968, p.1). Another journalist from 1931 is quoted as having written that, 'Mr Churchill loves war and violence' and that he is 'devoured by a perpetual *besoin de faire*' – (Gardner, p.2), meaning a need to be constantly active. 'There was a widespread feeling in the 1930s,' summarises Gardner, 'that the nation had got wise to Churchill at last – and just in time.' He was 'a political adventurer, a swashbuckler of the most dangerous kind' (p.2).

As far as Lord Beaverbrook (1879-1964), who was later a minister in Churchill's government, was concerned, '[*Churchill*] does not carry any conviction . . . He has held every view on every question . . . He is utterly unreliable in mental attitude' (pp.2-3). In other words, Churchill had no real principles. He simply did whatever was necessary to achieve attention, money, status or a sense of adventure, just as Storr suggested. Prime Minister Neville Chamberlain (1869-1940) was reluctant to give Churchill a place in his cabinet precisely because of Churchill's Narcissistic need to be the centre of attention: 'If I take him into the cabinet,' Chamberlain wrote to his sister, 'he will dominate it, and he won't give others a chance of even talking' (p.6). For those who knew him well, Churchill had clear psychopathic traits: no principles, a sense of entitlement, a domineering nature, a lack of empathy, recklessness and restlessness. This should be in no way surprising. One character-trait analysis found that 2% of scientists, 14% of thinkers, 20% of writers and 25% of artists can be classified as sub-clinically psychopathic, the ordering is the same, though the percentages higher, among 'eminent' members of these categories (Post, 1994). Churchill was an eminent writer and pursued art as a hobby. In addition, analyses of charismatic politicians generally concur that they combine very high intelligence with psychopathic traits. Such a psychological profile provides them with hypnotic though often superficial self-confidence, incredible bravery, and other attractive qualities (see Aberbach, 1996 or Dutton, K., 2012). Narcissism is related to psychopathology and involves, among other related traits, fantasies of power, a self-perception that one is superior, a need for admiration, exploitative behavior, and poor empathy (Campbell & Miller, 2011). Churchill evidently desired power, apparently perceived himself as heroically battling Hitler, exploited others (as we will see below), needed to be the centre of attention, and was clearly deficient in empathy.

Chartwell

Churchill's Finances

Churchill's finances were deeply problematic. As would be expected of somebody high on the psychopathic spectrum, impulsive, entitled Winston was not living anywhere near within his means. Even at St George's he was constantly running out of money to spend in the tuck shop and so writing home for more (Sandys, 1994, p.66). Money was a particularly acute problem between 1929 and 1939, because he was out of government office, meaning he had to survive on his meagre salary as an MP, which was just £500 per year. Being an MP at that time was very much a matter of public service, so British MPs did not receive anything like the generous salaries which they receive today. On this salary, Churchill had to maintain Chartwell — his estate in Kent, with all its staff — as well as the lavish lifestyle of champagne, wining and dining and socialising which he pursued (see Lough, 2015). Chartwell is a red brick mansion dating back to the sixteenth century, though largely rebuilt in the early 1920s, which Churchill had purchased in 1924. Keeping it was crucial to Churchill. He adored the place, once remarking to one of his secretaries, 'a day spent away from Chartwell is a day wasted.' Chartwell's gardens and surroundings, which were particularly beautiful, inspired Churchill to paint, and provided him with a source of peace. The estate included a heated swimming pool, an orchard, a forest, a lake, an arboretum, a tennis court, a croquet court (which doubled up as a cemetery for his beloved pets), and a walled garden, Churchill having built the wall himself (White, 2012). It also boasted stunning views of the Surrey Hills, officially an area of 'outstanding natural beauty.' Churchill commented that, 'I bought Chartwell for the view' (Feddon, 2014, p.8).

The View from Chartwell

Churchill managed to maintain Chartwell, while out of government office, in a variety of questionable ways. Churchill became involved in a group called The Focus. Churchill's involvement in this organisation has been discussed by John Charmley (1993) in *Churchill: The End of Glory* and in Paul Addison's (2013) *Churchill on the Home Front.* The Focus was funded by groups such as the Trades Union Congress and the Jewish Board of Deputies. The Focus started funding Churchill in exchange for Churchill turning his energy and oratorical skill towards prosecuting the case for war with Germany. In *No More Champagne: Churchill and His Money*, David Lough (2015) presents detailed evidence for Winston's parlous finances and profligacy. Lough reveals the staggering financial risks which Churchill took — such risk-taking, we might note, being consistent with Churchill's relatively high psychopathy — and his uncanny ability to write or orate himself out of trouble. Churchill was friends with the Irishman Brendon Bracken (1901-1958), a Conservative MP who became Churchill's Minister of Information. Bracken helped to negotiate vital funding sources for Churchill to deal with his periodic financial difficulties.[48] As Lough demonstrates,

Bottlescape by Winston Churchill, on display at Chartwell

Churchill spent large amounts of money on alcohol. Indeed, when I visited Chartwell, I found that one of the many Churchill pictures on display was a collection of the former owner's empty wine bottles and glasses. He had, apparently, sent his children searching around the house to find them, so he could set up the composition.

---

[48] Bracken was an extraordinary man. When the ambitious Irishman arrived in England in 1920, he wanted to have attended a public school, because he felt it would help him get into politics alongside Churchill, who was his idol. Accordingly, he turned up at Sedbergh School, a public school in West Yorkshire, claiming to be a 15-year-old Australian orphan (he'd spent time in Australia) with a family connection to the headmaster of Winchester. He was admitted and spent one term at the school. Through connections made at the school, Bracken became a public school master, then a publisher, and then Churchill's election campaign manager, an MP, and a minister in Churchill's government (see Lysaght, 1979).

It might be argued that Churchill was religious, as has been explored in detail in *God and Churchill* (Sandys & Henley, 2016) and theistic religiousness, in part because it means you feel you are constantly being watched by a moral God, is negatively associated with psychopathic personality traits even in societies which are not especially religious (e.g. Gebauer et al., 2014). However, his religiousness is debatable. Churchill's daughter, Mary Soames (1922-2014), stated that Churchill 'had a strong belief in a providential God' but 'was not religious in the conventional sense.' Sir Desmond Morton (1891-1971), who was Churchill's personal assistant in 1940, was certain that Churchill did not believe that 'Christ was God' (quoted in Roberts, 2010). It is fairly clear that Churchill suffered from depression and anxiety, though not as strongly as some have suggested, something he referred to as his 'Black Dog' (Attenborough, 2014). Even in somebody relatively high on the psychopathology spectrum, this kind of mood disorder would predict periods of intense religiousness (see Hills et al., 2004), which would help provide life with meaning and direction and accordingly alleviate the intensity of the symptoms. Indeed, if the person was high on the psychopathology spectrum, we would expect a purely deistic rather than moral god. These are precisely the kinds of gods worshipped by pre-agricultural peoples in relatively unchallenging ecologies where intense cooperation is less vital, a point made by the Lebanese psychologist Ara Norenzayan (2013). So-called 'Big Gods' — who are strongly moral — develop in parallel with complex societies of strangers, because belief in such moral gods provides people with a reason to cooperate, making the society more likely to survive.

Churchill's Alcoholism

Even positive biographers are forced to implicitly concede that Churchill was an alcoholic, though they play down the extent of the problems which it caused. Alcoholism is, of course, an obvious sign of poor impulse control (see Nettle, 2007). Key signs of being an alcoholic include the inability to control intake after starting to drink, binge drinking, obsessing about alcohol, and being unable to imagine life without alcohol, drinking every day, and people expressing concern about your drunkenness (Benton, 28th April 2009). Far more serious markers include the realistic possibility of alcohol withdrawal symptoms, such as seizures (Mehta et al., 2017, p.312), and the need to drink in the morning. As we will now see, Churchill presented all of these indicators. He was an archetypal alcoholic.

Churchill had a reputation as a drunk, something which Hitler referred to when lambasting him in speeches in the Reichstag (Wilt, 1990, p.22). Admiral Sir Andrew Cunningham (1883-1963) turned up at a night time meeting during the War to find that, 'There is no doubt the PM was in no state to discuss anything. Very tired and too much alcohol' (p.8). Historian Alan Wilt argues that Churchill's drinking 'did not seem to affect his conduct of the war' (Wilt, 1990, p.8). But that assumes that the war was fought optimally, which many historians would vociferously dispute (see Knight, 2012 and below). Perhaps the War would have gone considerably better if Churchill hadn't been heavily inebriated at meetings with his admirals.

Wilt (1990, p.8) insists that Churchill merely 'enjoyed a drink, or even quite a few in many instances' and that perhaps 'on occasion he had too much to drink.' This is an unacceptable understatement. According to a friend of Randolph Churchill's, Winston Churchill's first whiskey of the day was by 9.30am at the latest (Gardner, 1968, p.5). During a luncheon with the King of Saudi Arabia in 1945, no alcohol was served due to the king's strict Islamic faith. Churchill, via an interpreter, went so far as to remonstrate with the king about this. The king didn't seem offended, but such behaviour is further evidence of alcohol-dependence (Best, 2005, p.198). According to Churchill's (sympathetic) biographer, William Manchester, there was 'always some alcohol in his bloodstream.' When Churchill was knocked over by a car in New York in 1931, his doctor issued a medical note stating that his illustrious patient simply had to have alcohol at set times of the day and especially at all meal times (Langworth, 2017, p.87). This implies that Churchill drank alcohol with breakfast and that he was so addicted that his doctor was concerned about dangerous withdrawal symptoms, such as seizures, if his dependence on alcohol was not accommodated, even in Prohibition Era America. It is fascinating that some biographers can present highly convincing proof of Churchill's alcoholism and then conclude that Churchill displayed, in a wonderful and biased euphemism, 'more or less normality with respect to a good drink' and then add that it couldn't have 'hindered' him anyway, because he was, by implication, such a brilliant man (Langworth, 2017, p.90), which is irrelevant to the fact or otherwise of his alcoholism.

Field Marshal Sir Alan Brooke (1883-1963), Chief of the Imperial Staff, was summoned to Churchill in the middle of the day, during World War II, and recorded what he found in his diary: 'I found him very much the worse for wear, having consumed several glasses of brandy at lunch.' One evening at Chequers — the Prime Minister's Buckinghamshire country residence — Brooke was aghast at the way that Churchill poured himself 'one strong whiskey after another' (Manchester, 2015). In other words, Churchill was intoxicated at work, and his work was leading a country during a war. McKenzie King (1874-1950), the Canadian Prime Minister, wrote in his diary that President Franklin D. Roosevelt (1882-1945) had informed him, 'Chamberlain and Churchill were the only two in the Government who really saw the magnitude of the problems ahead . . . Churchill was tight most of the time.' US Under Secretary of State Sumner Welles (1892-1961) told King about how he had met Churchill at Downing Street and found him completely sloshed, with King adding how 'shameful' this was (Reardon, 2012, p.100). Like others, historian Terry Reardon (2012, p.101) argues that there's no evidence that Churchill's insobriety impacted his performance, to which it can be countered, at the very least, that a British Prime Minister should be in a state to have a serious discussion with the American Under Secretary of State when he comes to see him at Downing Street, especially during a war. The serious medical conditions from which Churchill suffered in adulthood — pneumonia, conjunctivitis, a heart attack, and two strokes (Weisbrode, 2013, p.194) — would make sense if he were a heavy drinker, as heavy drinking leads not only to heart problems and strokes but increased proneness to viral infections (Davis, 19th February 2018).

The argument that being at least moderately pissed most of the time would have made no difference to Churchill's performance as Prime Minister is really not a very persuasive one. Biographers seem to hold Churchill to different standards than they would anyone else; obvious evidence of his lionized status. For any one else, such evidence implies alcoholism, but for Churchill, it merely means that he was a jolly chap and a lover of life. Alcoholism is substantially a reflection of poor impulse control and high Neuroticism, as alcohol can make one feel better (Nettle, 2007). Churchill possessed both of these traits. Alcoholism is, therefore, comorbid with other addictions. It is, accordingly, unsurprising to find that Churchill was a chronic gambler, who lost large amounts of money frivolously betting (Cohen, 2013, p.400, note 47). Churchill was manifestly overweight by the time he was Prime Minister (noted in Perry, 2010, p.133), and thus a glutton, addicted to food. Sneyd-Kynnersley specifically commented on Churchill's gluttony, even as a child. Churchill was also a 'heavy smoker' even by the standards of the time, so clearly addicted to nicotine (Taylor, 1969, p.270).

Churchill's Syndrome

Historians who are willing to delve into the myths of the Churchill Cult have found abundant evidence consistent with the great man being relatively high on the psychopathic personality spectrum. Clive Ponting's (1994) *Churchill* shows that the great leader was an alcoholic who was happy to scrounge off his publishers as well as off wealthy friends. Churchill's arrogance led him into numerous military and political blunders, with much of his voluminous writing being attempts to justify or downplay these mistakes. This inability to accept blame — as well as his obvious sense of entitlement — would be consistent with the bloated ego that is an aspect of psychopathic personality. Churchill also wanted to sterilise what he regarded as degenerate groups within the working class, a view which would have been considered extreme even among the eugenics movement in the 1930s. He was considered to be untrustworthy by his colleagues, having crossed the floor of the Commons twice: defecting from the Conservatives to the Liberals and back again. Callousness and duplicity are further signs of being high on the psychopathology spectrum.

In *Churchill: The Greatest Britain Unmasked* (Knight, 2012), Nigel Knight gives us another more realistic portrait of the wartime leader. It highlights his numerous failings. In World War I, as First Lord of the Admiralty, he was in charge of the disastrous Gallipoli Campaign, which led to 140,000 allied deaths. When Chancellor of the Exchequer, he kept Britain on the Gold Standard, which made industry uncompetitive and prolonged the Depression. As First Lord of the Admiralty again, under Chamberlain, Churchill was behind the botched attempt to invade Norway. As war-leader, Knight argues, Churchill made blunder after blunder, which led to unnecessary deaths and lost opportunities to finish the war more quickly. Knight summarises that Churchill, 'was not mad or simple; his misguided decisions were the product of his personality — a mixture of arrogance, emotion, self-indulgence, stubbornness' — all signs of the personality disorder which seems best to explain Churchill's behaviour.

John Charmley has produced a series of books which are highly critical of Churchill. In *Chamberlain and the Lost Peace,* Charmley (1999) defends Churchill's predecessor, refuting the perception that he was hopelessly naïve and misled. He observes that there was no unified desire for war in Britain in 1939. The Peace Movement was very popular and Chamberlain's views were shared by diplomats and leading politicians of the day. Chamberlain, avers Charmley, was a careful, cautious servant of the British Empire in stark contrast to the hot-headed Churchill who was fully prepared to gamble the British Empire. It might be added that Churchill, similarly, gambled with money and his own health; recklessness being an aspect of psychopathic personality. In *Churchill: The End of Glory,* Charmley (1993) systematically sets out Churchill's numerous errors of judgement and their consequences. He argues that Churchill represented the reactionary politics of nostalgia and this could be seen both in his counter-productive crushing of the Indian Home Rule movement before the War and in his desire to wage war on Germany, such that Britain could control the balance of power in Europe. Charmley observes that those who were most implacably opposed to war, such as former Prime Minister Stanley Baldwin (1867-1947) and Lord Halifax (1881-1959), were those who best understood how fragile Britain's imperial power was and how easily it could slip. Churchill, argues Charmley, led Britain into all-out war, and so played a leading part in Britain's decline as a world power. This is a fundamental point. If the war was unnecessary, then Churchill was simply a warmonger, an obvious marker of psychopathic personality, and the Empire could have been saved were it not for the nature of Churchill's personality.

War Monger

We have already observed that during his own life time people commented that Churchill had a kind of lust for war, meaning we might expect him to direct his country into an unnecessary conflagration. Churchill was obsessed with war from a very young age, even being particularly interested in playing with toy soldiers. He was rejected from Sandhurst twice, but wouldn't give up, being absolutely determined to be an army officer. Churchill was accepted on his third attempt (Lee & Lee, 2010, p.68). Having graduated, he pulled some strings to get himself posted to various war zones. An enthusiastic supporter of the Great War, as First Lord of the Admiralty he directed particularly bloody and disastrous battles, such as the Gallipoli Campaign, and then spent six months on the front line himself. He was 'eager to meet force with force' (Weidhorn, 2003, p.24).

Consistent with high psychopathology was Churchill's desire for war in 1940. When Churchill became Prime Minister there was no point to the War from Britain's perspective. There was no question of Britain nor any part of its Empire being invaded, and the Nazi extermination camps were only discovered *after* the War anyway (Hirsch, 2010). In private, in 1941, Hitler did not want to attack Britain; such an attack would have, naturally, massively increased support for the war among the sceptical British public, as Churchill well knew. Hitler was prepared to withdraw from all but the territories that had been taken from Germany by the Treaty of Versailles after World War I, as long as he got a free hand to invade Russia, a point demonstrated by historian Peter Padfield (2013). However, Churchill seemed to want war. It might be argued that somebody like Hitler would surely have turned on the British Empire eventually, meaning the war was necessary. But there is simply no evidence for this. Hitler made clear in 1936 that he would much prefer an alliance with Britain than with Italy; having fought the British in World War I, he had a great deal of respect for them: 'I know the Englishmen from the last war, they are hard fellows' (quoted in Weber, 2010, p.328). Hitler was plain, in the 1920s, that Germany should not work against Britain's interests. It was France who had helped to cripple Weimar Germany by insisting on ruinous reparations and even occupying the German industrial area, the Ruhr, when these were not forthcoming and it was the Soviet Union, who had to be dealt with so that the Germans could expand their 'living space' (Kershaw, 2001, p.247). Hitler (1939, p.279) also stated in *Mein Kampf* in 1925 that:

> 'The British nation will therefore be considered as the most valuable ally in the world as long as it can be counted upon to show that brutality and tenacity in its government, as well as in the spirit of the broad masses, which enables it to carry through to victory any struggle that it once enters upon, no matter how long such a struggle may last or however great the sacrifice that may be necessary or whatever the means that have to be employed; and all that even though the actual military equipment at hand may be utterly inadequate when compared with that of other nations.'

Consistent with this, Hitler did all that he could to avoid a war with Britain, whose people he regarded as close ethnic kin. Based on the philosophy of testimony, we should accept testimony at face value unless there is a sound reason not to. There is no reason to think that Hitler would lie about his views on Britain to fellow Germans in the 1920s or even in the 1930s.

Also, if Hitler had wanted to invade Britain — to whom he had massively superior military power — he could have done so.

During the evacuation of Dunkirk, in May-June 1940, Hitler ordered his tanks to stop at a certain point, permitting the fleeing British expeditionary force to escape. Had he not done so, he could have crippled the British army. This superficially inexplicable decision would only seem to make sense if Hitler had 'wanted to provide the British with a face-saving outlet to encourage them to enter into peace negotiations' (Ward, 2004, p.85). There is no rational reason to think Hitler would have invaded Britain. He respected the British, regarded them as an ally, and simply wanted to create a Reich which covered all German-speaking populations and expand eastwards. After the Dunkirk debacle, with Germany in the dominant position, Hitler continued to do all he could to achieve peace with the new Prime Minister. In June 1940, a month after Churchill had become Prime Minister, Hitler made a peace offer but Churchill would not accept it (Douglas-Hamilton, 2012). By the summer of 1940, no British cities had been bombed, which was a serious problem for Churchill, because his backers wanted a proper war with Germany and Churchill required more support for it among the British public in order to prosecute such a war. Only the bombing of civilians could crush the UK's vocal peace movement. Churchill's lucky break came on the night of 24th-25th August, when a stray bomb, meant for oil tankers in Rotherhithe, fell on the East End, killing a few civilians. Churchill was able to present this as the most heinous aggression against the British people and so neuter the peace movement. He was thus able to persuade parliament and the public to get behind a full-on war with Germany (White, 2009, p.38).

Desperate for peace with Britain, Hitler seemingly sent his deputy, Rudolf Hess (1894-1987), to fly to Scotland to meet his acquaintance, the 14th Duke of Hamilton (1903-1973), in an attempt to use this high level contact to present Hitler's peace offer to Churchill. Either that or Hess, who was increasingly being side-lined by Hitler, realised that he could gain the Führer's favour if he could broker the peace which his boss was so desperate to achieve. Hess had to bail out of the plane. He parachuted down to a farm just 12 miles from his destination. Hess was interned and Hitler had to publically present him as a rogue agent who had simply gone mad (Douglas-Hamilton, 2012). In other words, the carnage of World War II could easily have been avoided. It was not avoided, in part, due to the psychology of the man who was First Lord of the Treasury by 1940.

It might be argued that going to war was necessary to defend democracy, such as in Poland, but this is simply untrue. After World War I, Poland became a multi-party democracy. However, it had to deal with economic crises, highly unstable government, and a multi-ethnic state. Only two thirds of its roughly 27 million people — in 1920 — were Polish. There were four million Ukrainians, a million Germans, a million Jews, a million Belarussians and a substantial number of Lithuanians, all under a highly centralized government. Multiethnic states tend to degenerate into ethnic conflict, as Finnish political scientist Tatu Vanhanen (1929-2015) has demonstrated statistically (Vanhanen, 2012). With the Polish state collapsing into chaos, in 1926 the country's war hero, Marshal Jozef Pilsudski (1867-1935), led a military coup, after which Poland was a violent military dictatorship in which opposition leaders were sent to camps and tortured (Lee, 2016, p.329). Pilsudski left most of the running of the country to a group of colonels. When Pilsudski died, in 1935, the dictatorship of the colonels continued right up until Poland was invaded by Germany in 1939 (see Leslie, 1983). In addition, Poland at the time was a ferociously nationalistic state which aimed to create an ethnically homogenous country. The German minority were continuously persecuted. The Polish government expropriated their land, nationalized German businesses, forced them to speak Polish even in the German areas (in contravention of the Geneva Convention), and fired Germans who worked for the government, replacing them with Poles.

In October-November 1930, the Polish government held a special 'Anti-German Week' which resulted in widespread mistreatment of Germans. Propaganda posters openly incited violence against the German minority. They portrayed a fat, helmeted, beer-swilling Prussian held back by a slim Polish knight who encouraged Poles to 'Repeat the scenes at Grunwald,' this being the place where the Poles routed the Teutonic knights in a fifteenth century battle. German shops were boycotted, German newspapers publically burnt, and Germans were attacked in the street, with the police rarely intervening. The result, as desired, was that many Germans in Poland fled to Germany (Demshuk, 2012, pp.47-49). One might go so far as to argue that the treatment of the German minority in Poland meant that Germany had little choice but to invade and take back control of German-speaking areas of Poland which had been part of Germany until Versailles. The Poles retaliated so, obviously, the Germans had to invade the entire country in order to protect the German minority. Poland could hardly take the moral high ground, considering that, in 1920, it had invaded areas of Ukraine, which were part of the Soviet Union, and added them to its territory. It then proceeded to repress and persecute the Ukrainian-speaking inhabitants, just as it did its German minority (Copsey, 2016, p.87).

Nazi Germany was a nationalistic dictatorship which persecuted its minorities, with a view to making them leave the country. Poland was a nationalistic dictatorship which persecuted its minorities to the extent of making them leave the country and, in doing so, was obviously going to infuriate Germany. Britain's going to war with Germany was clearly nothing to do with 'defending democracy.' It was defending one nationalistic dictatorship from another, which is hardly a justifiable reason to take Britain into a war or remain in the war. As an aside, Czechoslovakia — which was 48% Czech, 28% German and only 14% Slovak — was similarly unpleasant to its German minority, the Sudetan Germans, placing Germany's 1938 invasion of the Sudetenland in a rather different light. The Czech-dominated government forced all administration and schooling in the Sudetenland to be in Czech (against treaty guarantees to the contrary), it shut down all the German schools, gave all towns and streets Czech names, and expropriated land from Germans to give it to Czechs. If land hadn't been held by Germans since before 1620 it was 'restored' to the Czech people (Benacek, 2001; Glassheim, 2016).

Austrian-American historian Manfred Weidhorn (1994) has criticised the thesis that Britain should have made peace with Hitler in 1941, arguing that it assumes that Hitler would want peace, that the British coalition government would allow Churchill to negotiate with Hitler, that Hitler would have kept his side of the deal, and that the British Empire had a long way to go. However, we have already presented direct evidence that Hitler definitely wanted peace. Churchill was, of course, the most hawkish member of the government, so there is no reason to think that his cabinet would not have allowed him to negotiate. There is no reason to think that Hitler would have reneged on a deal that he manifestly wanted, and, obviously, the British Empire would have continued for longer if Britain had not been left bankrupted and psychologically shattered. When all else fails, opponents of Charmley's thesis simply resort to fallacious appeals to insult, asserting that it is, 'absurd . . . that instead of going to war Britain could, and should, have lived with Wilhelmine Germany's domination of western Europe. This is glibly clever but actually preposterous as is his claim . . . that Britain could and should have unilaterally withdrawn into neutrality in 1940–41' (Barnett, 2002, pp.519-520).

Chapter Ten

The Unnecessary War & the

Collapse of the West

Pat Buchanan's Churchill, Hitler and the Unnecessary War

THE MOST DAMNING picture of Churchill is presented by the American politician and writer Pat Buchanan in *Churchill, Hitler and the Unnecessary War: How Britain Lost Its Empire and the West Lost the World* (Buchanan, 2008). Buchanan's guiding purpose in writing the book was to destroy the foundations of the 'Churchill Cult' which he argues exists in the USA, and, to a great extent, the book accomplishes this aim. More recently, a very similar set of arguments, specifically with regard to World War II, have been presented by the British journalist Peter Hitchens in his book *The Phoney Victory* (2018).

Buchanan's central thesis is that both World Wars — although there is an extent to which they were a single war punctuated by a lengthy ceasefire — were monumentally disastrous for the Western powers and that they were especially so for Britain. He argues that World War I was entirely unnecessary for the UK. Regarding German naval expansion as a threat to the British Isles, the British government returned much of its Navy to Europe, which left it tied to Europe and dragged it into the Great War, he maintains. Buchanan also shows that Churchill, from his army days onwards, appeared to have a deep-seated 'lust for war' (Buchanan, 2008, p.65), which we have seen considerable evidence for already. This War left Britain and Europe financially crippled and emotionally exhausted. Any British person with an interest in genealogy will almost certainly find that their family lost somebody during World War I. This situation of exhaustion and financial malaise helped to create conditions where the USA could displace Britain as the dominant world power. Churchill, Buchanan shows, was an integral and hawkish part of the government which created this situation, of the government that imposed a terrible food blockade on Germany, and of the government that played its part in the German national humiliation and financial impoverishment that constituted the Treaty of Versailles. In effect, Churchill significantly contributed to creating the conditions in Germany which led to so many Germans voting for the Nazis and the Nazi Party ultimately taking control of the country and destroying the democratic Weimar Republic.

Buchanan insists that there were many opportunities, before the Nazis sunk the Weimar Republic, to revise the Versailles Treaty, which placed communities of Germans under the rule of anti-German or nationalistic governments in Poland, Czechoslovakia, and France. Buchanan avers that, considering the consequences, Churchill was clearly wrong to reject the German government's attempts to broker peace in 1940, citing various historians, such as Alan Clark (1928-1999), for his view that these overtures to peace were genuine (Buchanan, 2009, p.362). In addition, Buchanan shows that Churchill played a key part in the move to cut military spending in 1919, and that Churchill helped to disarm Britain during the 1920s, leaving her ill prepared for the very war which Churchill so avidly pushed for in the 1930s. Buchanan also observes, among other salient criticisms of Churchill, that the mass murder of Jews only took on the scale it did due to Hitler's invasion of Poland and the Soviet Union, putting millions of Jews under Nazi control. If Churchill had negotiated with Hitler to return to him the territories lost under Versailles, the war would not have happened and the Jewish loss of life would have been far less. Buchanan also draws upon various eminent historians, such as Ian Kershaw and Richard Evans, to argue that Hitler actually wanted an anti-Soviet alliance with Britain, *not* war with Britain. He summarises that, 'For that war one man bears full moral responsibility: Hitler . . . But this was not only Hitler's war. It was Chamberlain's war and Churchill's war . . .' (Buchanan, pp.292-293).

Churchill the Barbarian

The West's 'return to barbarism,' demonstrates Buchanan, was entirely the fault of Churchill. It was Churchill who flattened German cities, cities that had no military or other strategic sites, simply to kill German civilians and spread terror. Indeed, Churchill personally ordered the destruction of Dresden in 1945; an act which served no military purpose beyond wiping out thousands of enemy civilians and traumatising the survivors. Churchill then callously turned over the small independent nations of Eastern Europe to Stalin's tyranny.

The damage to Britain and the Empire, argues Buchanan, was terminal. He quotes Alan Clark's (2nd January 1993) review of Charmley's *Churchill: The End of Glory*. Clark went much further than Charmley, stating that the War:

'went on far too long, and when Britain emerged the country was bust. Nothing remained of assets overseas. Without immense and punitive borrowings from the US we would have starved. The old social order had gone forever. The empire was terminally damaged. The Commonwealth countries had seen their trust betrayed and their soldiers wasted (quoted in Buchanan, p.316).

Buchanan's book does not use any primary sources, and was criticised for this reason by one journalist (Kitsch, 11th June 2008). But this is a non-criticism. There is nothing unscholarly — indeed it is perfectly academically acceptable — to engage in a secondary analysis in the pursuit of demonstrating or critiquing a scientific or historical hypothesis. Such criticisms really only go to labour the point that the critic is biased and is desperate to find something with which to besmirch the book in the eyes of less thoughtful potential readers. Another reviewer (Bahnsen, 7th June 2008) termed Buchanan's book, for some reason, an 'anti-Semitic piece of garbage.' This is the fallacy of 'appeal to insult' and fallacies indicate bias on the part of those who employ them. We are all evolved to have various cognitive biases (see Boyer, 2001). They aid survival but not necessarily reasoned argumentation. Also, it might be argued that Britain could not possibly have kept out of the War if Hitler had started invading the countries of the East. But it can be countered that if Eire and Sweden could keep out of the War then so could Britain. To argue that it is simply not in the nature of Britain to act in such a way is no more than a fallacious appeal to tradition.

The Death of the West

So, we can conclude that Churchill, more than anyone else, can be blamed for the fall of the British Empire and the bankrupting of Britain. This was an Empire that Churchill's expensive public school education was meant to have inculcated him into loyally serving, but he brought about its destruction. And Churchill's war indirectly led to the destruction of Britain and perhaps even the West itself.

This thesis has been set out very fluently by Alan Clark (2nd January 1993), as we have already discussed. Indeed, a number of thinkers have presented strikingly convergent models of how Britain, and the West more generally, has reached its current situation, including Pat Buchanan in *The Death of the West* (Buchanan, 2001), English libertarian thinker Sean Gabb in *Culture Revolution, Culture War: How the Conservatives Lost England and How to Get It Back Again* (Gabb, 2007) and English journalist Douglas Murray in *The Strange Death of Europe: Immigration, Identity, Islam* (Murray, 2017). Distilling the different interpretations of thinkers such as these, we can reach the following essential model of what has happened: World War II left Great Britain bankrupt, short of labour to rebuild its bomb-damaged infrastructure, and, to a certain extent, just worn out. In particular, its ruling class was exhausted and demoralised; unable or unwilling to fight for its position. The British people had been made to endure considerable hardship and they wanted change. They wanted the 'Land Fit for Heroes;' they felt they deserved something better. It was also clear that the old system must have had very serious flaws. Why else had this very system got Britain into two catastrophic World Wars? In other words, the trauma of two cataclysmic conflicts left people questioning the traditions that had long held society together. With its rationing and the strong sense of nationalism it had induced, the War had also had a levelling effect. Many people felt as though the nation had come together as one during the War, and this relative equality should continue now that Britain had peace. So in the jubilation of just having triumphed over the Axis Powers, the British people kicked Churchill's Conservative Party out and embraced the socialist Labour Party of Clement Attlee (1883-1967), Churchill's wartime deputy in the coalition government.

With a clear and pressing need to rebuild the country, and a shortage of labour, the Attlee government passed the 1948 Immigration Act, which allowed citizens of the Commonwealth — as the Empire and former Empire was now being termed — to come and work in Britain. At the same time as Commonwealth citizens were beginning to come to Britain, Britain was starting her withdrawal from her collapsing Empire. India, the jewel of the imperial crown, was given independence in 1947. Eire, which already had Home Rule and had wisely stayed out of the War, declared itself to be a republic in 1949. Throughout the 1950s, the 'wind of change' blew through Africa and the rest of the Empire as it slowly fell apart. Britain was now a socialist economy and immigration was ensuring that certain parts of British cities were gradually becoming unrecognisable foreign ghettos. This would have helped to reduce a sense of community and reduce a sense of trust. It has been shown that immigration reduces trust even among the native community, because there is now a group to which the less loyal of the natives can defect (Putnam, 2007). This new system also made Britain far more meritocratic than it had previously been, ensuring that, to a much greater extent, people could reach (or fall to) the socioeconomic status merited by their intelligence and personality; in other words, it created a process of cognitive stratification (Herrnstein & Murray, 1994). Where once qualities such as intelligence were more equally distributed across the social classes — as, although IQ is 80% genetic in general, highly intelligent people are sometimes born into the working class just by genetic chance and are held back by nepotism — now this was decreasingly the case. This led to an elite that was increasingly out of touch with the instincts of most of its people. Intelligence predicts certain preferences: novelty, political liberalism, altruism, even a trusting nature (Dutton & Woodley of Menie, 2018).

With this new system — of socialism critiquing much that had previously been accepted with little question, such as wealth differences, the social class system, the monarchy and even the power of the Church — the semi-sacred symbols of national unity began to lose their sense of awe. The system upon which Britain's Empire had been built was being picked apart and the traditional ruling class were too exhausted or too short-term focused to do anything about it. It has been argued elsewhere that World War I disproportionately killed the sons of the English upper class, compared to the other social classes, because the upper classes were so much more likely to be officers, leading the troops into battle. During World War I, recruits who had been to public school were, assuming they were sufficiently fit, automatically made officers, as they had generally attended Officer Training Corps at school. Around 8% of British soldiers who fought in World War I were killed. However, among the officers, the fatality rate was 16% (Winter, 2012). German psychologist Heiner Rindermann (2018, p.243) has dug out the various studies which prove this in his useful reference work *Cognitive Capitalism*. These studies demonstrate that the British army lost 4 IQ points between 1938 and 1944, as did the Dutch army, and it has been quantitatively shown that, during World War II, higher IQ men were more likely to be killed on active service than lower IQ men. So, perhaps this disproportionate decline of the intelligence of the ruling class — partly caused by Churchill, as a hawk in the government during the Great War — explains, in part, this failure to act.

Once socialism was accepted, then those who wished to leverage social status would virtue-signal, or try to showcase their intelligence and bravery, by questioning ever more aspects of the traditional society, leading to an arms race where more and more foundations of the 'traditional' society which had made Britain 'rule the waves' were undermined, a point which has been discussed more broadly by the German psychologist Volkmar Weiss (2007). As people became more comfortable, with religiousness predicted by stress (Norenzayan & Shariff, 2008), they became decreasingly religious and stopped caring about religiously-sanctioned views of how they should live their lives. At the same time, some members of the educated classes attempted to play for status by mocking and pulling apart the established religion. In 1963, the Bishop of Woolwich, John A.T. Robinson (1919-1983) published *Honest to God* (Robinson, 1963), in which he denied every key doctrine of the Church of England and effectively denied that God existed at all. And those who wished to leverage social status by virtue-signalling helped to create an arms race through which the welfare state became ever more lavish, meaning there was no reason at all to follow the traditional model of the family. This helped to undermine the traditional model of the family, which had existed for so long, because it meant that there was no longer any financial disincentive to have children outside of marriage. This arms race — this constant move to question everything, at least within just about acceptable boundaries — led to a constant drift away from everything which had held the country together before the War.

The Left then moved on to the rights of ethnic minorities whom, it was argued, should be considered just as English as those families who had lived in the country for thousands of years. Indeed, 'Multiculturalism' — that Britain should play host to diverse cultures who should not have to conform to the majority culture — was an excellent idea and anyone who disagreed was condemned as 'racist' and a latter day supporter of Hitler. In this atmosphere of fear and conformity, mass-immigration was able to continue unchecked, because very few people wanted to open themselves up to criticism from the self-righteous mob by questioning it and calmly exploring the negative dimensions of it for the British people. These would include, of course, declining trust, a sense of alienation in their own land, a lack of positive ethnocentrism due to this lack of trust, and a lack of negative ethnocentrism in the face of aggressors due to inculcation with the idea that all cultures are somehow equal and due to the questioning of Anglicanism — with religiousness tending to predict ethnocentrism — partly brought about by religious diversity. This same snowball effect further encouraged people to question Christianity, leading to a less united society with far less of a sense of its own eternal importance, digging its way into ever deeper Nihilism (Sarraf et al., 2019). This problem has led to the English philosopher Sir Roger Scruton (2000) arguing that Westerners need to learn to live 'as if' their lives have eternal importance. In a similar vein, the Canadian psychologist Jordan Peterson (2018) has argued that religion is adaptive because it describes and practices what has worked for humanity in the past. He maintains that if we assess our actions — rather than what we think we think — then we will realise that we *do* believe that our lives have eternal meaning and we do believe in God and we need to come to realise and embrace an eclectic form of religiosity based on Christianity and other religions. In addition, Multiculturalism taught people that they shared in the guilt of their colonial forefathers, their dull 'egg and chips' culture could only be 'enriched' by immigration, and that their way of life was not worth defending. Those who disagreed, and they tended to be the working class whose communities were transformed by immigration, were dismissed as pathological and uncultured, requiring some form of re-education (see Murray, 2017 for a more detailed discussion).

The professional classes had a deep fear of being accused of 'racism' and an abhorrence of the pathological white working class. With cognitive and personality stratification, there was now a cultural and intellectual chasm between the white working class and themselves. The working class, many believed, had had every opportunity to better themselves, but they hadn't, and they were, therefore, low in diligence, low in intelligence, and 'other.' The Nazis were strong believers that personality and intelligence were mainly hereditary, so the War had also helped to suppress this substantially empirically accurate view (see Dutton & Woodley of Menie, 2018) in favour of the inaccurate, but more virtuous, view that these differences were overwhelmingly environmental. So, there was a degree to which the working class *could* help themselves but *chose* not to, leaving the intelligentsia with little but contempt for them

– especially as their values were so divergent from those of the intelligentsia.

None of this had happened in Japan, because Japan did not adopt socialism and it did not permit mass-immigration. Eastern Europe has avoided much of this, partly through being under the permafrost of Communism for the second half of the twentieth century. But Western Europe has not. Other Western European countries saw what the British government had done in allowing mass non-white immigration, thought it seemed like an efficient idea, and then followed suit. And the virtue-signalling status game only continued, moving from immigrants to refugees.

However, as the arms race only intensified, refugees from poor, unstable countries — that were in that condition partly because of the low average intelligence of their inhabitants, as has been demonstrated in detail (see Lynn & Vanhanen, 2012) — had to be permitted entry, then there had to be family reunification, then permitting entry to people who were 'fleeing poverty.' Poverty is significantly a reflection of the average intelligence of an individual and of his or her community (see Rindermann, 2018), so it is very difficult to flee it. And, of course, the frenzy of status-gaining, self-righteous virtue-signalling concomitantly moved on to the rights of homosexuals, and then transsexuals . . .

The Cycle of Civilization

It could be argued that the collapse of Britain would have occurred even if Churchill hadn't taken it into the War. Philosophers of History have long observed the way that civilizations seem to follow a predictable cycle. The Islamic philosopher, Ibn Khaldun (1332-1406), conceived of a quality he termed *asabiya,* meaning 'solidarity' or 'group consciousness.' Civilizations would be established by poor desert tribesmen who struggled under harsh conditions, and who were strongly religious and high in *asabiya.* They would build flourishing, wealthy cities but the relatively high level of luxury which these afforded them reduced their *asabiya.* Consequently, their civilization declined and they were invaded by new desert

237

tribesmen — deeply jealous of the civilization's wealth — who were high in *asabiya* (see Dutton & Woodley of Menie, 2018).

The first prominent 'modern' advocate of social cycle theory was the Italian historian Giambattista Vico (1668-1744). Vico developed the thinking of theorists like Ibn Khaldun by conceiving of the 'desert tribesman' as internal to the civilization. Vico maintained that states pass through three stages: The Age of Gods, the Age of Heroes and the Age of Men. After the Age of Men, society collapses back into the Age of Gods and the cycle occurs all over again. The three ages of the cycle, argued Vico, clearly took place in Ancient Greece and Rome. They began as simple, brutal societies whose anxieties were allayed by the gods, whom they deeply feared. The aristocracy ruled over these societies and controlled them through religion or, as Vico puts it, 'poetic wisdom.' From this, they developed into more complex societies where there was a much clearer divide between the 'nobility' (the heroes) and the 'plebeians,' who battled to gain some of the privileges held by the nobility but were ruled by them. So, society became less united. In the Age of Heroes, there is a conspicuous and highly distinct ruling class whose members fight with each other for control and to display their strength. In the Age of Men, the heroes cede some of their power to the plebeians. In the previous ages, humanity was ruled by religion and ritual and this upheld the power of the nobility. The plebeians advance their own interests, and undermine the power of the nobility, by advocating a rational way of thinking. This empowers the plebeians, but also undermines religion and, in so-doing, shatters cultural unity. Religiousness inspires people to work for the common good but now they focus only on the individual. Society splinters into 'the barbarism of reflection' in which civil wars are fought solely for personal gain. It duly collapses back to the Age of Gods. Vico argued that this can be seen in the Fall of Rome. In the Dark Ages, we then have a new 'Age of Gods.' Medieval Europe is the Age of Heroes and the Renaissance can be understood as the beginning of the Age of Men, in which society reaches an intellectual, cultural and technological peak which is also its own undoing (Rossides, 1998).

Vico's process is precisely what happened in the ancient world. For example, as Ancient Greece aged and became comfortable, there arose people like Socrates, who began questioning its religion and all other traditions, leading to rationalism and religious diversity. There was a similar process in ancient Rome. It was around the eighteenth century — with sceptical philosophers — and even more so into the nineteenth century that people, often wealthy but of middle class origin like Charles Darwin, started questioning traditional beliefs. Similarly, the German philosopher Oswald Spengler (1880-1936) argued that all civilizations grow and decline, following the same pattern as the seasons of the year. In Spring, the civilization is born; this parallels the West's Dark Ages and it is strongly religious. In Summer, we see the height of its creative achievements – its epics and poems. As in the late Medieval or Early Modern period, the society is optimistic and does not question itself. Moving into the Autumn, the society brings in the harvest, meaning that it is urbanized and wealthy. But, with levels of luxury so high, it begins to lose its religiousness and it starts to question itself. There comes a Socrates figure. The society questions religion, aristocratic rule, tradition . . . everything which has got it to this high state of civilization.

At first this induces optimism about a better future. But eventually, as everything is questioned, life becomes about nothing more than money. With no religion to hold it together, society becomes fragmented and a general sense of despair becomes all pervading. This is especially so among the more intelligent, such as the more educated. Having developed contraception by this stage, they stop having children, with intelligence being negatively associated with fertility in the modern West (Dutton & Woodley of Menie, 2018, Ch. 11). There is no unity against external invaders, with no religion to promote ethnocentrism. This process of rationalization continues, and every idea is questioned, then everything is rationalized down to money (even having children), all of the old ways are despised, and there is no longer any optimism or soul holding society together. Society is strongly individualist and we enter the winter of civilization. The constant critique, and artificial attempt to create meaning, leads to a nihilistic, pessimistic world and a gulf between the money-focused elite and the masses, because there is no longer any religious belief that the position of the elite is somehow deserved. Society becomes fragmented, democracy and order break down and demagogues take over, leading an increasingly alienated mass. This is the Age of Emperors. These Emperors are given extraordinary powers to sort out the mess of conflict that society has degenerated into, including problems of external invaders. The society collapses into dictatorship and war (Spengler, 1991, Dutton & Woodley of Menie, 2018, Ch. 11).

It has been argued that, ultimately, it is simply intelligence which underpins this process (Dutton & Woodley of Menie, 2018, Ch. 11). As the civilization grows, it is under conditions of Darwinian selection and these select for intelligence, because intelligence allows you to become rich, meaning that more of your children will survive. Indeed, it has been documented from wills and parish records that until the Industrial Revolution, the richer half of European populations had about double than number of surviving offspring than the poorer half (Clark, 2007). The Industrial Revolution — or a high level of luxury close to this point — brings this to an end by reducing environmental harshness through superior medicine and healthier living conditions. It also creates a situation of low stress, where some people (the more intelligent) start questioning religion, including the exhortation to go forth and multiply, and tradition. The more intelligent, therefore, start limiting their fertility and high fertility becomes an accident, associated with impulsivity and the inability to use contraception and so low intelligence, as is now true of Western societies (Dutton & Woodley of Menie, 2018, Ch. 7). Accordingly, intelligence — and civilization — decline, and it has been shown that this is for genetic reasons (see Dutton & Woodley of Menie, 2018, Ch. 7). German biochemist Gerhard Meisenberg (2007) argues that the West took until the Industrial Revolution to start questioning religion and using contraception — rather than doing so on the cusp of it as previous civilizations had — because of the unique intolerance for questioning religious dogmas that was inherent in Christianity — with dissenters being executed — and the strong Jewish taboo on contraception which Christianity inherited.

Churchill's War and the Winter of Civilization

It is likely true that the decline of civilization is inevitable. But there is a case for arguing that World War II was a turning point; a huge national trauma which caused the British – and others involved — to question tradition like never before. This has had numerous knock-on effects, creating a cascade of decline. In other words, Churchill's war sped up the process of degeneration. As already discussed, the key factor behind the reversal of the positive association between intelligence and fertility in previous civilizations has been the development of contraception and the decline of religiousness among the highly intelligent, specifically the upper class and the intelligentsia, in part due to their low stress life-styles. This has led to the more intelligent questioning religious demands to be fertile, and people realising that they can have smaller families and so a better lifestyle if they use contraception. Accordingly, large families become a product of impulsivity or the inability to correctly use contraception, both markers of low IQ (Meisenberg, 2007). However, the arms race of cultural critique and sanctimoniousness set off by World War II will have substantially sped up this process.

Firstly, the war itself — just as World War I did — disproportionately killed men of high intelligence, because they were more likely to become officers and display altruistic traits, which are associated with high IQ, such as gallantry.

Secondly, the rise of the welfare state reversed a previous situation where there was a very strong disincentive for the very poor — something predicted by their low IQ (Jensen, 1998) — to have children, due to the poverty in which they would find themselves if they did. The welfare state is now so generous that, in the UK, it is only families where both parents are on welfare that are breeding at above replacement fertility (Perkins, 2016), meaning that the future is in the hands of those with an IQ of around 80, insufficient to hold down a job in a technological society.

Thirdly, the process has led to equality for females, something that, despite what critics may say, is statistically demonstrable (see Williams, 2017). This has meant that the more intelligent women tend to heavily delay and limit their fertility in order to pursue careers.

For this reason, the negative correlation between IQ and fertility in the USA is higher among women than men (Meisenberg, 2010). Women with low IQ not only have more children than those with high IQ but, because they start so much younger, more generations as well.

Fourthly, the process has led to high immigration with the descendants of these immigrants having markedly higher fertility than the natives. For example, in the UK on the 2001 census, the white British had an average of 1.6 children whereas Pakinstanis, Bangladeshis and Somalis had an average of 5 (Lynn, 2011, p.269). There is abundant proof that general intelligence is in decline based on proxies for it which can be measured across time such as lengthening reaction times and declining per capita major innovations since the nineteenth century. Research from Iceland has found that the percentage of the population who carry polymorphisms (forms of a gene) which predict high intelligence has declined across the last three generations (Dutton & Woodley of Menie, 2018).

These are the key factors, though the process has probably set off others that are more complex. For example, the undermining of traditional values may lead to more intelligent people — who will be higher in the trait Openness — being less inculcated with the importance of the family and having children. But the central issue is that Churchill's war sped up the decline. Churchill is ultimately the reason why *we* are living through it rather than our descendants, some of whom will likely live through far worse. Churchill was born in the Autumn of civilization and he helped to ensure that it entered its winter much earlier than it could have by creating a nuclear winter towards the end of Autumn. If there had been no Churchill it is very probable that we would not be this far into the snow and ice of our civilization's winter. The trees would merely be bereft of leaves. Considering the views Churchill expressed in his lifetime, this is a mark of his failure. In Churchill's *The Story of the Malakand Field Force,* he roundly condemned Islam:

> 'But the Mahommedan religion increases, instead of lessening, the fury of intolerance. It was originally propagated by the sword, and ever since, its votaries have been subject, above the people of

all other creeds, to this form of madness. In a moment the fruits of patient toil, the prospects of material prosperity, the fear of death itself, are flung aside' (Churchill, 1898, Ch. III).

In a later chapter, he added:

'How dreadful are the curses which Mohammedanism lays on its votaries! Besides the fanatical frenzy, which is as dangerous in a man as hydrophobia in a dog, there is this fearful fatalistic apathy. The effects are apparent in many countries. Improvident habits, slovenly systems of agriculture, sluggish methods of commerce, and insecurity of property exist wherever the followers of the Prophet rule or live' (Churchill, 1898, Ch. X).

Yet the enormous growth of Islam in Europe (see Murray, 2017) can be traced back to the consequences of Churchill's war. In 1910, he expressed deep concern about the decline of average intelligence in Britain:

'I propose that 100,000 degenerate Britons should be forcibly sterilized and others put in labour camps to halt the decline of the British race' (quoted in Ponting, 1994).

However, his two wars indirectly accelerated its decline.

Churchill, in other words, can be understood as the central character in the movement of Western civilization from its Autumn to its Winter. This is what his long life accomplished. By contrast, his prep school headmaster — now remembered as nothing more than 'a particularly revolting sadist,' 'a perverted sadist,' a 'snob,' and a 'fanatic' — dedicated his very short life, as we will now see, to delaying the onset of Winter.

Chapter Eleven

'Never, never, never give up'

Communion at the Altar

WE EARLIER LOOKED at the petition which Sneyd-Kynnersley signed as an undergraduate at Trinity College, Cambridge, in May 1868. The petition had demanded that communion always happen on Sundays, and on Ascension Day, and only be given to people kneeling at the altar rail. As we observed, this issue was of great symbolic importance, because the lax attitude towards communion, and towards administering it in the traditional fashion, betokened the influence of the Low Church — of evangelicals — at Trinity College, at Cambridge, and in the UK more broadly. The Evangelicals, at that time, were, in certain respects, the ideological ancestors of the postmodernists which Churchill's war unleashed and who have done so much to snow Western civilization into a deeper and deeper winter.

We have already seen that there is fairly wide agreement among what are known as 'social cycle' theorists with regard to the indicators that civilization has reached its summer and is making its way into Autumn. Societies, in the Summer, are characterised by aristocratic rule and by a form of religiousness which binds the society together and is highly ritualistic in nature. This form of religiousness promotes positive and negative ethnocentrism; these qualities themselves being central to societies which triumph over other societies. As such, this society's God (or gods) regards the society as somehow uniquely chosen, with all other societies less godly to varying degrees. Societal membership is, therefore, effectively a matter of bonds of ancestry, though people who refuse to abide by the society's rules — which are divinely ordained — will be exiled or executed. This Cult is crucial to holding the society together, because it promotes cooperation as God's will and exposes those who might defect.

Accepting the Cult's beliefs and rituals implies that you are cooperative and can be trusted. Failure to do so means that you are a rogue agent who cannot be relied upon. Further, due to the importance of positive ethnocentrism in societal survival, if you are a rogue agent then you are a potential defector in times of war and, so, you are thoroughly dangerous. Ritual is, therefore, vital for such a society. Engaging in a religious ritual involves not only a sacrifice — of time and, often, of money — but it shows that whatever you might believe, you want to be part of the community; you are prepared to 'commune' with it, to be in 'communion' with it. Attendance indicates your prosocial personality (see Vaas, 2009). This is why, for example, Elizabeth I made clear that she had no interest in what people actually believed, so long as they attended Anglican communion on Sundays (Loades, 2006, p.137).

Societies, therefore, begin to collapse when they question this form of religiosity; this Cult. This tends to be questioned by those of middling social status, because those of high status benefit from the current system while those at the bottom often have insufficient intelligence to question it. Vico notes this and so do others. During its Autumn, then, it seems to be clear that societal traditions become subject to critique, primarily by non-aristocrats; the intelligentsia. Lacking wealth or ancestry, they stress the importance of education and morality, these being central 'middle class' values which distinguish them from the working class and upper class. For the intelligentsia, education is a good in itself rather than a means to an end (Sawyer, 2005, p.130) and they tend to strongly believe in their own moral superiority (p.205). Accordingly, they leverage their own status through signalling their intellectual faculties and daring in criticising the Cult and signalling their virtue, in advocating a society of equality and kindness. If the social cycle is based around intelligence, there may be an inevitability to this collapse, but there are policies which can slow it down or make it more rapid and more extreme. The Fall of Rome may well have been inevitable, due to the evidence that Roman intelligence was in decline (Dutton & Woodley of Menie, 2018, Ch. 11; Meisenberg, 2007). However, the rise of Christianity is likely to have made the situation considerably worse. The Christians, like the Multiculturalists, attempted to leverage status through signalling their virtue and other desirable psychological qualities, setting off an arms race of the same kind that we see today. It is not accurate to argue that the early Christians were overwhelmingly poor. In reality, they were mainly drawn – as social cycle theories would predict – from the equivalent of the urban middle class: artisans and businessmen (Carroll, 1992, p.78).

The Early Church and Evangelicals

The early Christians refused to participate in the Roman Cult, shunning its rituals, failing to eat meat from animals which had been sacrificed to the Roman gods, and condemning Roman religion as idolatry and devil-worship (see Coutsoumpos, 2015). They insisted that it was not Roman ethnicity and engaging in traditional rituals, which made you part of the in-group. Instead, it was believing that certain dogmas — for which there was no empirical evidence — were true. This is best summarised in the Church Father Tertullian's (c.155-c.240) infamous phrase, 'I believe it because it's absurd.' In order to showcase their faith, adherence to Christianity became based less around ritual and more around virtue-signalling, as a means of showing that you really were somehow purer and more devout than others. As the French philosopher Alain de Benoist (2004) has observed, this led to a reversal of the values which had been normal for the entire history of Roman civilization, and an arms race to deviate from these values as strongly as possible, pushing the values of Rome further and further from those which it had held during the heights of its civilization. You demonstrated the extent of your Christian fervour by (overtly at least) eschewing material wealth; by rejecting sex, by quite openly embracing the poor and sick; by raising, rather than getting rid of, babies who were deformed and likely to die young; by keeping unwanted pregnancies; and by showing deep compassion and forgiveness to criminals and outcasts. For the Christians, people were not to be looked up to because of their ancestry, but only due to their Christian piety. This reversal of values meant that 'the last shall be first' and that foreigners should be permitted to enter the society, so long as they professed to be Christian. This kind of society — low in negative ethnocentrism due to the nature of its new religion — would, of course, lose its martial values, be invaded from outside and Balkanize, just as computer models have demonstrated. Rome was an exhausted yet relatively luxurious society, it began to question its Cult, it adopted Christianity, and this directly contributed to its decline, as it became a multi-ethnic state with religious belief — rather than ancestry and related ritual observance — as the key test of membership (see Thompson, 2002).

A new 'Christian' civilization emerged from the ashes of the Dark Ages. It had developed its own Cult through syncretizing aspects of monotheistic Christianity and polytheistic paganism (Maroney, 2006). Religious belief was more central to this Cult than it generally was in polytheistic societies, where, de Benoist observes, there is little in the way of religious dogma. However, broadly, beneath a monotheistic veneer, Europe had developed a new Pagan cult. Protestantism — with its puritanical, virtue-signalling, questioning nature — played a central role, it might be argued, in creating a movement back towards the Early Church. Rather than conform to the Cult, it stressed that salvation lay in the individual's personal relationship with God, which would be duly reflected in his strongly moral behaviour and even his being materially blessed by God (see McGrath, 2007). However, those countries which adopted Protestantism soon managed to syncretize it into, in essence, a new, albeit slightly more puritanical, Cult. For example, though England went through a phase, under Edward VI (r. 1547-1553), of being a pronounced Protestant society, it soon developed its own Cult once more. This was overtly theologically Protestant. However, it maintained most of the rituals and general feel of Roman Catholicism: this was the Anglican settlement. Under this Cult, England was uniquely blessed by God, Englishness was clearly a matter of blood and ancestry as ordained by God, society participated in Anglican rituals and the very nature of society was underpinned by the belief in and acceptance of this Cult. It was under this Cult — though there were Catholics and Non-Conformists who questioned the Cult — that the British Empire reached its heights. This is the Cult which has been so rapidly dismantled since Churchill's war.

The Victorian evangelicals who Sneyd-Kynnersley opposed with the petition to the master of his college, stood in opposition to the Cult which was so central to the British Empire. They were extreme Protestants; latter-day Puritans in many respects. They also tended to come from outside the aristocracy. They were mainly professional middle class people, playing for social status through campaigns against issues such as drunkenness (Kucich, 2009, p.55). For the evangelicals, you were not a member of the in-group by virtue of your participation in traditional ritual and adherence to traditional modes of behaviour. Just as with the Early Church, being a part of the in-group was a matter of accepting certain dogmas and your personal relationship with God, which meant that you accepted these dogmas. This — and middle class status more generally — would be evidenced by virtue-signalling behaviour such as not swearing, shunning alcohol, maintaining extreme sexual constancy, dressing modestly, expressing moral outrage when people deviated from this code and so on (see McEnery, 2006; Argyle, 1994: Dutton, 2007). This sanctimoniousness would extend to the political advocacy of equality: better prison conditions, fairer labour laws, extension of the voting franchise to working class men, the promotion of contraception, and the restriction of the influence of the Cult, with non-members being permitted to enter Oxford, Cambridge and Durham Universities by law as of 1871 (Barclay & Horn, 2002). Indeed, the Victorian age was punctuated by a series of 'moral panics' among the educated classes about such issues as drunkenness among the working class (see McEnery, 2006). This led to the usual arms race, with the result that by the end of the Victorian Era society was not only immensely puritanical but Non-Conformism was very influential, especially in the Labour Movement, which inherently questioned the tradition of aristocratic rule. Professional class, virtue-signalling and evangelical influence had pushed the so-called 'Overton Window' — the range of opinions that are acceptable in public — further and further away from the traditions that were normal during the summer of civilization.

The Victorian Feeling of Gloom

So, the 1868 petition can be understood, ultimately, as an attempt to preserve the traditions at the heart of a dominant civilization — and especially its religious traditions — against those who would question them in order to elevate their own status through displays of their supposed virtue. Sneyd-Kynnersley's entire career could be understood as an attempt to hold back the avalanche of civilization's descent into winter. He tried to achieve this in two ways. He would happily take advantage of improvements which aided society; in fact, he was a pioneer in so-doing, meaning aspects of his school were extremely fashionable. Electric light meant that you could read more easily while the ability to swim — swimming having only become fashionable in the 1870s (Love, 2013, p.xii) — would clearly be very useful for future Naval cadets and it was a way of keeping fit. Pupils should be intellectually stimulated, allowing them to reach their potential, so out went the learning by rote which is associated with Victorian schools. Under Sneyd-Kynnersley, you learnt by doing —gardening, acting, numerous fascinating school trips — and you were inspired to love literature by the headmaster's own enthusiasm and his 'sumptuous prizes.' In all these ways, he was a pioneer – but this would have been with a view to making British civilization even better, through stimulating its future leaders.

However, he also attempted to preserve civilization from degeneration by reviving earlier traditions, which he regarded as vital and which were already on the wane. At a time when schools were beginning to embrace science, Sneyd-Kynnersley wrote a number of books on how best to teach Latin and Ancient Greek. At a time when public schools were moving towards using the cane, Sneyd-Kynnersley used the birch. At a time when evangelicalism had strongly permeated society, Sneyd-Kynnersley's religious services were firmly High Church, and his pupils — the potential future leaders of the country — were inculcated with a deep loathing for the Liberal Party, a party which pushed acceptable opinion ever-leftwards, further and further away from the opinions held when English civilization had borne fruit during the heights of summer.

It must be remembered that by the 1860s, the intellectual elite in the UK were increasingly of the view that British society, whatever its power in the world, was in decline. It was abundantly clear to then famous scientists such as Charles Darwin and Sir Francis Galton that industrialization had made life far too comfortable. Until the Industrial Revolution, the wealthier 50% of the population had about double than number of surviving children than did the poorer 50% of the population, something which has been discerned from surviving wills and parish records, as we have already noted (Clark, 2007). Given the robust association, of about 0.3, between income and intelligence (Jensen, 1998), it follows that pre-Industrial conditions — which, effectively, were conditions of strong Darwinian selection — selected for intelligence, as intelligence meant you could provide better conditions for your children, due to your wealth, making it more likely they'd survive into adulthood. Child mortality was about 40% on average — even higher among the poor — meaning that only the fittest, and most intelligent, survived into adulthood. Society became more and more intelligent, until the breakthrough of the Industrial Revolution. Consistent with this, markers of intelligence — such as literacy, numeracy, and low levels of violence — rose from the Medieval period to 1800, despite little increase in living standards. Per capita levels of important inventions, underpinned by per capita very high IQ people, also increased (Dutton & Woodley of Menie, 2018, Ch.4).

However, industrialization — with its resultant better living conditions, superior medicine and vaccinations — changed this. People were noticing that the less well off — whom they (correctly) felt were in that state due to deficiencies in 'wit' and 'character' (Jensen, 1998) — seemed to have the most children, while men from the higher classes appeared to have the fewest. Believing, correctly as it turned out, that these qualities were largely inherited (see Lynn, 2011), they feared the eventual collapse of civilization. And they were perfectly clear that Britain was, by then, an old civilization. In *Descent of Man*, Charles Darwin (1871) argued that as societies become more advanced they become more compassionate towards their weaker members, leading to the society's decline.

> 'With savages, the weak in body or mind are soon eliminated; and those that survive commonly exhibit a vigorous state of health. We civilised men, on the other hand, do our utmost to check the process of elimination; we build asylums for the imbecile, the maimed, and the sick; we institute poor-laws; and our medical men exert their utmost skill to save the life of every one to the last moment. There is reason to believe that vaccination has preserved thousands, who from a weak constitution would formerly have succumbed to small-pox. Thus the weak members of civilised societies propagate their kind. No one who has attended to the breeding of domestic animals will doubt that this must be highly injurious to the race of man. It is surprising how soon a want of care, or care wrongly directed, leads to the degeneration of a domestic race; but excepting in the case of man himself, hardly any one is so ignorant as to allow his worst animals to breed (Darwin, 1871, p.501).

Galton (1865, p.325) noted in 1865 that:

> 'One of the effects of civilisation is to diminish the rigour of the application of the law of Natural Selection. It preserves weakly lives that would have perished in barbarous lands. The sickly children of a wealthy family have a better chance of living and rearing offspring than the stalwart children of a poor one.'

He added that 'the weak members of civilized societies propagate their kind' leading to 'degeneration.' Galton (1869, p.414) wrote that:

> 'there is a steady check in an old civilisation upon the fertility of the abler classes: the improvident and unambitious are those

who chiefly keep up the breed. So the race gradually deteriorates, becoming in each successive generation less fit for a high civilisation.'

In other words, in an old civilization — just as happened in ancient Rome — the comfortable upper class and intelligentsia are so low in stress that they start questioning religion and tradition, including even the expectation to have children, 'natalism' as they term it, in such books as *Debating Procreation: Is it Wrong to Reproduce?* (Benatar & Wasserman, 2015). They become individualistic, solely intellectually-inclined, career-focused and disinterested in having children. Certainly, intelligence does indeed correlate with not wanting to have children in contemporary Western societies (Kanazawa, 2012, pp.179-180). This, among other factors, results in, as Galton argued, children being a product of the less intelligent. Sneyd-Kynnersley lived in a society in which the educated increasingly felt this sense of pessimism about the future. His career involved attempting to turn back the tide, or at least buying some time before it broke through the defences, both by reviving traditions at the heart of civilization and taking full advantage of the occasional useful piece of autumn fruit. This is, in so many ways, a preferable legacy to Churchill's one, of marching civilization to its winter as quickly as possible.

Getting the Balance Wrong

As we have discussed, the public school system was supposed to turn 'barbarous young men' into responsible 'gentlemen' — capable of running the Empire — through a system of pronounced but controlled violence and other forms of discipline. A high functioning psychopath, like Churchill, with little natural care for the feelings of others and a low desire to follow the rules, would have required a particularly harsh and constant regime in order to be 'broken' into an English gentleman. This is what he needed and this is what Sneyd-Kynnersley was more than happy to provide.

The headmaster got the balance slightly wrong, with incalculable consequences for the British Empire and its motherland. Had Sneyd-Kynnersley been slightly more original, perhaps employing the electrocutions favoured by his brother-in-law, and had he paid more attention to Churchill's health, then Churchill's wounds wouldn't have been severe enough to be of note, he may not have become unwell, he would likely not have been withdrawn from the school, and he could have been fully broken down; reducing his psychopathic tendencies to the minimum and likely sparing Britain World War II and all that has followed on from that. As Churchill (1931, p.243) himself wrote:

> If I had to live my life over again in the same surroundings no doubt I should have the same perplexities and hesitations; no doubt I should have the same sense of proportion, my same guiding lights, my same onward thrust, my same limitations. And if these came in contact with the same external facts, why should I not run as the result along exactly the same grooves? Of course, if the externals are varied, if accident and chance flow out through new uncharted channels, I shall vary accordingly. But then I should not be living my life over again, I should be living another life in a world whose structure and history would to a large extent diverge from this one.'

'Come Friendly Bombs and Fall on Slough . . .'

Sneyd-Kynnersley was too engrossed in shepherding the first division boys onto the train that July day to notice Maurice Baring passing through the station. The headmaster sparkled with excitement; even more so than his pupils. He was taking them to London; to the capital of the Empire! They were going to visit the Tower . . . and Sneyd-Kynnersley already found himself imagining that he was a sixteenth century courtier, dashing across the ancient cobbles carrying an urgent message for Henry VIII himself. He could not wait. And then afterwards, he'd booked a table at a hotel for a dinner that would be Heaven on a plate. The boys were going to be thrilled.

As the train pulled in and the air filled with smoke, he looked over Slough, where he'd once taught. Eighty years later, lady representatives of the people of Slough would be at the home of a passionately pro-Empire politician, who had demanded an end to the nation-changing influx of South Asian Muslim immigrants, brandishing a petition in support of him (Schwartz, 2011, p.40). One hundred and thirty years hence, some of these immigrants to Slough would be jailed for plying teenage English girls with alcohol before persuading them to have sex (*Slough and Bucks Observer*, 16th February 2015). And it could all be traced back to one former pupil of his whom he simply hadn't had quite enough time to tame.

Never, in the history of human civilization has so much rested on what one headmaster did or didn't do to one boy's arse.

References

Abbott, M. (1993). *Family Ties: English Families, 1540-1920.* London: Routledge.

Abel, R.L. (1998). *The Making of the English Legal Profession, 1800-1988.* Washington, DC: Beard Books.

Aberbach, D. (1996). *Charisma in Politics, Religion and the Media: Private Trauma, Public Ideals.* London: Palgrave Macmillan.

Abrantes, R. (1997). *Dog Language: An Encyclopedia of Canine Behavior.* Wanatchee: Wakantanka.

Addington-Dawson, C.A. & Gettys, W. (1935). *An Introduction to Sociology.* New York: Ronald Press.

Addison, P. (2017). Churchill and Women. In Toye, R. (Ed). *Winston Churchill: Politics, Strategy and Statecraft.* London: Bloomsbury.

Addison, P. (2013). *Churchill on the Home Front, 1900-1955.* London: Faber & Faber.

Addison, P. (2006). *Churchill: The Unexpected Hero.* Oxford: Oxford University Press.

A. G. B. (1900). H.F. Sneyd-Kynnersley. *The Marlburian,* XXXV: 546.

Ainslie, D. (1922). *Adventures Social and Literary.* New York: E.P. Dutton.

Akins, C. (2004). The Role of Pavlovian Conditions in Sexual Behavior: A Comparative Analysis of Human and Nonhuman Animals. *International Journal of Comparative Psychology,* 17: 241-262.

Alberini, C. & Le Doux, J. (2013). Memory reconciliation. *Current Biology,* 23: 1-7.

Almanach de Gotha. (1900). Gotha: Justus Perthes.

American Psychiatric Association. (2013). *Diagnostic and Statistical Manual of Mental Disorders (5th ed.).* Arlington, VA: American Psychiatric Publishing.

Antony, M. (2009). *The Masculine Century, Part Two: From Darwinism to Feminism: The Rise of Ideologies of Aggression.* Bloomington, IN: iUniverse.

Appleton's Journal of Literature, Science and Art. (30th April 1870). Table Talk.

Argyle, M. (1994). *The Psychology of Social Class.* London: Routledge.

Attenborough, R. (Dir.). (1972). *Young Winston.*

Attenborough, W. (2014). *Churchill and the 'Black Dog' of Depression: Reassessing the Biographical Evidence of Psychological Disorder.* London: Palgrave Macmillan.

Backhouse, E. (2017). *The Dead Past.* Jordaan, P. (Ed). Alchemy Books.

Badcock, C. (2003). Mentalism and mechanism: Twin modes of human cognition. In Crawford, C. & Salman, C. (Eds.). *Human Nature and Social Values: Implications of Evolutionary Psychology for Public Policy.* Mahwah, NJ: Erlbaum.

Bahnsen, D. (7th 2008). *Churchill, Hitler, and the Unnecessary War* by Patrick Buchannan. *Red Country.* (This reference was found via a Wikipedia page on Buchanan's book).

Bakewell, M. (1996). *Lewis Carroll: A Biography.* London: Mandarin.

Baldwin, D. (2015). *Richard III.* Stroud: Amberley Publishing.

Balmer, R. (2004). *Encyclopedia of Evangelicalism.* Waco, TX: Baylor University Press.

Balon, R. (2016a). Introduction to the Realm of Paraphilias. In Balon, R. (Ed). *Practical Guide to Paraphilia and Paraphiliac Disorders.* New York: Springer.

Balon, R. (2016b). General Information: History, Etiology and Theory (e.g., Courtship), Diagnosis, Comorbidity and Prevalence. In Balon, R. (Ed). *Practical Guide to Paraphilia and Paraphiliac Disorders.* New York: Springer.

Barclay, O. & Horn, R. (2002). *From Cambridge to the World: 125 Years of Student Witness.* Leicester: Intervarsity Press.

Baring, M. (1934). *C.* London: William Heinemann.

Baring, M. (1922). *The Puppet Show of Memory.* London: William Heinemann.

Barnett, C. (2002). *The Verdict of Peace: Britain Between Her Yesterday and the Future.* London: Pan Books.

Baron-Cohen, S. (2002). The extreme male brain theory of autism. *Trends in Cognitive Sciences,* 6: 248-254.

Barton, A. (2012). *Alfred Lord Tennyson's 'In Memoriam.'* Edinburgh: Edinburgh University Press.

Barton, C. & Douglas, G. (1995). *Law and Parenthood.* Cambridge: Cambridge University Press.

Beard, M. (2010). *Pompeii: Life in an Ancient Roman Town.* London: Profile Books.

Bebbington, D. W. (1989). *Evangelicalism in Modern Britain: A History from the 1730s to the 1980s.* London: Routledge.

Benacek, V. (2001). History of Czech Economic and Political Alignments Viewed as Transition. In Salvatore, D., Svetlicic, M. & Damijan, J. (Eds.). *Small Countries in a Global Economy: New Challenges and Opportunities.* London: Palgrave Macmillan.

Benatar, D. & Wasserman, D. (2015). *Debating Procreation: Is it Wrong to Reproduce?* Oxford: Oxford University Press.

Benes, R. (20th April 2017). How the Catholic priesthood became an unlikely haven for gay men.*Slate,* http://www.slate.com/blogs/outward/2017/04/20/how_the_catholic_priesthood_became_a_haven_for_many_gay_men.html

Benson, E.F. (1916). *David Blaize.* New York: George H. Doran Company.

Benton, S. (28th April 2009). Social Drinkers, Problem Drinkers and Alcoholics. *Psychology Today,* https://www.psychologytodaycom/us/blogthe-highfunctioning-alcoholic/200904social-drinkers-problem-drinkers-and-alcoholics

Berkshire Chronicle. (7th April 1883). Stealing Rabbits at Sunninghill.

Best, G. (2005). *Churchill and War.* London: A.&C. Black.

Best, G. (2001). *Churchill: A Study in Greatness.* London: Hambledon Continuum.

Bexhill-On-Sea Observer. (25th February 1911). A Snail's Wooing.

Bicester Herald. (16th August 1912). Marriages.

Bird, S. (1st July 2018). Winston Churchill was 'probably sexually abused' as a boy, House of Cards creator claims. *Daily Telegraph,* https://www.telegraph.co.uk/news/2018/07/01/winston-churchill-probably-sexually-abused-boy-house-cards-creator/

Blanchard, R. (2008). Review and theory of handedness, birth order, and homosexuality in men. *Laterality,* 13: 51-70.

Blanchard, R. (2000). Fraternal Birth Order and Sexual Orientation in Pedophiles. *Archives of Sexual Behaviour,* 5: 463-478.

Bluck, S. (2003). Autobiographical memory: Exploring its functions in everyday life. *Memory,* 11: 113-123.

Bloch, M. (1992). *Prey Into Hunter: The Politics of Religious Experience.* Cambridge: Cambridge University Press.

Boden, A. & Hedley, P. (2017). *The Three Choirs Festival: A History.* Woodbridge: The Boydell Press.

Boyer, P. (2001). *Religion Explained: The Human Instincts that Fashion Gods, Spirits and Ancestors.* London: William Heinemann.

Bowen, J. (1975). *A History of Western Education: Civilization of Europe, Sixth to Sixteenth Century.* Vol. 2. London: Routledge.

Bradby, H.C. (1900). *Rugby.* London: George Bell & Sons.

Bradley, G.G. (1858). *Mr Bradley's Testimonials.* Rugby.

Brainerd, C. & Reyna, V. (2005). *The Science of False Memory.* Oxford: Oxford University Press.

Brasenose College Register. (1909). Volume I. Oxford: Basil Blackwell.

Brenan, G. (1979). *A Life of Ones Own: Childhood and Youth.* Cambridge: Cambridge University Press.

Brendon, V. (2009). *Prep School Children: A Class Apart Over Two Centuries.* London: Bloomsbury.

Briggs, J. (2007). *Virginia Woolf: An Inner Life.* London: Penguin.

Brown, R. (2002). *Church and State in Modern Britain, 1700-1850.* London: Routledge.

Buchanan, P.J. (2008). *Hitler, Churchill, and the Unnecessary War: How Britain Lost Its Empire and the West Lost the World.* New York: Crown Publishers.

Buchanan, P.J. (2001). *The Death of the West: How Dying Populations and Immigrant Invasions Imperil Our Culture and Civilization.* New York: St Martin's Griffin.

Buck, N. (12th September 2011). To Spank or Not to Spank? Is that Really Still a Question? *Psychology Today,* https://www.psychologytoday.com/us/blog/peaceful-parenting/201109/spank-or-not-spank-is-really-still-question

Burke's Landed Gentry. (1912). London.

Burke, B. (1898). *A Genealogical and Heraldic History of the Landed Gentry of Great Britain and Ireland.* London: Henry Colburn.

Burke, B. (1882). *A Genealogical and Heraldic History of the Landed Gentry of Great Britain and Ireland.* London. London: Harrison.

Burke, B. (1879). *A Genealogical and Heraldic History of the Landed Gentry of Great Britain and Ireland.* London. London: Harrison.

Burke, B. (1852). *A Genealogical and Heraldic Dictionary of the Landed Gentry of Great Britain and Ireland for 1852.* London: Colburn & Co.

Burke, J. (1835). *A Genealogical and Heraldic History of the Commoners of Great Britain and Ireland, Enjoying Territorial Possessions or High Official Rank but Uninvested with Heritable Honours.* London: Henry Colburn.

Burke, P. (2005). *History and Social Theory.* Cambridge: Polity Press.

Buss, D. (1989). *The Evolution of Desire: Strategies of Human Mating.* New York: Basic Books.

Campbell, A. (1885). *Records of Argyll: Legends, Traditions and Recollections of Argyllshire Highlanders.* Edinburgh: William Blackwood & Sons.

Campbell, J. (2011). *Margaret Thatcher: Volume One: The Grocer's Daughter.* New York: Random House.

Campbell, W.K. & Miller, J. (2011). *The Handbook of Narcissism and Narcissistic Personality Disorder: Theoretical Approaches, Empirical Findings, and Treatments.* Hoboken, NJ: John Wiley & Sons.

Cannon, J. (1987). *Aristocratic Century: The Peerage of Eighteenth-Century England.* Cambridge: Cambridge University Press.

Carroll, M. (2005). *The Cult of the Virgin Mary: Psychological Origins.* Princeton: Princeton University Press.

Carson, D., Foster, J. & Tripathi, N. (2013). Child sexual abuse in India: Current issues and research. *Psychological Studies,* 3: 318-325.

Cartledge, P. (2003). *Spartan Reflections.* Berkeley: University of California Press.

Charmley, D. (1999). *Chamberlain and the Lost Peace.* London: Ivan R. Dee.

Charmley, D. (1993). *Churchill: The End of Glory: A Political Biography.* London: Faber & Faber.

Cheshire Observer. (16th July 1904). Death of Mr C.W. Sneyd-Kynnersley.

Chisholm, H. (Ed). (1911). Douglas, John. *Encyclopædia Britannica. 8 (11th ed.).* Cambridge: Cambridge University Press.

Christian, P. & Annal, D. (2014). *Census: The Family Historian's Guide.* London: Bloomsbury.

Churchill, R. (1966). *Winston S. Churchill: Youth, 1874-1900.* New York: Houghton Mifflin.

Churchill, W.S (1931). A Second Chance. *The Strand Magazine.* Volume 81.

Churchill, W.S. (1930). *My Early Life: A Roving Commission.* London: Oldham's Press.

Churchill, W.S. (1898). *The Story of the Malakand Field Force: An Episode of Frontier War.* London: Dover Publications.

Cinalli, G., Maixner, W. & Sainte-Rose, C. (Eds.). (2012). *Pediatric Hydrocephalus.* New York: Springer.

Clark, A. (2nd January 1993). A reputation ripe for revision. *The Times.*

Clark, G. (2014). *The Son Also Rises: Surnames and the History of Social Mobility.* Princeton: Princeton University Press.

Clark, G. (2007). *A Farewell to Alms: A Brief Economic History of the World.* Princeton, NJ: Princeton University Press.

Clayton, P. & Rowbotham, J. (2009). How the mid-Victorians worked, ate and died. *International Journal of Environmental Research and Public Health,* 6: 1235-1253.

Coates, R. (1998). Onomastics. In Romaine, S. (Ed). *The Cambridge History of the English Language, 1776-1997.* Cambridge: Cambridge University Press.

Cohen, D. (2018). *Churchill and Attlee: The Unlikely Allies Who Won the War.* London: Bite Back Publishing.

Cohen, M. (2013). *Churchill and the Jews, 1900-1948.* London: Routledge.

Colarusso, C. (2010). *The Long Shadow of Sexual Abuse: Developmental Effects Across the Life Cycle.* New York: Jason Aronson.

Coles, P. (2015). *The Shadow of the Second Mother: Nurses and Nannies in Theories of Infant Development.* London: Routledge.

Committee on Understanding Premature Birth. (2007). *Preterm Birth: Causes, Consequences and Prevention.* Washington, DC: National Academies Press.

Conry-Murray, C. (2015). Children's Judgments of Inequitable Distributions That Conform to Gender Norms. *Merrill-Palmer Quarterly,* 61: 319-344.

Conway, M. & Pleydell-Pearce, C. (2000). The Construction of Autobiographical Memories in the Self-Memory System. *Psychological Review,* 107: 261-288.

Copsey, N. (2016). *Public Opinion and the Making of Foreign Policy in the 'New Europe': A Comparative Study of Poland and Ukraine.* London: Routledge.

Corfield, P. (1996). The Rivals: Landed and Other Gentlemen. In Harte, N.B. & Quinault, R. (Eds.). *Land and Society in Britain, 1700-1914.* Manchester: Manchester University Press.

Coss, P. (2005). *The Origins of the English Gentry.* Cambridge: Cambridge University Press.

Coutsoumpos, P. (2015). *Paul, Corinth, and the Roman Empire.* Eugene, OR: Wipf & Stock Publishers.

Cowan, J.D. (1914). *An Ancient Irish Parish: Past and Present, Being the Parish of Donaghmore, County Down.* London: David Nutt.

Cox, C. & Luddy, M. (2010). *Cultures of Care in Irish Medical History, 1750-1970.* London: Palgrave Macmillan.

Crake, A.D. (1883). *The Last Abbot of Glastonbury: A Tale of the Dissolution of the Monasteries.* London: Mowbray.

Crisp, F. (1919). *The Visitation of England and Wales, Volume 20.* Privately Printed.

Crockford's Clerical Directory. (1908). Macdonald, Robert Estcourt. Oxford: Oxford University Press.

Cukic, I. & Bates, T. (2015). The association between Neuroticism and heart rate variability is not fully explained by cardiovascular disease and depression. *PLoS One,* 10(5): e0125882.

Cust, L. (1899). *A History of Eton College.* London: Duckworth & Co.

D'Este, C. (2009). *Warlord: A Life of Winston Churchill at War, 1874-1945.* New York: HarperCollins.

Darwin, C. (1871). *The Descent of Man.* London: John Murray.

Dahl, R. (1984). *Boy.* New York: Cape.

Davidoff, L. & Hall, C. (1987). *Family Fortunes: Men and Women of the English Middle Class, 1780–1850*. London: Routledge.

Davies, M. (1970). Blood pressure and personality. *Journal of Psychosomatic Research*, 14: 89-104.

Davis, K. (18th February 2018). Ten health risks of chronic heavy drinking. *Medical News Today*, https://www.medicalnewstoday.com/articles/297734.php

Davis, M., Zautra, A. & Smith, B. (2004). Chronic Pain, Stress, and the Dynamics of Affective Differentiation. *Journal of Personality*, 72: 1133-1159.

De Benoist, A. (2004). *On Being a Pagan*. Atlanta, GA: Ultra.

De Fruyt, F. & Mervielde, I. (1996). Personality and interests as predictors of educational streaming and achievement. *European Journal of Personality*, 10: 405-425.

De Lisle, G. (Ed.). (1870). *Marlborough College Register, From 1843 to 1869 Inclusive*. Marlborough, Wiltshire: Marlborough College.

De Symons Honey, J.R. (1977). *Tom Brown's Universe: The Development of the Victorian Public School*. London: Millington.

Deary, T. (2016). *Villainous Victorians: Splats, Hats and Lots of Rats*. London: Scholastic Books.

Debrett's Peerage. (1879). The Earls of Charleville. London.

Dell, A. (2007). Joseph Sandars, Quaker. *Magazine of the Buckinghamshire Family History Society*, 31: 117-120.

Dellamora, R. (1990). *Masculine Desire: The Sexual Politics of Victorian Aestheticism*. Chapel Hill: University of North Carolina Press.

Demshuk, A. (2012). *The Lost German East: Forced Migration and the Politics of Memory, 1945–1970*. Cambridge: Cambridge University Press.

Derby Daily Telegraph. (25th August 1905). Fatal Trap Accident: Minister's Wife Killed.

Derbyshire Advertiser and Journal. (4th March 1859). Uttoxeter.

DeSalvo, L. (1990). *Virginia Woolf: The Impact of Child Sexual Abuse On Her Life and Work*. New York: Ballantine Books.

Disraeli, B. (1982). *Benjamin Disraeli Letters: 1842-1847*. Toronto: University of Toronto Press.

Dobbs, M. (2003). *Never Surrender – A Novel of Winston Churchill*. New York: HarperCollins.

Dorset County Chronicle. (24th April 1879). A Remarkably Good Tea.

Douglas-Hamilton, J. (2012). *The Truth About Rudolf Hess*. New York: Random House.

Dozier, E. (1954). *The Hopi-Tewa of Arizona*. Berkeley: University of California Press.

Dundee Courier. (12th August 1930). Best Sellers of a Bygone Day.

Dutton, E. (2019). Why are Non-Heterosexuals Attracted to Religious Celibacy? A Case for the 'Gay Shaman' Theory. *Mankind Quarterly*, 59: 2.

Dutton, E. (July 2018). Exploring Ancestors' Ages. *Family Tree*.

Dutton, E. (2018). Women marry up. In Shackelford, T. & Shackelford-Weeks, V. (Eds.). *Encyclopaedia of Evolutionary Psychological Science*. New York: Springer.

Dutton, E. (2015). *The Ruler of Cheshire: Sir Piers Dutton, Tudor Gangland and the Violent Politics of the Palatine*. Northwich, Cheshire: Léonie Press.

Dutton, E. (2008). *Meeting Jesus at University: Rites of Passage and Student Evangelicals*. Aldershot: Ashgate.

Dutton, E. (2007). "Bog off Dog Breath! You're Talking Pants!" Swearing as Witness Evangelism in Student Evangelical Groups. *Journal of Religion and Popular Culture*, XVI.

Dutton, E. & Madison, G. (2019). The Evolution of Punishment. In Shackelford, T. & Shackelford-Weekes, V. (Eds.). *The Encyclopedia of Evolutionary Psychological Science*. New York: Springer.

Dutton, E. & Woodley of Menie, M.A. (2018). *At Our Wits' End: Why We're Becoming Less Intelligent and What It Means for the Future*. Exeter: Imprint Academic.

Dutton, E. & Madison, G. (2018). Why do middle-class couples of European descent adopt children from Africa and Asia? Some Support for the Differential *K* Model. *Personality and Individual Differences*, 160-156 :130.

Dutton, E., Madison, G. & Lynn, R. (2016). Demographic, economic, and genetic factors related to national differences in ethnocentric attitudes. *Personality and Individual Differences*, 101: 137-143.

Dutton, E. & Charlton, B. (2015). *The Genius Famine: Why We Need Geniuses, Why They're Dying Out and Why We Must Rescue Them*. Buckingham: University of Buckingham Press.

Dutton, K. (2012). *The Wisdom of Psychopaths*. New York: Random House.

Easton, L.M. (2011). *Journey to the Abyss: The Diaries of Count Harry Kessler, 1880-1918*. New York: Alfred A. Knopf.

Easton, L.M. (2002). *The Red Count: The Life and Times of Harry Kessler*. Los Angeles: University of California Press.

Electrical Review. (18th December 1891). Volume 29.

Epstein, S. (1971). *Winston Churchill: Lion of Britain*. New York: Gerard Publishing.

Erickson, A. (2002). *Women and Property in Early Modern England*. London: Routledge.

Essex Winter, W. & Chetwood, T. (Eds.). *Epsom College Register, From October, 1855 to July, 1905*. London: Richard Clay & Sons.

Exeter and Plymouth Gazette. (24th August 1887). Wedding at St James' Church.

Farrell, A. (1964). *Winston Churchill*. New York: G.P. Putnam's Sons.

Feddon, R. (2014). *Churchill at Chartwell*. London: Pergamon Press.

Ferguson, C.L. (1931). *A History of the Magpie and Stump Debating Society, 1866-1926*. London: W. Heffer & Sons.

Feist, G. (1998). A Meta-Analysis of Personality in Scientific and Artistic Creativity. *Personality and Social Psychology Review*, 2: 290-309.

Fern, S. (2014). *The Man Who Killed Richard III*. Stroud: Amberley Publishing.

Festinger, L. (1957). *A Theory of Cognitive Dissonance*. Stanford, CA: Stanford University Press.

Feyn, K., MacCann, C., Tilopoulos, N. & Silvia, P. (2015). Aesthetic Emotions and Aesthetic People: Openness Predicts Sensitivity to Novelty in the Experiences of Interest and Pleasure. *Frontiers in Psychology*, doi: 10.3389/fpsyg.2015.01877

Foley, J. (1998). *The Road to Chartley: Ghosts, Legends and Stories of the A518*. Stafford: Jim Foley.

Forster, E.M. (1965). *Two Cheers for Democracy*. London: Penguin.

Foster, J. (1891). *Alumni Oxonienses*. Oxford: James Parker & Co.

Foster, J. (1885). *Men at the Bar*. London: Hazell, Watson & Viney.

Fox-Davies, A. (1929). *Armorial Families: A Directory of Gentlemen of Coat Armour*. London: Hurst & Blackett.

Fox-Davies, A. (1900). *The Right to Bear Arms*. London: Elliot Stock.

Fraser, G. (5th February 2017). Like John Smyth's accusers, I bear the scars of a muscular Christian education. *Guardian*, https://www.theguardian.com/commentisfree/2017/feb/05/john-smyth-public-school-christianity-brutality-thrashings-evangelical-decency

Fraser, N. (2012). *The Importance of Being Eton: Inside the World's Most Powerful School*. London: Short Books.

Freemon, F.R. (2012). *Organic Mental Disease*. Lancaster: MTP Press.

Fremantle, A. (27th October 1967). Review: *Long Shadows* by Shane Leslie. *The Commonweal*.

Friedman, H., Tucker, J., Tomlinson-Keasey, C. et al. (1993). Does childhood personality predict longevity? *Journal of Personality and Social Psychology*, 65: 176-185.

Frost, G. (2008). *Victorian Childhoods*. Westport, CT: Praeger.

Frydman, M. & Lynn, R. (1992). The general intelligence and spatial abilities of gifted young Belgian chess players. *British Journal of Psychology*, 83: 233-235.

Fuchs, T. (2000). *A Concise Biography of Adolf Hitler*. London: Penguin.

Furnivall, F. (Ed). (1868). *The Babees Book*. London: The Early English Text Society.

Gabb, S. (2007). *Culture Revolution, Culture War: How the Conservatives Lost England and How to Get It Back Again*. London: The Hampden Press.

Gadd, D. (1974). *The Loving Friends: A Portrait of Bloomsbury*. London: The Hogarth Press.

Galanter, M. (1998). *Cults: Faith, Healing and Coercion*. London: Routledge.

Galton, F. (1906). *Noteworthy Families (Modern Science): An Index to Kinships in Near Degrees Between Persons Whose Achievements Are Honourable, and Have Been Publicly Recorded*. London: John Murray.

Galton, F. (1869). *Hereditary Genius*. London: Macmillan.

Galton, F. (1865). Hereditary talent and character. *MacMillan's Magazine*.

Gathorne-Hardy, J. (1978). *The Old School Tie: The Phenomenon of the English Public School*. New York: The Viking Press.

Gathorne-Hardy, J. (1972). *The Rise and Fall of the British Nanny*. London: Hodder & Stoughton.

Gardner, B. (1968). *Churchill in His Time: A Study in Reputation, 1939-1945*. London: Methuen.

Gebauer, J., Bleidorn, W., Gosling, S. et al. (2014). Cross-Cultural variations in Big Five relationships with religiosity: A sociocultural motives perspective. *Journal of Personality and Social Psychology*, 107: 1064-1091.

Gibson, I. (1978). *The English Vice: Beating, Sex, and Shame in Victorian England and After*. London: Duckworth.

Gilbert, G. (2014). *Psychodynamic Psychiatry in Clinical Practice, Fifth Edition*. Washington, DC: American Psychiatric Publishing.

Giuliani, S. (5th July 2018). Abusi e violenze, la terribile infanzia di Churchill secondo il creatore di House of Cards. *Il Giornale*, http://www.ilgiornale.it/news/cultura/abusi-e-violenze-terribile-infanzia-churchill-secondo-1549085.html

Glassheim, E. (2016). *Cleansing the Czechoslovak Borderlands: Migration, Environment, and Health in the Former Sudetenland*. Pittsburgh: University of Pittsburgh Press.

Gleadle, K. (2001). *British Women in the Nineteenth Century*. Basingstoke: Palgrave.

Goldfrank, E. (1945). Socialization, Personality, and the Structure of Pueblo Society (with Particular Reference to the Hopi and Zuni). *American Anthropologist*, 47: 516-539.

Gottfredson, L. (1997). Editorial: Mainstream science on intelligence. *Intelligence*, 24: 13-24.

Graham Hall, J. (2003). *Yes, Lord Chancellor: A Biography of Lord Schuster - Permanent Secretary to 10 Lord Chancellors*. London: Barry Rose Law Publishers.

Griffith, E.J. (1913). *Report of the Departmental Committee on Reformatory and Industrial Schools*. London: HMSO.

Grim, J. (1987). *The Shaman: Patterns of Healing Among the Obibway Indians*. Norman: University of Oklahoma Press.

Gronn, P. (1999). *The Making of Educational Leaders*. London: A. & C. Black.

Guardian. (19th August 1891). Marriages.

Guest, J. (Ed.). (1989). *The Best of Betjeman.* London: Penguin Books.

Gunderson, J. (2009). *Borderline Personality Disorder: A Clinical Guide.* Washington, DC: American Psychiatric Association.

Haig, A. (1984). *The Victorian Clergy.* London: Routledge.

Halsey, A. H., Sheehan, J. & Vaizey, J. (1972). Schools. In Halsey, A. H. (Ed.). *Trends in British Society Since 1900: A Guide to the Changing Social Structure of Britain.* London: The Macmillan Press.

Hamann, B. (2010). *Hitler's Vienna: A Portrait of the Tyrant as a Young Man.* London: Tauris.

Hammond, R. & Axelrod, R. (2006). The evolution of ethnocentric behaviour. *Journal of Conflict Resolution,* 50: 1-11.

Hartshorn, M., Katnatcheev, A. & Shultz, T. (2013). The evolutionary dominance of ethnocentric cooperation. *Journal of Artificial Societies and Social Simulation,* 16: 7.

Hatcher, V. (1910). *The Sneads of Fluvana.* Roanoke, VA: Mrs William E. Hatcher.

Heanley, R.M. (1888). *A Memoir of Edward Steere, D.D., LL.D., Third Missionary Bishop of Central Africa.* London: George Bell & Sons.

Heath, I. (2004). Editorial: Women in Medicine. *British Medical Journal,* 329: 412-413.

Heffer, S. (2013). *High Minds: The Victorians and the Birth of Modern Britain.* New York: Random House.

Hein, D. (2008). *Geoffrey Fisher: Archbishop of Canterbury.* Cambridge: James Clarke & Co.

Helms, M.W. & Mimardiere, A.M. (1983). SNEYD, William I (c.1614-95), of Keele, Staffs. In Henning, B.D. (Ed.). *The History of Parliament: The House of Commons 1660-1690.* Woodbridge: Boydell & Brewer.

Herman, A. (2010). *Gandhi and Churchill: The Rivalry That Destroyed an Empire.* New York: Random House.

Herman, A. (2007). *How the Scots Invented the Modern World: The True Story of How Western Europe's Poorest Nation Created Our World and Everything in It.* New York: Three Rivers Press.

Herrnstein, R. & Murray, C. (1994). *The Bell Curve: Intelligence and Class Structure in American Life.* New York: Free Press.

Herring, G. (2010). *What Was the Oxford Movement?* London: Continuum.

Herringer, C. (2014). *Victorians and the Virgin Mary: Religion and Gender in England 1830–85.* Oxford: Oxford University Press.

Hill, L. (1952). Infantile personalities. *American Journal of Psychiatry,* 109: 429-432.

Hills, P., Francis, L., Argyle, M. & Jackson, C. (2004). Primary personality trait correlates of religious practice and orientation. *Personality and Individual Differences,* 36: 61-73.

Hinchcliff, P. (1998). *Frederick Temple, Archbishop of Canterbury: A Life.* Oxford: Clarendon Press.

Hirsch, M. (2010). *The Liberators: America's Witnesses to the Holocaust.* New York: Random House.

Hitchens, P. (2018). *The Phoney Victory: The World War II Illusion.* London: I.B. Tauris.

Hitler, A. (1939). *Mein Kampf.* (Trans: Murphy, J.). London: Hurst & Blackett Ltd.

Holder, R.F. (1976). Smith, Shepherd (1835–1886). *Australian Dictionary of Biography.* National Centre of Biography: Australian National University

Holt, J. (2016). *Public School Literature, Civic Education and the Politics of Male Adolescence.* London: Routledge.

Hooper, D. & Whyld, K. (1996). *The Oxford Companion to Chess.* Oxford: Oxford University Press.

House of Commons Education Committee. (2012). *Great Teachers: Attracting, Training and Retaining the Best, Ninth Report of Session 2010-12, Vol. 2: Oral and Written Evidence, Volume 2.* London: HMSO.

How, F.D. (1904). *Six Great Schoolmasters: Hawtrey, Moberly, Kennedy, Vaughan, Temple, Bradley.* London: Methuen.

Howard, M. (1996). Churchill: Prophet of Détente. In Kemper, R.C. (Ed.). *Winston Churchill: Resolution, Defiance, Magnanimity, Good Will.* London: University of Missouri Press.

Hoyt, E. (1983). *Davies: The Inside Story of a British-American Family in the Pacific and its Business Enterprises.* TopGallant Publishing.

Hughes, K. (2001). *The Victorian Governess.* London: Hambledon & London.

Humes, J. (2003). *Winston Churchill.* London: DK Publishing.

Humes, J. (2001). *Eisenhower and Churchill: The Partnership that Saved the World.* New York: Forum Publishing.

Humphries, S. (1983). *Hooligans Or Rebels?: An Oral History of Working Class Childhood and Youth 1889-1939.* Oxford: Blackwell.

Hunter, A. (2007). *Power and Passion in Egypt: The Life of Sir Eldon Gorst, 1861-1911.* London: I. B. Tauris.

Hutchison, A. (1990) Kynnersley, Thomas Alfred Sneyd. *Dictionary of New Zealand Biography,* https://teara.govt.nz/en/biographies/1k18/kynnersley-thomas-alfred-sneyd (accessed 8th July 2018).

Jarvis, M. (2012). *In the Eye of All Trade: Bermuda, Bermudians, and the Maritime Atlantic World, 1680-1783.* UNC Books.

Jay, D. (1980). *Change and Fortune: A Political Record.* London: Hutchinson.

Jenkins, R. (2001). *Churchill.* London: Macmillan.

Jensen, A. (1998). *The g Factor: The Science of Mental Ability.* Westport, CT: Praeger.

Johnson, B. (2014). *The Churchill Factor: How One Man Made History.* London: Hachette.

Johnson, D. (1997). The Eating and Drinking. In Berkley, J. (Ed). *Leadership Handbook of Preaching and Worship.* Grand Rapids, MI: Baker Books.

Jones, R. & Lopez, K. (2014). *Human Reproductive Biology.* London: Academic Press.

Journal of Horticulture and Cottage Gardener. (27th November 1884). Awards.

Kanazawa, S. (2012). *The Intelligence Paradox: Why the Intelligent Choice Isn't Always the Smart One.* Hoboken, NJ: John Wiley & Sons.

Kershaw, I. (2001). *Hitler: 1889-1936 – Hubris.* London: Penguin.

Kessler, H. von. (1988). *Gesammelte Schriften: Volumes I-III.* (Ed.). Gerhard Schuster. Frankfurt a. M.: S. Fischer.

Kessler, H. von. (1935). *Gesichter und Zeiten.* Berlin: Fischer. Unpublished English translation by Simon Hall (2002).

Kiernan, R.H. (1942). *Churchill.* London: George G. Harkap & Co.

Kim, E. (2012). *The Rise of the Global South: The Decline of Western Christendom and the Rise of Majority World Christianity.* Eugene, OR: Wipf & Stock.

Klank, C., Daeschlein, G. & Schuett, C. (2008). Pneumonia as a long-term consequence of chronic psychological stress in BALB/c mice. *Brain, Behavior and Immunity,* 22: 1173-1177.

Kleinberg, S. (2002). Alfred, Lord Tennyson. In Aldrich, R. & Wotherspoon, G. (Eds.). *Who's Who in Gay and Lesbian History: From Antiquity to World War II.* London: Routledge.

Knight, N. (2012). *Churchill: The Greatest Britain Unmasked.* London: David & Charles.

Knowledge. (1886). *Latin Prose Composition.* By the Rev. Herbert W. Sneyd-Kynnersley, LLD.

Kodjebachava, G. & Sabo, T. (2015). Influence of premature birth on the health conditions, receipt of special education and sport participation of children aged 6–17 years in the USA. *Journal of Public Health,* doi: 10.1093/pubmed/fdv098.

Koenig, H. (2012). Religion, Spirituality, and Health: The Research and Clinical Implications. *ISRN Psychiatry,* http://dx.doi.org/10.5402/2012/278730

Krafft-Ebing, R. (1998). *Psychopathia Sexualis: With Especial Reference to the Antipathic Sexual Instinct: A Medico-Forensic Study.* (Trans. Klaf, F.S.). New York: Arcade Publishing.

Kucich, D. (2009). *Imperial Masochism: British Fiction, Fantasy, and Social Class.* Princeton, NJ: Princeton University Press.

Kura, K., te Nijenhuis, J. & Dutton, E. (2015). Why do Northeast Asians Win So Few Nobel Prizes? *Comprehensive Psychology,* 4. doi: 10.2466/04.17.CP.4.15

Labelle, L., Bourget, D., Bradford, J. et al. (2012). Familial Paraphilia: A Pilot Study with the Construction of Genograms. *ISRN Psychiatry,* http://dx.doi.org/10.5402/2012/692813

Langmore, D. (1981). *European Missionaries in Papua, 1874-1914: A Group Portrait.* PhD Thesis: Australian National University.

Langworth, R. (2017). *Winston Churchill, Myth and Reality: What He Actually Did and Said.* Jefferson, NC: McFarland Publishing.

Lansford, J., Deater-Deckard, K., Dodge, K., Bates, J. & Pettit, G. (2009). Ethnic differences in the link between physical discipline and later adolescent externalizing behaviors. *Journal of Child Psychology and Psychiatry,* 45: 801-812.

Larzelere, R. (2000). Child Outcomes of Nonabusive and Customary Physical Punishment by Parents: An Updated Literature Review. *Clinical Child and Family Psychology*, 3: 199-221.

Lawrence, B. (1972). *The Administration of Education in Britain*. London: Batsford.

Lee, S. (2016). *European Dictatorships 1918–1945*. London: Routledge.

Lee, C. & Lee, J. (2010). *The Churchills: A Family Portrait*. New York: St Martin's Press.

Lee, C. & Lee, J. (2007). *Winston and Jack: The Churchill Brothers*. London: Celia Lee.

Leeds Mercury, (27ᵗʰ December 1872). Dr. Hayward and Mr. Scott.

Leinster-Mackay, D. (2012). The nineteenth-century English preparatory school: cradle and crèche of Empire? In Mangan, D.A. (Ed.). *Benefits Bestowed? Education and British Imperialism*. Abingdon: Routledge.

Leinster-Mackay, D. (1981). Victorian Quasi-Public Schools: A Question of Appearance and Reality or an Application of the Principle of Survival of the Fittest? *British Journal of Educational Studies*, 39: 54-68.

Leinster-Mackay, D. (1971) *The English Private School 1830-1914, with Special Reference to the Private Proprietary School*. Durham University: PhD Thesis.

Leslie, A. (1969). *Lady Randolph Churchill: The Story of Jennie Jerome*. New York: Scribner.

Leslie, D. (2014). *Banged Up! Doing Time in Britain's Toughest Jails*. Edinburgh: Black & White Publishing.

Leslie, S. (1966). *Long Shadows: Memoirs of Sir Shane Leslie*. London: John Murray.

Leslie, R.F. (1983). *The History of Poland Since 1863*. Cambridge: Cambridge University Press.

Levy, M. (2000). A Conceptualization of the Repetition Compulsion. *Psychiatry*, 63: 45-53.

Lewis, I.M. (2003). *Ecstatic Religion: A Study of Shamanism and Spirit Possession*. London: Routledge.

Lewis Taylor, R. (1952). *Winston Churchill: An Informal Study of Greatness*. New York: Doubleday.

Loades, D. (2006). *Elizabeth I: A Life*. London: A. & C. Black.

Lockwood, E. (1893). *The Early Days of Marlborough College: Public School Life Between Forty and Fifty Years Ago.* London: Simpkin, Marshall, Hamilton, Kent & Co.

Loimier, R. (2009). *Between Social Skills and Marketable Skills: The Politics of Islamic Education in 20th Century Zanzibar.* Leiden: BRILL.

London Gazette. (30th July 1889). Statham and Cross.

London Gazette. (28th June 1859). Commissions signed by the Lord Lieutenant of the County of Stafford.

Lord, J. (1970). *Duty, Honour, Empire: The Life and Time of Colonel Richard Meinertzhagen.* New York: Random House.

Loris: A Journal of Ceylon Wildlife. (1973). Minutes of the 79th Annual General Meeting., 13.

Lough, D. (2015). *No More Champagne: Churchill and His Finances.* London: Head of Zeus.

Love, C. (2013). Introduction. In Love, C. (Ed). *A Social History of Swimming in England, 1800–1918: Splashing in the Serpentine.* London: Routledge.

Lovell, M.S. (2012). *The Churchills: In Love and War.* London: W.W. Norton & Co.

Lovell, M.S. (2011). *The Churchills: A Family at the Heart of History - From the Duke of Marlborough to Winston Churchill.* London: Hachette.

Lynch, S., Turkeimer, E., D'Onfrio, B. et al. (2006). A genetically informed study of the association between harsh punishment and offspring behavioral problems. *Journal of Family Psychology,* 20: 190-198.

Lynd, H.M. (1968). *England in the Eighteen-Eighties: Toward a Social Basis for Freedom.* New Brunswick, NJ: Transaction Publishers.

Lynn, R. (2011). *Dysgenics: Genetic Deterioration in Modern Populations.* London: Ulster Institute for Social Research.

Lynn, R. & Vanhanen, T. (2012). *Intelligence: A Unifying Construct for the Social Sciences.* London: Ulster Institute for Social Research.

Lysaght, D. (1979). *Brendan Bracken.* London: Allen Lane.

Långström N, Rahman, Q., Carlström, E. & Lichtenstein, P. (2010). Genetic and environmental effects on same-sex sexual behavior: a population study of twins in Sweden. *Archives of Sexual Behavior,* 39: 75–80.

Macdonald, A. & Macdonald, A. (1904). *The Clan Donald. Volume III.* Inverness: The Northern Counties Publishing Company.

Macdonald, R.E. (1905). Skating in Austria and Germany. In Aflalo, F.G. (Ed.). *The Sports of the World.* London: Cassell & Co.

MacKenzie, A.W. (1881). *History of the MacDonalds and Lords of the Isles: With the Principal Genealogies of the Principal Families of the Name.* Inverness: A.W. MacKenzie.

Mail Online. (16th May 2006). Royal Joy at Beatrice's Election Win. http://www.dailymail.co.uk/columnists/article-386707/Royal-joy-Beatrices-election-win.html

Manchester Courier and Lancashire General Advertiser. (21st August 1906). A Municipal By-election at Chester.

Manchester Guardian. (17th May 1886). Manchester Spring Assizes. https://www.corpun.com/ukj88605.htm

Manchester, W. (2015). *The Last Lion: Winston Spencer Churchill: Visions of Glory, 1974-1932.* New York: Pan MacMillan.

Mangan, J.A. (2004). Bullies, beatings, battles and bruises: 'great days and jolly days' at one mid-Victorian school. In Huggins, M. & Mangan, J.A. (Eds.). *Disreputable Pleasures: Less Virtuous Victorians at Play.* Abingdon: The Psychology Press.

Margretson, S. (1980). *Victorian High Society.* Teaneck, NJ: Holmes & Meier.

Marlborough College, School List. (1865). Junior Scholarships.

Maroney, E. (2006). *Religious Syncretism.* London: SCM Press.

Marriott, S. (1981). *A Backstairs Degree: Demands for an Open University in Late Victorian England.* Leeds University: Department of Adult Education.

Marshall, D. (2013). *Industrial England, 1776-1851.* London: Routledge.

Marshall, W., Fernandez, Y. & Cortoni, F. (1999). Rape. In Van Hassett, B. & Hersen, M. (Eds.). *Handbook of Psychological Approaches with Violent Offenders.* New York: Kluwer Academic.

Mason, P. (1962). *Prospero's Magic: Some Thoughts on Race and Class.* Oxford: Oxford University Press.

Mazurek, M. (2017). *The Unknown Relatives: The Catholic as the Other in the Victorian Novel.* London. Routledge.

McAdams, D. & Pals, J. (2006). A new Big Five: Fundamental principles for an integrative science of personality. *American Psychologist*, 61: 204-217.

McCain, J. & Salter, M. (2014). *Thirteen Soldiers: A Personal History of Americans at War.* New York: Simon & Schuster.

McCoy, M. & Keen, S. (2013). *Child Abuse and Neglect.* London: Psychology Press.

McEnery, T. (2006). *Swearing in English: Blasphemy, Purity and Power from 1586 to the Present.* London: Routledge.

McGrath, A. (2007). *Christianity's Dangerous Idea: The Protestant Revolution.* London: SPCK.

McKibbin, R. (1998). *Class and Cultures: England, 1918-1951.* Oxford: Oxford University Press.

Mehta, C., Rehman, M., & Varelas, P. (2017). Alcohol-Related Seizures in the Intensive Care Unit. In Varelas, P. & Claasen, J. (Eds.). *Seizures in Critical Care: A Guide to Diagnosis and Therapeutics.* New York: Springer.

Meisenberg, G. (2010). The reproduction of intelligence. *Intelligence*, 38, 220-230.

Meisenberg, G. (2007). *In God's Image: The Natural History of Intelligence and Ethics.* Kibworth, Leicestershire: Book Guild Publishing.

Melnyk, J. (2008). *Victorian Religion: Faith and Life in Britain.* New York: Praeger.

Mentor, I. (2016). Introduction. In Beauchamp, G., Clarke, L., Kennedy, A. & O'Doherty, T. (Eds.). *Teacher Education in Times of Change.* Bristol: Policy Press.

Mercurio, J. (1975). *Caning: Educational Ritual.* New York: Holt, Rinehart & Winston.

Metzen, J. (2012). *The Causes of Group Differences in Intelligence Studied Using the Method of Correlated Vectors and Psychometric Meta-Analysis.* Master's Thesis: University of Amsterdam.

Meyerbeer, G. (1999). *The Diaries of Giacomo Meyerbeer: The Years of Celebrity, 1850-1856.* (Trans. Letellier, R.I.). Teaneck, NJ: Farleigh Dickinson University Press.

Middleton, J. (2005). Thomas Hopley and Mid-Victorian attitudes to corporal punishment. *History of Education*, 34: 599–615.

Millard, C. (2016). *Hero of the Empire: The Making of Winston Churchill.* London: Penguin.

Miller, E. M. (2000). Homosexuality, birth order, and evolution: Toward an equilibrium reproductive economics of homosexuality. *Archives of Sexual Behavior*, 29, 1-34.

Mingay, G. (1976). *The Gentry: The Rise and Fall of a Ruling Class*. London: Longman.

Minutes of the Proceedings of the Institution of Civil Engineers. (1901). Henry Francis Sneyd-Kynnersley. 143: 322-323.

Mitchell, A. (Ed). (1902). *Rugby School Register, Volume II, August 1842, to January 1874*. Rugby: A.J. Lawrence.

Mitchell, S. (2009). *Daily Life in Victorian England*. Bolder, CO: Greenwood Press.

Moloney, L. (2015). St Vincent's and Its Mysterious Headmaster. *Eastbourne Local Historian*, 124: 14-26.

Monthly Notices of the Royal Astronomical Society. (1897). Thomas Gwyn Elger. Vol. 57.

Moore, J. (2018). Hopley, Thomas. *Dictionary of National Biography*, https://doi. org/10.1093/ref:odnb/93658

Moran, J. (2005). *Reading the Everyday*. London: Routledge.

Morning Chronicle. (18th June 1857). Births, Deaths and Marriages.

Morris, D. (1969). *The Human Zoo: A Zoologist's Study of the Urban Animal*. New York: Book Company.

Morris, J. (2016). *The High Church Revival in the Church of England: Arguments and Identities*. Leiden: BRILL.

Mosely, P. (1995). 'Father of Australian Soccer': John Walter Fletcher 1847-1918 - a Biographical Sketch. *ASSH Bulletin*, 3-7.

Mullen, R. & Munson, J. (2009). *The Smell of the Continent: The British Discover Europe*. London: Pan Books.

Murray, D. (2017). *The Strange Death of Europe: Immigration, Identity, Islam*. London: Bloomsbury.

Neill, J. (2011). *The Origins and Role of Same-Sex Relations in Human Societies*. Jefferson, NC: McFarland.

Nelson, C. (2007). *Family Ties in Victorian England*. Bolder, CO: Greenwood Publishing.

Nettle, D. (2007). *Personality: What Makes You Who You Are.* Oxford: Oxford University Press.

Newcastle Evening Chronicle. (26ᵗʰ June 1945). Triumphal Tour of Mr. Churchill.

Norenzayan, A. (2013). *Big Gods: How Religion Transformed Cooperation and Conflict.* Princeton, NJ: Princeton University Press.

Norenzayan, A. & Shariff, A. (2008). The origin and evolution of religious pro-sociality. *Science,* 322: 58-62.

Norris, C., Leaf, P. & Fenn, K. (2018). Negativity bias in false memory: moderation by neuroticism after a delay. *Cognition and Emotion,* doi: 10.1080/02699931.2018.1496068.

North Devon Journal. (27ᵗʰ February 1851). Deaths.

Northwestern University. (1864). *Catalogue of the Northwestern University, 1863-64.* Evanston, IL.

Norton R. (Ed.). (30ᵗʰ April 2017). Miscellaneous News Reports, 1848. *Homosexuality in Nineteenth-Century England: A Sourcebook,* http://rictornorton.co.uk/eighteen/1848news.htm

O'Connell, E. (2013). Quakers and Education. In Angell, S. & Dandelion, P. (Eds.). *The Oxford Handbook of Quaker Studies.* Oxford: Oxford University Press.

Observer. (1ˢᵗ June 1835). Front page. London.

Ocobock, P. (2017). *An Uncertain Age: The Politics of Manhood in Kenya.* Athens: Ohio University Press.

Onyeama, D. (1972). *Nigger at Eton.* London: Leslie Frewin.

Orme, N. (2006). *Medieval Schools: From Roman Britain to Renaissance England.* Yale University Press.

Orwell, G. (1955). Charles Dickens. In Morgan, S. (Ed.). *Reading for Thought and Expression.* London: Macmillan.

Our Schools and Colleges, 1883 & 1884. (1883). London: Simpkin, Marshall & Co.

Oxford Undergraduates' Journal. (29ᵗʰ January 1874). Dr Hayman and Rugby.

Padfield, P. (2013). *Hess, Hitler and Churchill: The Real Turning Point of the Second World War.* London: Icon Books.

Page, D. (1883). *Advanced Textbook in Physical Geography*. London: William Blackwood & Sons.

Pall Mall Gazette. (2nd June 1877). Advertisements.

Palmer, B. (8th February 2012). How Many Kids Are Sexually Abused by Their Teachers? *The Edge*, http://www.slate.com/articles/news_and_politics/explainer/2012/02/is_sexual_abuse_in_schools_very_common_html?via=gdpr-consent

Pearson, J. (2011). *Blood Royal: The Stories of the Spencers and the Royals*. London: A.&C. Black.

Pearson, J. (1991). *The Private Lives of Winston Churchill*. New York: Touchstone.

Pedraza, H. (1986). *Winston Churchill, Enoch Powell, and the Nation*. London: Cleveland Press.

Peel, M. (1996). *The Land of Lost Content: The Biography of Anthony Chenevix-Trench*. Edinburgh: Pentland Press.

Perkins, A. (2016). *The Welfare Trait: How State Benefits Affect Personality*. London: Palgrave Macmillan.

Perry, J. (2010). *Winston Churchill*. Nashville, TN: Thomas Nelson.

Perwick, P. (2018). *Telling Tales: The Fabulous Lives of Anita Leslie*. London: Bloomsbury.

Peterson, J.B. (2018). *12 Rules for Life: An Antidote to Chaos*. London: Allen Lane.

Pfeifer, J. & Allen, N. (2012). Arrested development? Reconsidering dual-systems models of brain function in adolescence and disorders. *Trends in Cognitive Science*, 16: 322-329.

Piffer, D. (2018). Correlation between PGS and environmental variables. *RPubs*, https://rpubs.com/Daxide/377423

Pilpel, R. (1978). *Churchill in America, 1895-1961: An Affectionate Portrait*. New York: Harcourt, Brace & Jovanovich.

Pinker, S. (18th June 2012). The false allure of group selection. *The Edge*, https://www.edge.org/conversation/the-false-allure-of-group-selection

Piper, L. (2006). *The Tragedy of Erskine Childers*. London: A.&C. Black.

Ponting, C. (1995). *Churchill*. London: Sinclair-Stevenson.

Post, F. (1994). Creativity and psychopathology. *British Journal of Psychiatry*, 165: 22-34.

Powell, A. (21st September 1991). Laughter and the Love of Friends. *The Spectator.* http://archive.spectator.co.uk/article/21st-september-1991/33/laughter-and-the-love-of-friends

Public Opinion. (20th April 1872). The Sentence of O'Connor for the Outrage on the Queen.

Punch Magazine. (18th December 1875). Even handed Flogging.

Putnam, R. (2007). *E Pluribus Unum*: Diversity and community in the twenty-first century. The 2006 Johan Skytte Prize lecture. *Scandinavian Political Studies*, 30: 137–174.

Raineval, Marquis of Ruvigny and. (1903). *The Plantagenet Roll of the Blood Royal.* London: E.C. & T.C. Jack.

Ratcliffe, S. (2018). The Art of Curling Up: Charles Dickens and the Feeling of Curl Papers. In Kingstone, H. & Lester, K. (Eds.). *Paraphernalia! Victorian Objects.* London: Routledge.

Reading Mercury. (30th June 1888). Ascot: St George's Sports.

Reading Mercury. (2nd June 1888). Trinity Ordinations.

Reading Mercury. (14th April 1888). Marriage.

Reading Mercury. (26th February 1887). Oxford.

Reading Mercury. (6th October 1883). Maidenhead.

Reading Observer. (7th April 1883). Robbery of Rabbits at Sunninghill.

Reardon, T. (2012). *Winston Churchill and Mackenzie King: So Similar, So Different.* Toronto: Dundurn.

Reed, J. (2000). *Glorious Battle: The Cultural Politics of Victorian Anglo-Catholicism.* Create Space Independent Publishing Platform.

Renton, A. (2017). *Stiff Upper Lip: Secrets, Crimes and the Schooling of a Ruling Class.* London: Hachette.

Reports from Commissioners. (1872). Volume 25. London: House of Commons.

Restarick, H. (1924). *Hawaii, 1778-1920, from the Viewpoint of a Bishop: Being the Story of English and American Churchmen in Hawaii with Historical Sidelights.* Honolulu, HI: Paradise of the Pacific.

Rideout, E. (1931). Rodney Street, Liverpool. *Historical Society of Lancashire and Cheshire,* 61-95.

Rindermann, H. (2018). *Cognitive Capitalism: Human Capital and the Wellbeing of Nations.* Cambridge: Cambridge University Press.

Ringrose, J. (2018). *Understanding and Treating Dissociative Identity Disorder (or Multiple Personality Disorder).* London: Routledge.

Roberts, A. (2010). *Hitler and Churchill: Secrets and Leadership.* London: Hachette.

Roberts, C.E.B. (1937). *Stanley Baldwin: Man or Miracle?* London. Greenberg.

Robertson, A. (22nd August 2018). Even a Prime Minister can't get away with term-time holidays! Letter reveals how William Gladstone asked if MP's son could be taken out of school 135 years ago... only for his 'indulgence' to be flatly refused! *Mail Online,* http://www.dailymail.co.uk/news/article-6087125/Letter-reveals-William-Gladstone-asked-MPs-son-taken-school.html

Robinson, J.A.T. (1963). *Honest to God.* London: SCM Press.

Rose, N. (2009). *Churchill: An Unruly Life.* London: I.B. Tauris.

Rossides, D. (1998). *Social Theory: Its Origins, History and Contemporary Relevance.* Lanham, MD: Rowman & Littlefield.

Round, J.H. (1901). *Studies in Peerage and Family History.* London: Constable.

Rowley, T. (2006). *The English Landscape in the Twentieth Century.* London: A.&C. Black.

Royal Calendar, and Court and City Register for England, Scotland, Ireland and the Colonies. (1846). London: John Varnham.

Royal Society of Literature. (1907). *Report of the Royal Society of Literature and List of Fellows.* London.

Rylands, W. H. (Ed.). (1906). *Ars Quatuor Coronatorum. Vol. XIX.* Margate: H. Keble.

Ryley Scott, G. (1968). *The History of Corporal Punishment.* London: Tallis Press.

Salter, F. (2006). *On Genetic Interests: Family, Ethnicity and Humanity in an Age of Mass Migration.* New Brunswick, NJ: Transaction Publishers.

Samuel, H. (3rd January 2017). France bans smacking, raising pressure on UK to follow suit. *Daily Telegraph*, https://www.telegraph.co.uk/news/2017/01/03/france-bans-smacking-raising-pressure-uk-follow-suit/

Sandnabba, N.K., Santtila, P., Alison, L. & Nordling, N. (2002). Demographics, sexual behaviour, family background and abuse experiences of practitioners of sadomasochistic sex: A review of recent research. *Sexual and Relationship Therapy*, 17: 1.

Sandys, C. (1994). *The Young Churchill: The Early Years of Winston Churchill*. New York: E.P. Dutton.

Sandys, J. & Henley, W. (2016). *God and Churchill: How the Great Leader's Sense of Divine Destiny Changed His Troubled World and Offers Hope for Ours*. London: SPCK.

Sarraf, M., Woodley of Menie, M.A. & Feltham, C. (2019). *Modernity, Nihilism and Mental Health*. London: Routledge.

Saturday Review. (5th May 1877). Sunninghill House. Front Page Advertisements.

Saunders, J. (2018). *Great Men at Bad Moments: Brief Lives of Some Aberrant Headmasters*. Bath: Brown Dog Books.

Sawyer, A. (2005). *The Moral Significance of Class*. Cambridge: Cambridge University Press.

Schaarwächter, J. (2015). *Two Centuries of British Symphonism: From the Beginnings to 1945. A preliminary survey*. New York: Georg Olms Verlag.

Schoeman, C. (2013). *Churchill's South Africa: Travels during the Anglo-Boer War*. Johannesburg: Penguin Random House South Africa.

Schwartz, B. (2011). *The White Man's World*. Oxford: Oxford University Press.

Scott, J. (2016). *Tracing Your British and Irish Ancestors: A Guide for Family Historians*. Barnsley: Pen & Sword.

Scott, J. (2014). *Who Rules Britain?* Hoboken, NJ: John Wiley & Sons.

Scruton, R. (2000). *Modern Culture*. London: Continuum.

Scudamore, C. (1913). *English Officers of the Nineteenth Century*. London: George Routledge & Sons.

Scudamore, C. (1912). *Heroic Lives of the Nineteenth Century*. London: George Routledge & Sons.

Scudamore, C. (1906). *Normandy.* London: Methuen.

Scudamore, C. (1901). *Belgium and the Belgians.* London. William Blackwood & Sons.

Scudamore, C. (Ed.). (1888). *Scenes from the War in La Vendée: Edited from the Mémoires of Madame De La Rochejaquelein.* London: Williams & Norgate.

Seaton, H. (1963). *Lion in the Morning.* London: John Murray.

Sebba, A. (2012). *Jennie Churchill: Winston's American Mother.* London: Hachette.

Sebright, A. (1922). *A Glance Into the Past.* London: Eveleigh Nash & Grayson Ltd.

Sela, Y., Shackelford, T. & Liddle, J. (2015). When religion makes it worse: Religiously motivated violence as a sexual selection weapon. In Sloane, D. & Van Slyke, J. (Eds.). *The Attraction of Religion: A New Evolutionary Psychology of Religion.* London: Bloomsbury.

Seligman, L. & Hardenburg, S. (2000). Assessment and treatment of paraphilias. *Journal of Counselling and Development,* 78: 107-113.

Sellar, D. (2011). The Family. In Cowan, E. & Henderson, L. (Eds.). *A History of Everyday Life in Medieval Scotland.* Edinburgh: Edinburgh University Press.

Senior, J. (2016). *Broken and Betrayed: The True Story of the Rotherham Abuse Scandal by the Woman Who Fought to Expose It.* London Pan Macmillan

Shanley, M. (1993). *Feminism, Marriage, and the Law in Victorian England.* Princeton, NJ: Princeton University Press.

Shariff, A. (2015). Does Religion Increase Moral Behavior? *Current Opinion in Psychology,* 6: 108-113.

Sherkat, D. (2002). Sexuality and Religious Commitment in the United States: An Empirical Examination. *Journal for the Scientific Study of Religion,* 41:313–323.

Shipping World Yearbook and Who's Who. (1909). Austria.

Silvester, C. (1993). *The Penguin Book of Interviews: An Anthology from 1859 to the Present Day.* London: Viking.

Simpson, R. (1983). *How the PhD Came to Britain: A Century of Struggle for Postgraduate Education.* Milton Keynes: Open University Press.

Singer, B. (2012). *Churchill's Style: The Art of Being Winston Churchill.* New York: Abrams.

Slough and South Bucks Observer. (16th February 2015). Slough men jailed for child sexual offences committed against 'vulnerable' teenage girls. http://www.sloughobserver.co.uk/news/13438566.Slough_men_jailed_for_child_sexual_offences_committed_against__vulnerable__teenage_girls/

Smyth, C. (1940). *Simeon and the Church Order.* Cambridge: Cambridge University Press.

Sneyd-Kynnersley, E. M. (1910). *A Snail's Wooing: The Story of an Alpine Courtship.* London: MacMillan.

Sneyd-Kynnersley, E.M. (1908). *HMI: Some Passages In the Life of One of HM Inspectors of Schools.* London: MacMillan.

Sneyd-Kynnersley, H.W. (1886). *Latin Prose Composition.* London: Relfe Brothers.

Sneyd-Kynnersley, H.W. (1877). *A Parallel Syntax: Greek and Latin for Beginners.* London: William Blackford & Sons.

Soble, A. (1997). *Sexual Investigations.* New York: New York University Press.

Somerset & Wood. (2018). Harriet Sneyd. https://somersetandwood.com/collections/harriet-sneyd

Soto, C., John, O., Gosling, S. & Potter, J. (2011). Age differences in personality traits from 10 to 65: Big Five domains and facets in a large cross-sectional sample. *Journal of Personality and Social Psychology,* 100: 330-348.

Spalding, F. (1980). *Roger Fry, Art and Life.* Berkeley: University of California Press.

Sparrow-Simpson, W. (1933). *The Contribution of Cambridge to the Anglo-Catholic Revival.* London: SPCK.

Spengler, O. (1991). *The Decline of the West.* Oxford: Oxford University Press.

Spiro, M. (2017). *Burmese Supernaturalism.* London: Routledge.

Staffordshire Advertiser. (28th September 1912). Uttoxeter: Death of Mr Sneyd-Kynnersley.

Staffordshire Advertiser. (18th March 1848). Stafford Spring Assizes.

Statham, S.M. (1938). *Immorality.* London: Charles Murray.

Statham, S.M. (1930). *The Wisdom of the Serpent.* London: A.H. Stockwell.

Statham, S.M. (1922). *Hephzibah: A Novel.* London: A.H. Stockwell.

Statham, S.P.H. (1925). *The Descent of the Family of Statham*. London: Times Book Company.

Steinberg, L. (2014). *Age of Opportunity: Lessons from the New Science of Adolescence*. New York: Houghton, Mifflin & Harcourt.

Stevens, A. (2015). *Archetype Revisited: An Updated Natural History of the Self*. London: Routledge.

Stevens, A. & Price, J. (2000). *Evolutionary Psychiatry: A New Beginning*. London: Routledge.

Steyn, R. (2018). *Louis Botha: A Man Apart*. Johannesburg: Jonathan Ball Publishers.

Storr, A. (1991). *The Dynamics of Creation*. London: Penguin.

Storr, A. (1989). *Churchill's Black Dog*. New York: HarperCollins.

Storr, A. (1972). *The Dynamics of Creation*. London: Secker & Warburg.

Storr, A. (1969). *Seksuaalinen poikkeavuus*. (Trans. Tolso, M.). Helsinki: Weilin + Göös.

Storr, A. (1965). *Sexual Deviation*. London: Penguin.

Tasman, A., Kay, J., Lieberman, J., First, M. & Riba, M. (2015). *Psychiatry. Fourth Edition. Volumes I and II*. Hoboken, NJ: John Wiley & Sons.

Taylor, A. (1969). *Churchill Revised: A Critical Assessment*. New York: Dial Press.

Taylor, J. (2004). The smacking controversy: what advice should we be giving parents? *JAN*, 46: 311-318.

The Army and Navy Gazette. (21st November 1899). Lieut. I.A. Broadwood.

The Biograph and Review. (1880). T. C. Sneyd-Kynnersley.

The Eagle. (1893). Obituary: Thomas Clement Sneyd-Kynnersley, MA. Volume 17.

The English Journal of Education. (1857). University Intelligence.

The Freemason's Chronicle. (13th October 1883). Laying the Foundation Stone of St. Agnes' Church Moseley.

The Gentleman's Magazine. (1841). Obituary: Clergy Deceased. London: W. Pickering.

The Globe. (29th March 1909). Marriages.

The Illustrated Sporting and Dramatic News. (3rd February 1877). Mr. Blagrove's Concertina Concerts. Volume 6.

The King's Royal Rifle Corps Chronicle. (1911). Captain D.H. Blundell-Hollinshead-Blundell.

The Meteor. (21st February 1885). Further Subscriptions for the New Big School.

The Monthly Record of Church Missions. (1884). London: Society for the Propagation of the Gospel.

The Morning Post. (21st April 1893). Front Page Advertisements.

The Morning Post. (26th January 1893). Winton House.

The Morning Post. (18th January 1893). Sales by Auction.

The Morning Post. (15th December 1892). Winton House – Prep School.

The Morning Post. (8th December 1892). Front Page Advertisements.

The Morning Post. (2nd June 1892). Front Page Advertisements.

The Morning Post. (24th February 1892). Wanted: Good Plain Cook.

The Morning Post. (6th November 1886). Deaths.

The Morning Post. (25th May 1885). University Intelligence.

The Morning Post. (28th April 1885). Marriages.

The Morning Post. (7th April 1862). University Intelligence.

The Musical Standard. (1883). Passing Events. Vol. XXIV.

The Naval and Military Gazette. (22nd August 1883). Instructor for St George's, Ascot.

The Strad. (1896). Volume 6. London: Orpheus.

The Sydney Morning Herald. (29th January 1868). Family Notices.

The Sydney Morning Herald. (31st January 1938). Family Notices.

The Westminster and Foreign Quarterly Review. (1st April 1878). Miscellanea.

Thompson, E.A. (2002). *Romans and Barbarians: The Decline of the Western Empire.* Madison, WI: University of Wisconsin Press.

Thompson, J. (2011). *Imperial War Museum Book of the War at Sea 1914-18.* London: Pan Books.

Thomas, R. (1980). *The Liverpool and Manchester Railway.* London: B.T. Batsford.

Thornton, T. (2000). *Cheshire and the Tudor State, 1480-1560.* Woodbridge: The Boydell Press.

Trevor-Roper, H. (1977). *The Hermit of Peking: The Hidden Life of Sir Edmund Backhouse.* New York: Alfred A. Knopf.

Truth. (1878). Volume 3.

Turner, V. (1969). *The Ritual Process: Structure and Anti-Structure.* New York: Aldine Publishers.

Tyerman, C. (2000). *A History of Harrow School, 1324-1991.* Oxford: Oxford University Press.

Tyrka, A., Wier, L., Price, L. et al. (2008). Childhood Parental Loss and Adult Psychopathology: Effects of Loss Characteristics and Contextual Factors. *International Journal of Psychiatry in Medicine*, 38: 329-344.

University of London. (2018). University of London Students, 1836-1938, https://www.senatehouselibrary.ac.uk/our-collections/special-collections/archives-manuscripts/university-of-london-students-1836-1934

Urban, S. (1862). *The Gentleman's Magazine. Volume 74.* London.

Urban, S. (July-December 1862). *The Gentleman's Magazine. Volume 213.* London.

Vaas, R. (2009). God, gains and genes. In Voland, E. & Schiefenhövel, W. (Eds). *The Biological Evolution of Religious Mind and Behavior.* New York: Springer.

Van Gennep, A. (2013). *Rites of Passage.* London: Routledge.

Vanhanen, T. (2012). *Ethnic Conflicts: Their Biological Roots in Ethnic Nepotism.* London: Ulster Institute for Social Research.

Venn, J. (1911). *Alumni Cantabrigienses: A Biographical List of All Known Students, Graduates and Holders of Office at the University of Cambridge, from the Earliest Times to 1900.* Cambridge: Cambridge University Press.

Vitebsky, P. (2001). *Shamanism.* Norman: University of Oklahoma Press.

Wadsworth, J. (2014). *Letters from the Trenches: The First World War By Those Who Were There.* Barnsley: Pen and Sword.

Wainewright, J. (Ed.). (1907). *Winchester College, 1836-1906 – A Register.* Winchester: P. & G. Wells.

Walford, G. (2012). *Life in Public Schools.* London: Routledge.

Walford's County Families of the United Kingdom. (1913). Innes-Cross. London: Spottiswoode & Co.

Walford's County Families of the United Kingdom. (1909). Cooke, Mrs, of Dartan, co. Armagh. London: Spottiswoode & Co.

Walvin, J. (1982). *A Child's World: A Social History of English Childhood, 1800-1914.* London: Penguin.

Ward, J. (2004). *Hitler's Stuka Squadrons: The JU 87 at War 1936-1945.* St Paul, MN: MBI Publishing.

Ward, J. (1843). *The Borough of Stoke-upon-Trent, in the Commencement of the Reign of Her Most Gracious Majesty Queen Victoria.* London: W. Lewis & Son.

Wardle, D. (1970). *English Popular Education, 1780-1870.* Cambridge: Cambridge University Press.

Wardrop, M. (29th July 2011). Judge tells sex offender: I don't criticise you for being attracted to children. *Daily Telegraph,* https://www.telegraph.co.uk/news/uknews/crime/8671235/Judge-tells-teacher-sex-offender-I-dont-criticise-you-for-being-attracted-to-children.html

Watson, A.E.T. (Ed.). (Jan-June 1901). The February Competition. *The Badminton Magazine of Sport and Pastimes,* XII.

Weber, M. (1991). The Sociology of Charismatic Authority. In Gerth, H.H. & Mills, C.W. (Eds.). *From Max Weber: Essays in Sociology.* London: Routledge.

Weber, T. (2010). *Hitler's First War: Adolf Hitler, the Men of the List Regiment, and the First World War.* Oxford: Oxford University Press.

Weidhorn, M. (2003). A contrarian's approach to peace. In Muller, J. (Ed.) *Churchill as Peacemaker.* Cambridge: Cambridge University Press.

Weidhorn, M. (1994). Salvaging Charmley. *Finest Hour.*

Weisbrode, K. (2013). *Churchill and the King: The Wartime Alliance of Winston Churchill and George VI.* London: Penguin.

Weiss, V. (2007). The Population Cycle Drives Human History: From a Eugenic Phase into a Dysgenic Phase and Eventual Collapse. *Journal of Social, Political and Economic Studies,* 317-358.

Welby, T.E. (2016). *The Victorian Romantics 1850-70: The Early Work of Dante Gabriel Rossetti, William Morris, Burne-Jones, Swinburne, Simeon Solomon and their Associates*. London: Routledge.

West Middlesex Herald. (2nd January 1893). St George's Gymnastic Club.

Weston-Smith, M. (2013). *Beating the Odds: The Life of E.A. Milne*. London: Imperial College Press.

White, J. (2009). *London in the Twentieth Century: A City and Its People*. New York: Random House.

White, P. (2012). *Churchill's Cold War: How the Iron Curtain Speech Shaped the Post War World*. London: Duckworth.

Who Was Who, 1916-1928: A Companion to Who's Who: Containing the Biographies of Those Who Died During the Period. (1967). Macdonald, Canon Frederick William. London: A. & C. Black.

Willemsen, A. (2008). *Back to the Schoolyard: The Daily Practice of Medieval and Renaissance Education*. Turnhout, Belgium: Brepolis Publishers.

Williams, J. (2016). *Academic Freedom In An Age of Conformity: Confronting the Fear of Knowledge*. London: Palgrave Macmillan.

Williams, R. (2007). *The Historian's Toolbox: A Student's Guide to the Theory and Craft of History*. London: M. E. Sharpe.

Wilson, D. & Sober, E. (1994). Reintroducing group selection to the human behavioural sciences. *Behavioral and Brain Sciences*, 17: 585–654.

Wilson, F. (2010). Mill: logic and Metaphysics. In Moyar, D. (Ed.). *The Routledge Companion to Nineteenth Century Philosophy*. London: Routledge.

Wilson, J. & Herrnstein, R. (1985). *Crime and Human Nature: The Definitive Study of the Causes of Crime*. New York: The Free Press.

Wilt, A. (1990). *War from the Top: German and British Military Decision Making During World War II*. Bloomington: Indiana University Press.

Wiltshire Archaeological and Natural History Magazine. (June 1929). Canon Frederick Macdonald. Vol. XLIV.

Windsor and Eton Express. (15th April 1905). St George's, Ascot.

Windsor and Eton Express. (31st December 1904). To Trustees and Investors: Slough.

Windsor and Eton Express. (24th September 1904). Ascot: Bankruptcy: Mr Edward Blair.

Windsor and Eton Express. (13th December 1902). Charles Gordon Shackle, Deceased.

Windsor and Eton Express. (10th July 1886). Windsor Union Board of Guardians.

Windsor and Eton Express. (3rd July 1886). Ascot.

Windsor and Eton Express. (21st November 1885). East Berks Election, 1885.

Windsor and Eton Express. (7th April 1883). Trial of Prisoners.

Winkelman, M. (2010). *Shamanism: A Biopsychosocial Paradigm of Consciousness and Healing.* Westport, CT: Praeger.

Winter, J. (2012). Demography. In Horne, J. (Ed.). *A Companion to World War I.* Oxford: Wiley-Blackwell.

Woodruff, P. (1971). *The Men Who Ruled India: The Founders.* London: Jonathan Cape.

Woolf, V. (1940). *Roger Fry: A Biography.* New York: Harcourt, Brace and Co.

Woodley of Menie, M.A., Fernandes, H., Kanazawa, S. & Dutton, E. (2018a). Sinistrality is associated with (slightly) lower general intelligence: A data synthesis and consideration of secular trend data in handedness. *HOMO: Journal of Comparative Human Biology,* 69: 118-126.

Woodley of Menie, M.A., Dutton, E. & Figueredo, A.J. et al. (2018b). Communicating intelligence research: Media misrepresentation, the Gould Effect and unexpected forces. *Intelligence,* doi.org/10.1016/j.intell.2018.04.002

Woodley, M.A. (2011). The cognitive differentiation-integration effort hypothesis: A synthesis between the fitness indicator and life history models of human intelligence. *Review of General Psychology,* 15: 228-245.

Young, F. (2015). *Inferior Office? A History of Deacons in the Church of England.* Cambridge: James Clarke & Co.

Ziomkiewicz-Wichary, A. (2016). Serontonin and dominance. In Shackleford, T. & Weekes-Shackleford, V. (Eds.). *Encyclopedia of Evolutionary Psychological Science.* New York: Springer.

Unpublished Primary Sources

Autograph Album. 200 autographs, letters and signatures addressed to the Rev. Herbert Sneyd-Kynnersley. In the hands of Sworders, Fine Art Auctioneers, 24th August 2018.

Bedfordshire Archive. Robert Estcourt Macdonald of Meinhard Strasse 10, Innsbruck, in the Empire of Austria, and others. 21st February 1906. X 877/3. Bedford.

Birth, Marriage, and Death Records of England and Wales, available at www.familysearch.org and the General Records Office, London.

Diary of Aubrey Jay. In the hands of Lord Jay of Ewelme.

The Duke of Wellington, Autographed Letter. Part of the Sneyd-Kynnersley Collection. In the hands of Sworders, Fine Art Auctioneers, 24th August 2018.

East Sussex Records Office. H.M. Cooke, St Vincent's, Eastbourne, 1893. ACC 8859/3/C/57. Brighton.

England and Wales Electoral Registers, 1832-1932. www.findmypast.co.uk

English Parish Baptism, Marriage, Marriage Licence, Burial Records and Bishop's Transcripts; available at www.familysearch.org

Grand Tour. Unpublished handwritten book by Thomas Clement Sneyd-Kynnersley. In the hands of Sworders, Fine Art Auctioneers, 24th August 2018.

Hampshire Archives and Local Studies. Bonham Carter. Letter from Arthur at St. George's School Ascot to his father. N.D [c. 1880]. 70M88/59. Winchester.

Illinois Cook County Deaths, 1878-1994, available at www.familysearch.org

Jay, Edward Aubrey Hastings. (1947). Unpublished Memoir. In the hands of the Hon. Peter Jay.

Liverpool Record Office. Document: 385 JAM/2/1, searchable at http://discovery.nationalarchives.gov.uk/

London Borough of Sutton: Archives and Local Studies. Copy of court roll, Manor of Carshalton. Presentation of the will of Clement Kynnersley of Carshalton, esq., admission of his heir, his nephew, Thomas Sneyd Kynnersley of Loxley, Staffs., and his surrender to the uses of his will. 16th October 1815. LG6/8/1/11.

National Library of Ireland, Genealogical Office, Dublin. Copy of royal licence to Arthur Charles Innes of Dromantine, Co. Down, to take the name Cross in addition to and after that of Innes and to bear the arms of Cross and Innes quarterly, July 12, 1888. MS 153, pp.605-610.

National Library of Ireland, Genealogical Office Dublin. Copy of grant of arms to Herbert Martin Cooke of Dromantine, Co. Down, husband of Sarah Jane Beauchamp Cooke otherwise Cross Innes [*sic.*] otherwise Cross on his assuming under Royal Licence and in compliance with the will of Col. William Cross of Dartan, Co. Armagh, the name and arms of Cooke Cross July 1, 1908. MS 111, pp.218-219.

National Census of England and Wales, available at www.familysearch.org

Probate Records for England and Wales, available at https://probatesearch.service. gov.uk/#calendar

St George's, Ascot, Archive: A List of St George's School, Ascot, for the Lent Term of 1883.

The National Archive. Divorce Court Case 9528. Appellant Dorothy Norah Macdonald otherwise Dorothy Norah Hutton. Respondent: Robert Estcourt Macdonald. Type: wife's petition for/of nullity. (wn). 1917. J77/1294/ 9528. Kew.

Warwickshire Archive. CR 2747/88, searchable at http://discovery.nationalarchives. gov.uk/

Interviews and Correspondence

Miss Aisling Lockhart. Manuscripts and Archive Research Library Trinity College, Dublin. 15th October 2018. By email.

Mr. Michael Kousah. Ely Books. Owner of the Sneyd-Kynnersley Family Photograph Album. 16th November 2018. By email.

Mrs Barbara Marke. Auxiliary Territorial Service conscript during World War II. 7th October 2018. By telephone.

Mr Michael Stansfield. Deputy Archivist, Durham University. 4th October 2018. By email.

The Rev. Christopher Turner. Anglican Minister of Hook Norton and Great Rollright near Chipping Norton, Oxfordshire. 7th July 2018. By telephone.

By the Same Author

At Our Wits' End: Why We're Becoming Less Intelligent and What It Means for the Future (with Michael Woodley of Menie) (2018).

J. Philippe Rushton: A Life History Perspective (2018).

How to Judge People By What They Look Like (2018).

The Genius Famine (with Bruce Charlton) (2015)

The Ruler of Cheshire: Sir Piers Dutton, Tudor Gangland and the Violent Politics of the Palatine (2015).

Race and Sport: Evolution and Racial Differences in Sporting Ability (with Richard Lynn) (2015).

Religion and Intelligence: An Evolutionary Analysis (2014).

Culture Shock and Multiculturalism (2012).

The Finnuit: Finnish Culture and the Religion of Uniqueness (2009).

Meeting Jesus at University: Rites of Passage and Student Evangelicals (2008).

Index of Names

A

B

D

E

F

Foster, E.M., 14, 48, 92, 135, 183

Francis, George, 136-137

Fraser, Giles, 144

Fraser, Nick, 169

Fry, Edward, 102

Fry, Roger, 25, 29, 38, 43-44, 56, 59, 61, 76-77, 85, 87, 89, 96, 100, 102-103, 107, 109, 113, 118, 125, 133-134, 139, 142, 144, 148, 158, 160-162, 168, 170-171, 189, 194, 196, 198-201

G

Gabb, Sean, 232

Galton, Francis, 53, 251

Gardner, Brian, 213

Gardner, Sir William, 17

Gathorne-Hardy, Jonathan, 28-29, 45, 123, 140, 143, 204

Gibson, Ian, 24, 30, 58, 142, 146, 165, 167, 204

Gladstone, William, 55, 79, 113, 161

H

Hadow, Flora Georgina, 50

Halifax, Lord, 223

Hallam, Arthur, 173

Hamilton, The Duke of, 225

Hamilton-Gordon, Arthur, 113

Hardy, Robert, 25, 295

Hawtrey, J.W., 69, 71-73, 76

Hayman, Henry, 70-72

Headfort, 2nd Marquess of, 45

Hess, Rudolf, 225

Hitchens, Peter, 229

Hitler, Adolf, 17, 212, 215, 219, 223-225, 227-232, 235

Hodgkin, Mariabella, 134

Holmes, Harry Arthur, 103, 122, 135, 137, 141, 163